Agent Orange and Rural Development in Post-war Vietnam

Vu tells the story of Vietnamese farmers who have survived a 30-year war of independence and unification, its damaging legacies in their living environment, and the unfamiliar pressure of the market economy.

Vietnamese famers are neither simply obedient beneficiaries of policy decisions made by higher authorities nor convention-ridden cyphers. Rather, they are sophisticated decision-makers capable of navigating the changes threatening to disrupt their lives over multiple generations. Vu's research pays particular attention to those farmers whose families have suffered from direct and indirect exposure to the toxic herbicides popularly known as Agent Orange. She demonstrates that their priority has tended to be the protection of their existing assets, rather than pursuing the promise of new riches, and that this tendency has helped them maintain stability in a turbulent economic and political environment.

A fascinating study for scholars of Vietnamese anthropology and society, the book will also be of interest to sociologists and economists with a broader interest in the impact of economic and political change on rural lifestyles.

Vu Le Thao Chi is Assistant Professor at the Faculty of Policy Management, Graduate School of Media and Governance, Keio University, Japan.

Routledge Contemporary Southeast Asia Series

The aim of this series is to publish original, high-quality work by both new and established scholars on all aspects of Southeast Asia.

Securitising Singapore
State Power and Global Threats Management
Syed Mohammed Ad'ha Aljunied

The European Union and Myanmar
Interactions via ASEAN
Edited by Ludovica Marchi Balossi Restelli

The State and Religious Violence in Indonesia
Minority Faiths and Vigilantism
A'an Suryana

Science and Development in Thai and South Asian Buddhism
David L. Gosling

The Arab Uprisings and Malaysia's Islamist Movements
Influence, Impact and Lessons
Mohd Irwan Syazli Saidin

Islam, Blasphemy, and Human Rights in Indonesia
The Trial of Ahok
Daniel Peterson

Agent Orange and Rural Development in Post-war Vietnam
Vu Le Thao Chi

Ethnographies of Development and Globalization in the Philippines
Emergent Socialities and the Governing of Precarity
Edited by Koki Seki

For more information about this series, please visit: www.routledge.com/Routledge-Contemporary-Southeast-Asia-Series/book-series/RCSEA

Agent Orange and Rural Development in Post-war Vietnam

Vu Le Thao Chi

Routledge
Taylor & Francis Group
LONDON AND NEW YORK

First published 2020 by Routledge

2 Park Square, Milton Park, Abingdon, Oxon OX14 4RN
605 Third Avenue, New York, NY 10017

Routledge is an imprint of the Taylor & Francis Group, an informa business

First issued in paperback 2021

Publisher's Note

The publisher has gone to great lengths to ensure the quality of this reprint but points out that some imperfections in the original copies may be apparent.

British Library Cataloguing-in-Publication Data
A catalogue record for this book is available from the British Library

Library of Congress Cataloging-in-Publication Data
Names: Vu, Le Thao Chi, author.
Title: Agent Orange and rural development in post-war Vietnam / Vu Le Thao Chi.
Description: Abingdon, Oxon ; New York : Routledge, 2020. | Series: Routledge contemporary Southeast Asia series | Includes bibliographical references and index.
Identifiers: LCCN 2019052682 (print) | LCCN 2019052683 (ebook) | ISBN 9780367898458 (hardback) | ISBN 9781003021377 (ebook)
Subjects: LCSH: Rural development—Vietnam. | Agriculture and state—Vietnam. | Farmers—Vietnam—Economic conditions. | Farmers—Vietnam—Social conditions. | Agent Orange—Health aspects—Vietnam. | Vietnam—Rural conditions.
Classification: LCC HD2080.5 .V77 2020 (print) | LCC HD2080.5 (ebook) | DDC 338.109597—dc23
LC record available at https://lccn.loc.gov/2019052682
LC ebook record available at https://lccn.loc.gov/2019052683

ISBN: 978-0-367-89845-8 (hbk)
ISBN: 978-1-03-217338-2 (pbk)
DOI: 10.4324/9781003021377

Typeset in Galliard
by codeMantra

Contents

Figures

Tables

Acknowledgements

My sincerest appreciation goes to the families and children in Phu Cat, Vietnam. The stories about their life, often told in simple narratives, are the precious inspiration and valuable materials that I used to write this book. I dedicate it to these honest and hard-working people. Thank you for embracing me and making me feel at home whenever I am wandering in your community.

I owe a special debt to the late Professor Trinh Van Bao and Professor Tran Duc Phan, who helped me to build the very first foundation for my long-term commitment to the research in Phu Cat. I am grateful to Dr Truong Quang Dat for his untiring support for over 15 years and the friendship that blossomed as a result.

My deepest gratitude goes to Professor Michio Umegaki, my teacher and colleague, for numerous conversations and discussions in the classes, in the field, and in the whole process of making this book since its conception. Then there are the current and former students from Chi-kenkyukai (Lab) at Keio University who have accompanied me on nearly every trip to Phu Cat, especially since 2014, and helped me with data collection. Their tireless research efforts are an indispensable source of energy for me. Many of them have continued to extend their support for the project, even after their graduation. Their support has come whenever I needed it.

Speaking of support to my work, I wish to thank an unlikely family from afar, the Campbells in Denver, Colorado, for being faithful readers of my works, big and small.

As always, my own family has never failed to push me to pursue life, as an educator or as a scholar, that is worth living.

Finally, I wish to express my appreciation to Simon Bates at Routledge, who, from the initial meeting in early 2019, has supported the publication of this project, and to Tan Sheng Bin, who has been very crisp and efficient in our exchanges through the final phase of the book's publication.

Acknowledgements

Introduction

Agent Orange, rural development, and enduring farmers

This book is about how Vietnamese farmers faced and coped with uncertainties – risks – in the years after the *Doi Moi* reforms in the second half of the 1980s, which unleashed significant social, political, and economic changes. Among them, a small group of families stand out because of their children and their various mental and physical disabilities. The disabilities are suspected to have been induced by direct and indirect exposure to the wartime use of toxic chemicals popularly known as "Agent Orange". This group of families is unique in the specific difficulties they face, but these do not prevent them from representing a larger group of Vietnamese farmers. The group's uniqueness is not as prominent when we carefully examine their behaviour.

The Vietnamese farmers, in turn, represent more than themselves. The changes they have embraced are not an exception to the micro or macro changes that others face and need to adjust to in order to survive. They are laden with uncertainties, regardless of who may have designed them. They are another way in which risks present themselves. Whatever course of action one may take, it runs the risk of not leading to what one expects or hopes for. Every course of action is the embodiment of risks that impose the pressure of decision-making on anyone for whom uncertainties are the rule. However, the changes do not leave many merely stunned and standing by. Noted sociologists Peter Berger and Thomas Luckmann observed that men do many things to make the changes before them look "unproblematic" so that they can embrace them without fear of pushing themselves to go through an "extreme transition". Our everyday life is a consummate form of these efforts.[1]

The Vietnamese farmers exhibit a remarkable consistency in their behaviour, which some brush off as a sign of their unfounded stubbornness, or ignorance, or as the result of the irresponsiveness to the appeals of professionals and experts in various areas, responding to the demands of the farmers' well-being.

Certainly, there are some who, for one reason or another, are unable to make sound judgement. However, the changes they encounter in their living environment are not something they can stand idly by and let the professionals manage. The farmers were consistently successful in their efforts to cope with the rapid and often disabling changes. It is this consistency that breathes life into the tenacity that the farmers rely on, often unknowingly.

The book is about the source of the tenacity of the farmers. Our observation begins with scenes we have become familiar with.

Local drama

Mai and Binh meet at least once a week. Both had been born with physical and mental deficiencies caused by damage to their brains. Binh is 30 years old, and Mai is 20. Within the past two or three years, Mai has grown taller than Binh. Indeed, Binh has not grown much taller than 130 cm since our first meeting in 2004.

They are sisters. They did not know of each other until 2006 when we brought them together. When Binh was born in 1988, Tran T. H.,[2] her mother, was only a few steps away from getting married to Binh's father. She gave her up to another woman in the same commune for reasons we can only guess. The mother was under heavy pressure from her family, who may have felt ashamed or hoped that she would consummate her marriage if the disabled child was not around; she herself may have thought that living alone was hard enough for a single mother in a rural community. Binh's adopted mother is also unmarried. She had let her husband go because they could not have children. The adopted mother used to spend a great deal of time working in coffee plantations in Buon Ma Thuot, some 150 km south-west of Phu Cat, leaving the care of Binh in the hands of her neighbours and relatives. After all, the effects of the country's astonishing economic growth since the early 1990s have not "trickled down" to these mothers yet.

Mai was born ten years later. Her mother was unmarried, again. This time, she kept her daughter. Her physical disabilities, more pronounced than Binh's, do not usually deter Mai from moving around the neighbourhood. She spends time with the neighbours' children. Occasionally the mother's relatives in the commune take her in to keep an eye on her. Mai has no other choice because her mother needs to tend the paddy and help others for a small amount of extra income whenever opportunities present themselves.

Binh and Mai are among the many disabled children with defects induced by direct or indirect exposure to Agent Orange, the dioxin-yielding herbicides sprayed during the war. The sisters are from the 48 original families in Phu Cat suggested by Hanoi Medical University for our research.

They meet in a classroom at a local primary school together with close to 20 "children" with various types of birth defects. Of these 20-some students, the oldest is a 32-year-old "girl", and the youngest is an 8-year-old deaf girl, the cause of whose disability is unknown but is probably unrelated to the effects of Agent Orange.

In 2012, we initiated, and have since helped run, weekend classes at a few primary schools in different communes in Phu Cat District, Binh Dinh Province, in central coastal Vietnam. Early on at Cat Trinh Primary School II, the volunteer teachers tasked with monitoring, overseeing, and "teaching" these children decided to call the class *Lop hoc Uoc Mo*, a Dream Class. There are four Dream

Classes within the district, and a fifth is on its way. Altogether, over 100 disabled children gather in these classes every weekend. Some of them are siblings. They represent a fraction of over 32,000 disabled people (not including the invalid war veterans) in the province.[3]

Among these children are a few who came to the regular primary school classes before. None lasted long. They did not know what to do with themselves in the classroom. Neither did the teachers. In Dream Classes, their activities range from a set of simple physical exercises to singing and dancing to colouring a picture book to learning simple alphabets. Binh, as it turned out, is an excellent painter, a surprising talent for a girl who usually sits within a radius of 20 or 30 m from her tiny shack with the neighbours' kids, smiling and laughing. Luyen, a boy with learning disabilities and a speech impediment who is a student of Dream Class II in Cat Tanh Commune, even won first prize in a painting competition held in Qui Nhon, a prosperous port town he had never even thought of visiting before.

There are always a few parents or siblings watching over these children in the classroom. Sometimes, an accompanying father nervously looks on as his child struggles with a drawing pen, or pokes at a nearby child. Sometimes, an older sister gives a helping hand to her brother to draw something, which looks like a flower or a house or an animal.

The children know it is time to go home when the teachers begin distributing snacks along with a pint of milk. They grab them and tuck them in their backpacks, and begin looking around for their parents or siblings, who give them a lift home on the backs of small motorcycles, or nod at another child to start the short walk home together.

Of the four, Dream Class I in Cat Trinh Commune is next to the central section of the district, Ngo May, a hub of business-government-medical services. These children rarely, if ever, visit this section. Neither do their families. "Oh, uh, I have nothing to do there", said Ninh, a farmer who has taken care of 32-year-old Tam, a Dream Class student and younger sister with complex mental and physical disabilities. Their father passed away when they were still young. Until recently, their mother lived in Ho Chi Minh City to make a living on her own. Ngo May remains almost as distant as Ho Chi Minh City is to him and Tam or, for that matter, to the majority of the farmers we have met. The chores of a farming family utterly consume Ninh's and his wife's time – raising their own three children, tending the rice paddies, growing peanuts and other vegetables, in addition to caring for Tam. Among the farmers in Cat Trinh, Ninh, who sees no point in spending much time in Ngo May, is not an exception.

It has been over one generation, 30 years at least, since the Vietnamese farmers ceased to be a sort of assembly line workers in a factory: namely the rice paddies managed by agricultural cooperatives. The *Doi Moi* of 1986 and the accompanying reforms released the farmers from the rigid division of labour on the agricultural production line. The end to the collective farming style restored the familiar mode of agricultural life where a family is the primary and autonomous agent of action. The family-centred productive life also embraces community-wide cooperation. "Oh, I was helping out our neighbour". More than once, Ninh casually mentioned at some of our unannounced visits as he rushed back into the front yard of his house on his bike to greet us. "They needed some hands in their rice paddy".

Then, we remembered earlier scenes. In the busiest time for the farmers, that of rice harvesting, there were patches of rice paddies where no one was to be seen while the patches next to them were filled with people reaping rice. The farmers probably found it more efficient to concentrate their helping hands on one patch at a time, then shift to another. This and other reciprocal practices may be left over from the days of collective farming. We suspect that they might go even further back, beyond the collective farming era.

With the market economy penetrating even this rural community, signs of a widening income gap are hard to miss. But these signs appear pale against those of the improvements made, such as the paved roads crisscrossing the lowland district. Ninh, who recently finished building a large 300 m^2 house, still exhibits no sign of material wealth; neither does his mother, for whom he built another house. The villagers all agree that he works hard. He wears the same look and raggedy clothes as he did the first time we met 15 years ago. The only explanation for his building these new houses is that he finally decided to move away from the home of his birth and establish his own family home.

The mother of Binh and Mai, probably at the other end of the rich-poor spectrum, is always willing to provide her services to somebody else at harvest time. Her house, no bigger than a room in Ninh's new home, is a home to herself and Mai. She works on her own small land and often as a menial labourer. Nothing remotely indicative of surplus assets can be seen. She looks at Mai with a mother's caring eyes.

Dream Class children are from families who are somewhere between Ninh's and Tran T. H.'s, income-wise. There is an air of equality among the families of the children of the Dream Class.

Over time, we have detected changes in the children in the Dream Class. Some of them have begun forming a small group of children they like. From the look of it, the children occupy their seats in the classroom not just because they are instructed to do so but because they are seated next to their *friends.* Vu, a child of a single mother living with her and her aged parents and a newcomer to Dream Class I, rarely mingles with anyone at home and usually isolates himself and immerses himself in whatever his arms can grab. In the Dream Class, he exchanges his "opinions" with his friends next to him and pushes and shoves them with hearty laughter.

In another Dream Class in Cat Tanh Commune, a year after it opened in 2016, we watched a small group of children methodically instructing the rest to be seated and distributing the materials to be used in class. The leader of the group was a boy with learning disabilities who had been nominated by the teachers as the head of the class. One of the teachers informed us that he divided his work among some of the others "at his own volition".

Some of the children are no longer accompanied by their parents. They come and leave with the "classmates" of their choosing. Some of their behaviour has surprised their parents. "You know what?" one of the parents confided to us in Dream Class I, a year after its opening. "These days, the night before Dream Class, my daughter goes through her clothes, not that she has many to choose from". These Dream Class children are among the children whom medical experts have conclusively characterized as "disabled" to engage in "normal" conduct of life and to establish the routines of everyday life on their own accord. These changes are indicative of improvements in the broader context of their everyday lives. Or so they seemed, at least, to us.

Our approach

However, as we deciphered the parents' narratives from our frequent visits, we also detected something else in the ways in which most of them react to the improvements. They are certainly aware of these changes and are very happy about them. Yet, in their eyes, it has not made their children *less* disabled: their "disabilities" remain an unchanged constant in their parents' and families' everyday lives. This subtle difference in our reactions to the children's improvements alerted us to something that touches on the very core of the way these farmers have lived. The fact that they do not see their children as less disabled has driven them to deal with their misfortune in more ways than one.

Our first reaction to the difference was sympathy. Many of the parents have gone through several steps of medical consultations and treatments for their disabled children, starting with a local Commune Clinic and progressing to a major children's hospital in Ho Chi Minh City, though only a few ever took that final step. We realized that a greater disappointment followed each step as each was another, and firmer, confirmation that the Agent Orange-induced disabilities or birth abnormalities "have no cure". Their children's disabilities are beyond the reach of human efforts in the parents' eyes.

If the parents make efforts now to visit the District Health Centre or the provincial general hospital – respectively a 10–20-minute and a 40–60-minute bike ride away – the primary purpose is to secure a certificate confirming that their son or daughter *is* disabled due to the Agent Orange-induced complications. The document guarantees them the payment of a "government pension", amounting to between $15 and $50 a month.

"Naa, we don't take our kid(s) to the Clinic" is the answer that pops up with alarming frequency as we have added more families to visit beyond the original 48. The parents have decided to live with their disabled children as an integral part of their life, as something neither they nor medical specialists can change or remove. To them, those improvements exhibited in the Dream Class are the reward for the families embracing and enduring the misfortune, and not the proof of the efficacy of their choice to improve the health conditions of the children. The Dream Classes are not there for change; they are for the rest of the family to have a brief reprieve once a week.

Our second reaction was empathy, which has made our observations of their life a little more involved. Over the years, we have tried to imagine what it is like to be a part of the families. Our visits have become occasions for the empathetic reconstruction of their lives.

To nearly all parents, everyday life is filled with routine. A deviation from any one part of this could easily impinge on the rest. Tending rice paddies, or peanut or cashew nut farms, alone is immensely time-consuming, especially since Phu Cat usually maintains a twice-a-year or even thrice-a-year harvesting of rice. This frequent harvesting of rice does not make the farmers that much richer. It merely consumes more labour and opportunities, and leaves less time to tend to other parts of the daily routine. Liberation from the collective mode of farming since the late 1980s multiplied the pressure on families to keep up with production. The collective farming of pre-*Doi Moi* Vietnam may have provided a safety net for the livelihood of the members. The liberation from it meant that the responsibility of producing and marketing the produce fell squarely on the individual farming families, even though the very basic framework for cooperation remains intact among the farmers.

Away from the rice paddies and farms of various produce, there are many ceremonial occasions; some are seasonal and others such as funerals and weddings are unpredictable. Almost none of these are strictly family affairs. They engage their neighbours in the preparations. These are additions to the daily demands such as securing education for the "normal" siblings, of whom there are usually many, of the disabled children.

The families do not or cannot afford to allocate their scarce resources specifically for the disabled children in need of special care. Resources such as time, opportunities, and others are fully mobilized, whereas the demands on them stemming from the care for their disabled children are irregular and often unpredictable. The parents have very little margin for tailoring the use of the resources to the unpredictable demands of the disabled children. An exception may prove the rule. Here are these parents who are not farmers, even though they have the right over the farmland that the husband had acquired through post-*Doi Moi* changes. The husband of one couple in Cat Minh Commune with a boy with a severe case of brain damage quit his job to look after, and provide the needed care to, the child. We do not know of any other cases like this family among over 80 families we have investigated in the past 15 years in Phu Cat. Embracing the disabled children *as they are* is the inevitable reality faced by the parents as farmers, however difficult it may be.

We have also discovered, however, that the same reality is the inventor of something else. The reality has pushed the parents to develop, perhaps unbeknownst to themselves, ways in which everything appears to them less challenging so as not to make their life in dire need of an "extreme transition".[4]

Resigning herself to her son's mental defects at his birth as her "fate (*so phan*)", a mother quickly added that "it is good that he is healthy and can communicate verbally". After a pause, she smiled and said, "That family [five-minute drive away in the same commune] also has a disabled son, but unlike my son, their son can't speak and no one can understand what he wants". We do not know which of the two boys is more seriously disabled. She was making light of the burden of having a disabled child by comparison. She was describing her burden as *less* severe than the other mother's as if she were comforting the "other self" in her who may actually be experiencing the pain of that burden. The hardship is securely locked in that comparative narrative. We are sure that she has developed this dual self, a narrating self and an experiencing self, through many occasions when others expressed their sympathy for her unfortunate son.

It may be because of the same necessity that these parents rarely link their children's misfortune to the principal cause, namely Agent Orange and the war that brought the substance to their backyard. The war seems to have faded into the distant past and with it the link between the cause of their children's misfortune and the war. Together, the problem of having disabled children has become something they live with, rather than something they can remove or change.

Only when prodded did the father of a girl with Down's syndrome say he had fought on the side of the army of the Republic of Vietnam near Phu Cat Airport. Early on in the research, he talked about how he lost his leg below his knee as he caressed the poorly made wooden leg. The link between the war, Agent Orange, and the daughter's disability never entered his narrative, or crossed his mind. That is, at least, was the appearance he maintained.

When the residents talk about the war, they usually do so with a light touch, as if they had been a safe distance from it. A local clinic staff member loves to relate a story involving Nui Ba Mountains, large hills in the middle of the district that are known to have been heavily sprayed with Agent Orange. "Each of the soldiers in the Korean unit [deployed in Phu Cat Airport] carried one soldier on his back in an operation to help the southern army to wipe the National Liberation Front soldiers off the mountains". He paused, grinning for effect. "The idea was so that the NLF unit in the mountains would underestimate the approaching unit's strength". There is no hint of remorse about the Mountains as a persistent source of Agent Orange-induced ailments or birth abnormalities long after the war's end.

Sporadic references to the effects of Agent Orange *and* the war may indicate that the residents are resigned to the fact that the health damages have been done and cannot be undone. Throughout the years of our research, major operations were carried out by the government, jointly with the United States, aimed at neutralizing the contamination around Phu Cat Airport, over 20 km south of the Mountains, were carried out. None of the families, or for that matter the Commune Clinic staff, brought the operations to our attention, even casually.[5] To them, Agent Orange, like the war itself, is far removed from their life. Anything disruptive needs to be ignored or, if it cannot be ignored, tucked away in comforting narratives that can make light of it.

Bewilderment, of a sort, was our third reaction. It began to appear off and on through our early contacts with the families, especially when the visits led to lengthy conversations. This bewilderment became a puzzle that has kept our research afloat. Are the Agent Orange families merely, and blindly, enduring the unendurable?

"There's nothing we can do about it" is the usual and natural response of the families with the disabled children as they are exposed to casual remarks such as "no cure for Agent Orange-induced defects" by a local clinic staff and to a more refined and hence more conclusive diagnosis at higher-level medical establishments such as the District Health Centre or provincial general hospital in Quy Nhon. It is an expression facing a chasm whose depth the families cannot fathom – the possibility, nearing the impossibility, of removing or undoing the health consequences of Agent Orange contamination. There is "no choice" other than living with the disabilities since such medical innovations are too far away from the present and too costly. To the families, even limited efforts to accommodate the needs of disabled children such as special schools for handicapped children do not come into their daily thinking: "Too expensive for us to send our children to". These facilities, or making use of them, are not among the choices available to them.

Do they, then, suspend their life just because they have only these impossible choices – really no choice – for the disabled children? How do they embrace the disabled children before the "problem" is removed? What is their life in the *interim*? But they do have other things they need to tend to. Or is their life really that of the interim?

Over years of research, we have observed that not all behaviours of the farmers align with justifiable reasons. Some of them were clearly out of line with what one may expect, such as having more children after having one, or even two, disabled children. Others, though less dramatic, are not that different as they casually, or so it appears to us, leave their disabled children alone for a period of time while they earn quick cash elsewhere as a menial labourer.

Behaviour deviating from our expectation is also found in farmers without the burden of children with birth defects. A "land millionaire" up on the Nui Ba Mountains never stops acting as if he is just another farmer living barely above the subsistence level. He takes on every bit of the production process all by himself with help from his wife, including the construction of a small reservoir further up the hill. There are no machines, nor a group of hired hands, in sight.

Puzzles

The bewilderment has led to ask ourselves: what if there are valid reasons for all the actions that the farmers have taken? This exercise in interpretation has prompted us to put a spin on the usual recipe for observing the farmers: throw away the notion that only actions that are meant to maximize their intended outcome are rational and bring in a new idea that all, or nearly all, actions are taken for good reasons.

Two thoughts crossed our mind. First, all actions and behaviours only collectively constitute a farmer's life. When captured in that constitution, an action may have sufficient reason to be taken, even though that action appears to be irrational when viewed alone. The other is that the consequence(s), or utility, of an action is usually offered by others in the form of possibility and probability only. The freedom of how to interpret the probability is left solely to the one who reads that probability: X% that an undesirable outcome may occur is (100 – X)% that a desirable outcome may be achieved.

These thoughts helped shift our view of the farmer: he is a decision-maker first and foremost, and *not* a beneficiary of one single action designed and promoted by somebody else. He would not see an action as a path to one goal *independent of* others dispersed around different demands of his life. Therefore, he does not choose a course of action solely for its intended merit or consequence. Facing many demands on, and concerns about, his life, the only reliable source for his action is what he has learned and earned, the tangible and intangible assets. Any suggestion to change, or even implicating a change in, his life would be a threat to these assets. And the threat looms large in his examining eyes, before he acts.[6]

The shifted view towards the farmers led to a third thought or question: how do these farmers recognize the effectiveness of their chosen action? Our observations are informed of this third thought, which is more a hypothesis: the farmers' everyday life is the efficacy test of their action.

These farmers choose actions that are meant only collectively to satisfy the demands of their life. In this demand-action equation, each action is acceptable, or "reasonable" (in bounded rationality parlance),[7] to the farmers as long as they collectively meet the demands of everyday life. A net result is that the farmers are "satisficing"[8] themselves, even if each of the actions falls short of the expectation of its advocate. In real life, the advocates may be many and ubiquitous in the areas of medicine, food production, and education, among others. The farmers' everyday lives that are spared of, or have survived, a major disruption or change is the evidence that their actions are passing that efficacy test.

To some, the farmers' uncanny use of narratives, the above-mentioned "dual self" narratives, or their cryptic ways of tucking the war and Agent Orange away in the remote past are merely acts of escapism. But for us, they are the making, thus the evidence, of the farmers' tenacity in living through the years of constant changes, various adverse developments, and other instances of uncertainty.

There are several themes that run through the body of the text. One is a somewhat revised view towards rational behaviour. Our view that the farmers are the primary decision-makers of their own life places them in a light different from one that casually treats them as simply the beneficiaries of expert knowledge from various sources. The second theme comprises the two broad areas of action from which we develop our observations and interpretations of farmers' behaviour: wealth and health. From a general perspective, these are the two areas where one is inclined to see readily the expected utility of action: for the former, an increase in profit by means of cost-efficient production, and for the latter, health free of sickness and weaknesses by means of a certain regimen and cautious use of certain materials. These are the areas, however, where our farmers deviate from the usual expectations. Between the two areas of wealth and health, our observations tend to lean more towards the latter, because of our initial interest in Vietnam, due to the dire consequences of the wartime use of toxic chemicals on humans. Those on the former, nonetheless, provide important supporting insights.

The third is the attention we paid to the narratives of the farmers. The key medium between us and the farmers is the latter's narratives. They are sometimes prompted by our prodding; sometimes they come out in a form that comprises nothing more than disjointed utterances, sandwiched by long silences. Piecing them together is, in and of itself, an act of our reconstructing their life into a coherent whole.

This attention was born out of our initial suspicion about the frequent use of phrases such as "it's our fate (*so phan*)". The phrase often prefaces their responses to our question of how they took the initial realization of their children's misfortunes. Our understanding of it gradually transformed into something else. The phrase, of course, signals the resignation that there are things beyond their control. But that does not mean that everything else is out of their control. The phrase may well signal the farmers' resolve to face life either because of or in spite of the misfortune that had struck some of them. It often signals their resolve to live a life worth pursuing. Observing the farmers over the past 15 years, we have become especially alert to this gap between what they say and their possible sub-textual message: the latter tells us more about how the farmers live.

Our research at its initial stage from 2004 to 2008, on the human consequences of Agent Orange contamination, needed to be authorized by Hanoi Medical University and the Ministry of Health of Vietnam. They also selected areas for the research, where local District Health Centres and Commune Clinic staff assisted us with their detailed local knowledge about the health conditions of the residents. In the three areas, we initially investigated over 120 families with children with defects induced by Agent Orange. We visited some of these families many times. The three areas were Kim Bang, a semi-rural district within commuting distance of Hanoi; Thanh Khe, an urban district in Da Nang; and Phu Cat, a rural district in central coastal Binh Dinh Province.

Kim Bang has a heavy concentration of former North Vietnamese Regular Army soldiers who fought along the Ho Chi Minh Trail; Thanh Khe is located next to Da Nang Airport, which played a strategically critical role during the war and was also the storage site for Agent Orange and other toxic herbicides. Finally, Phu Cat, a central coastal community, has the strategic Phu Cat Airport and Qui Nhon, a seaport. The last two are the sites of the Vietnam-U.S. joint soil clean-up operations.

The late Dr Trinh Van Bao, of Hanoi Medical University, originally conducted extensive medical research in these areas and asked us to follow up with social research. Of the three focus areas, Phu Cat is away from any major emerging industrial complex, especially since the second half of the 1990s, and thus offers a site where the impact of Agent Orange on human health remains relatively isolated and intact. The landscape of this site – mostly rice paddies, thick bushes surrounding separate groups of small red-brick houses, and a few farmers bending over or swinging hoes over their heads – is a picture-perfect representation of the scene of "peasants by day and Viet Cong by night", as U.S. soldiers put it. This is also the site where Dr Bao left the strongest impression among the local medical staff through his down-to-earth style of contact with Agent Orange-affected families. Therefore, it is no coincidence that we focussed our research on Phu Cat, especially for the later rounds of research and beyond.

We began the second phase of research, which we are still conducting, in Phu Cat in 2010. We have added about 40 families to the original 48, along with scores of primary school teachers and local clinic workers. The second stretch of research has provided an invaluable perspective on the changes – and/or their absence – in the families and the district. It is a perspective that catches the families not at stationary moments but in the moving moments of everyday life over many years. A disabled ten-year-old boy whom we met in 2004 has grown into a 25-year-old man. His father has aged, and so has his mother. Many of the parents of the disabled children are now becoming close to, or are over, 60 years old and are surrounded by grandchildren, if they are fortunate.[9]

During the second phase of research we began to find meaning in what we witnessed in the first phase as we re-evaluated the bases of the farmers' behaviours as well as what they signify. Through the interactive works of the two phases, one reinforces the findings of the other.

Notes

1 Peter L. Berger and Thomas Luckmann, *The Social Construction of Reality: A Treatise in the Sociology of Knowledge*, New York, Penguin Books, 1966, especially pp. 33–42.
2 We use occasionally shortened names or given names only for some of the interviewees and disabled children when we find it necessary to protect their anonymity.
3 The Red Cross Binh Dinh office provided the following figures: 32,372 handicapped people, accounting for 2.12% of the population, with 3,689 aged under 16; 18,389 aged from 16 to 59; and 10,294 aged 60 or above.
4 Berger and Luckmann, *op. cit.*, p. 37.
5 On the operation, and for that matter overall post-war clean-up efforts by the government with and without U.S. cooperation, see Le Ke Son and Charles R. Bailey's *From Enemies to Partners: Vietnam, the U.S. and Agent Orange*, Chicago, IL, G. Anton Publishing, 2017.
6 Here we have Daniel Kahneman's critical view of an expected-utilitarian mode of thinking. See his *Thinking Fast and Slow*, New York, Farrar, Straus and Giroux, 2011. We develop the point here later in Chapter 7. See also a succinct presentation of Kahneman's decision-making analysis by Jack S. Levy, *Annual Meeting Focus: The Decade of Behavior Lecture*, "Daniel Kahneman: Judgement, Decision, and Rationality," https://pdfs.semanticscholar.org/47b0/312fb97a83e3f9bb639f3309e960e5037664.pdf
7 Herbert Simon has been a consistent advocate of the "bounded rationality" notion, as opposed to the more rigid, rationalist framework for evaluating people's behaviour. See Herbert Simon, *Administrative Behavior: A Study of Decision-Making Processes in Administrative Organizations*, New York, Macmillan, 1947 and for a fuller development, "Rational choice and the structure of the environment," *Psychological Review*, Vol. 63, No. 2, 1956, pp. 129–138. Also, Daniel Kahneman, "Maps of bounded rationality: Psychology for behavioral economics," *The American Economic Review*, 2003, Vol. 93, No. 5, pp. 1449–75.

8 Simon, *ibid.*, and "Rational decision making in business organizations," *The American Economic Review*, Vol. 69, No. 4, 1978, pp. 493–513. See also Michael Byron, "Satisficing and optimality," *Ethics*, Vol. 109, October 1998, pp. 67–93.

9 We usually visited the research sites three to four times a year for the first round of research between 2004 and 2008, and twice a year for the second round between 2009 and 2019. The duration of the visit varied from three days to two weeks. For the sake of keeping the text kempt, we minimized the reference to the month and year of our visits to the research sites.

Part I

Rural life in changing Vietnam

1 Transformation of Vietnam and its farmers

The following pages discuss the changing parameters of life for the farmers in Vietnam. The country's transformation has included several phases that have cumulatively reduced the prominence of agriculture in its economy, yet farmers still account for the greatest portion of its population. First, we briefly outline the timeline of developments, providing a survey of key events in Vietnam for the decades before and after 1975, before moving on to discuss the following years more closely.

This section will be followed by a brief discussion of an alternative framework for capturing the change in Vietnamese farmers' behaviour. They were in constant turmoil, regardless of whether they were in the North or the South. One theme that runs throughout this chapter is how the farmers managed their behaviour when acting in one way was often replaced by another without really seeing its consequences. What are they likely to listen to when they are confronted by pressure to deviate from their familiar courses of action?

The final section introduces the "problem" that this book addresses: the farmers' behaviour under pressure to make the right decision.

The purpose of this historical survey is twofold. First, it places Vietnam in a broader context of national and international development. It will stress the point that, since the end of the Second World War, this country has had no significant period of time during which a generation could enjoy life without the turmoil of political, economic, and social upheavals. This reminder serves as a warning that the term "transition" carries a special meaning for the Vietnamese.

Second, the survey will help direct attention to the conditions under which individual farmers and communities face and adapt, within the context of local life, to changes that are traceable primarily at the national or the macro level. It will help clarify the point that the life of farmers in the period with which we are concerned lies in the broad context of the constant changes that collectively constitute Vietnam's post-Second World War development.

Since 1986, Vietnam has transitioned from a centrally planned economy to a market-based one. This transitional phase began ten years after the unification of North and South Vietnam, and was preceded by a period in which a planned economy prevailed, following the conclusion of the war of unification in 1975. Under the communist regime, the newly unified Socialist Republic of

Vietnam embarked upon the difficult task of installing a production system in which control was centralized in order to reach all levels and phases of production throughout society. This period of planned economy came to an end ten years later as a result of the introduction of the *Doi Moi* reforms. *Doi Moi* was a new radical economic reform, a version of a similar, if less dramatic, course of development followed by the neighbouring Lao People's Democratic Republic (PDR). Both countries have remained under socialist rule – i.e., a system where communists monopolize power – and yet are undergoing a subtle but profound internal transformation.

The beginning of this transition coincided with another: that of the Eurasian giant, i.e., the Soviet Union under Gorbachev. The end of socialist rule here prompted the rest of the world to lump together all the cases of socialist transformation into one unified theme: the end of divisive competitions among the modern forms of rule. Francis Fukuyama's *The End of History?* (1989) reinforced and expanded its implications beyond the North Atlantic region with the assertion that the post-French Revolution contest between the liberal-capitalist and authoritarian-socialist systems had ended with the decisive victory of the former.[1]

What is lost in this euphoria especially in the West is that Vietnam, and Lao PDR, had a very limited period that could justifiably be called a socialist era: between 1954 and 1986 for the northern half of Vietnam, and between 1976 and 1986 for the whole country. Moreover, most of these decades included years of war in the backyards of most Vietnamese people. If we add the uncertain years between the conclusion of the Pacific War and the siege of Dien Bien Phu, Vietnam fought a 30-year war. Nonetheless, the attention of development specialists has often been fixed almost exclusively on what may *await* Vietnam at the other end of its transition, leading them to design nearly all policies from that fixed perspective.

What is often lost in the 30-year war perspective is the attention to its impact on the country's population: Vietnam, throughout the post-Second World War era, faced waves of war and constant exposure to various forms of external and armed interventions, and thus there was only a limited window in which socialism could take root. Very little room has been left for questioning what lay in the beginning of the transition and *its* influence on the population, which has been under pressure due to constant changes. "The beginning" may not be the socialist mode of production for the Vietnamese; it may well be the changes themselves that never seemed to stop.

The attention given to farmers is even more lopsided: the bulk of the burden of the transition usually falls to them. As will be discussed later, nonetheless, farmers are viewed almost exclusively in terms of their ability and willingness to respond to the promises at the far end of the transition, and to incentives to increase their productivity. This raises a fundamental issue that will be discussed in this book: the lure, or absence, of an obvious gain in wealth and in other areas of concerns essential to life.

Since the end of the Second World War, Vietnamese farmers have been exposed to pleas as well as the social and economic pressure accompanying the war for independence, socialist justice (the North after 1954), liberal democracy (the South after Diem's Republic), and unification, and, later, were pressured further for efficient agricultural production. In other words, changing Vietnam meant for the majority of Vietnamese constant confrontations with alternative courses of action from which everyone had to choose. The farmers were forced to consider not only what they might gain but also what they might lose as a result of choosing one course of action over another. How does a farmer formulate the basis of his choice when he receives constantly shifting pleas and pressures, of which the increase in productivity may be but one?

The official shift towards a market economy, facilitated by the *Doi Moi* reforms, has merely complicated the basis for calculating the correct choice, opening up even more opportunities for decisions to be made: the farmers have been given more freedom to decide what and how to gain from their newly acquired rights to use the land, and a much wider margin of autonomy and responsibility has been given to individual farmers as they were released from the cooperative mode of production in determining what might secure their well-being.

Incentives for higher productivity now need to be carefully balanced with other concerns. One particularly important concern is health as opening agriculture to a market economy also means pressure for higher productivity *and* freer use of agricultural inputs, including herbicides and other agrochemicals, which can pose elevated risks to the health of those using them. However, healthy farmers may find it difficult to identify and prevent health risks because one tends to value health only in its absence.

How do the farmers survive these shifts in the "national" goals and the corresponding changes in the basic characteristics of rural life? One very basic proposition in this work is that incentives for higher productivity alone, or for health security alone, do not interest the farmers. There are things the farmers do that *collectively* help them navigate their life during the transition. Calculation of the utility of one action in one area of concern, in isolation from the rest, borders on a mere abstract mental exercise.

Attention to the local context is especially important for the following reason. Changes, by definition, mean departure or deviation from the past. Therefore, they are also disruptions of life that present a degree of uncertainty for an individual or community. Thus, a decision by individuals or communities to go along with, or be part of, changes designed elsewhere is *not* solely a result of what the changes promise to bring about. It is also a result of balancing the cost of deviating from past, familiar courses of action on the part of the farmers.

In short, the survey is intended to illuminate the conditions of life in the middle of transition, during which time the farmers may be conscious of both the costs and the benefits of deviating from familiar behaviour: the conditions that subtly and persistently influence the behaviour of the largest portion of the population – farmers – in their daily encounters with promises of a better life on *the other* end of the transition – promises, as presented, elaborated, and articulated by "professionals", of higher productivity, of a healthy life, of commercial activity, and of a society engaged in globalization.

War and society

In the mid-1950s, Geneva played a crucial role in shaping the course of development in Indochina, thousands of miles away. At the Geneva Conference (April 26–July 20, 1954), the major powers, including the United States and the Soviet Union, worked out a political framework in which the indigenous actors were expected to overcome their differences and establish stable nation-states in the region.[2]

The appearance of the ensuing non-interference was nothing more than a facade. The following decades witnessed the unfolding of internal wars typical of the Cold War era: the local warring parties were openly and/or illicitly supported by the United States, the Soviet Union, and the People's Republic of China, unwittingly earning themselves the name of "proxies". Indochina became a theatre where the actors' movements and conversations strictly conformed to the expectations of the Cold War audience.

In this unfolding drama, the year 1975 represented a clear turning point. It marked the beginning of socialist rule throughout Vietnam in the eyes of an audience who was much too accustomed to the Cold War purview. Ironically, the spotlight had shifted since the 1972–1973 Paris Peace Talks between the United States and North Vietnam (and the Provisional Revolutionary Government of the South). The Talks confirmed that the de-Americanization of the war was irreversible, leaving the unmistakable impression that the Vietnam War began fading away from the Cold War's main stage. The developments towards unification appeared almost a foregone conclusion.

A consequence of this anti-climactic (in the eyes of many of those who were outside Vietnam) turn of the war was, perhaps, an ungrounded relief: Indochina was finally free from foreign intrusion. Washed away with the relief was the question of how wartime exigencies had influenced, and still continue to influence, the relationship between the top echelons of the government in the capital and people at the local level.

In the following, we briefly examine the relationship between war and society during the period when the internal divisions in the region conveniently coincided with the international, Cold War, divisions. It is a necessary step towards understanding how ordinary people shaped the foundations for their behaviour on their own terms when the divisions ended.

1954 Geneva Accord and the aftermath

In the summer of 1954, decisions made by the major powers in Geneva effectively expelled France from Indochina and granted independence to Vietnam, Laos, and Cambodia.[3] The decisions concerning Vietnam, however, were an odd reflection of the local political conditions – such as Viet Minh's decisive victory over the French army in Dien Bien Phu only a few months earlier – and the power politics of the time. Vietnam was granted independence but was divided into the North and the South along the 17th Parallel (DMZ); its unification would be achieved during the general election held two years later in 1956 as a means of "peaceful" unification. At this time 300 days were assured for those who wished to move and settle on either side of the parallel.

The prospect of a "peaceful" unification evaporated in 1955 as the United States installed Ngo Dinh Diem, a Catholic and anti-French nationalist, in Saigon as caretaker for the interim two years. Diem wasted no time hardening his grip on his reign. His efforts to win the support of tenant and small farmers by redistributing lands produced only negligible results.[4] At the same time, Diem stopped short of nothing when it came to uprooting nearly all anti-Diem elements in the South. Frontal attacks on the private armies of the sects Cao Dai and Hoa Hao were just the beginning of a systematic elimination of anyone suspected of being remotely unsympathetic to the Saigon regime.

Facing the ruthless Diem, the remainder of the Viet Minh and their sympathizers in the South needed to regroup while building with utmost caution their rural bases of resistance. Their efforts eventually culminated in the formation of the National Liberation Front (NLF) in 1961, with the blessing of Hanoi. This became the only lever for turning political events against the Diem regime in the South. An amalgamation of urban intellectuals with nationalist leanings, pro-North socialists, tenant farmers, owners of small- to medium-sized land, and the like, the NLF was hardly a unified front, and it lacked the resources needed to confront Diem's overwhelming power; it could barely contain the divisive and premature moves towards the armed uprisings sent to challenge it.

With a quickly diminishing prospect of peaceful unification, the anti-Diem forces in the South represented a special kind of difficulty for the North. No action could mean Diem had achieved increasingly firmer footing. The direct support of the North towards armed action could betray the North's own, albeit remote, hope for peaceful unification. Direct support might also deprive the North of the precious time and resources needed for its efforts to consolidate its rule internally and could offer a timely opportunity for the United States to increase its support for Diem. Thus, one of the key leaders in the North, Le Duan (General Secretary, Labour Party, 1960–1976 and Communist Party, 1976–1986), a native of Quang Tri, just south of the 17th Parallel, with a brilliant record of anti-colonial movement, is reported to have argued that the choice for the North had to be based primarily on the consolidation of its socialist rule first.[5] The least the North could do was help forge the anti-Diem forces in the South into a coherent organization, the NLF, and then keep it under tight control.

The North needed to deal with the delicate situation in the South, though its hands were already full with the urgent need to install and secure economic foundations for the new socialist state. The land reform, i.e., the redistribution of farmland among tenant farmers, was a crucial policy choice. Confiscation of land from landowners and its reallocation were the most that the North could do without risking external intervention. They drastically decreased large landholdings and increased the smaller ones. However, these changes disrupted rural order as overzealous party cadres often pushed the ruling Party to neglect the household-based production practices customarily followed among the farmers in the North.[6]

Farmers had to stop being farmers. At the outset, the land reform was no more than a reorganization of rural order into a network of mutual-help organizations (*to doi cong*) and "lower-level cooperatives" (*Hop Tac Xa Bac Thap*). As a result, productivity increased. These early attempts at socialist intervention in production still honoured the families as the basic units of agricultural production. The shift towards "higher-level cooperatives" (*Hop Tac Xa Bac Cao*) in the late 1950s changed all this. Farmers were reorganized into production brigades (*Doi san xuat*) of 40–100 members.[7] They were evaluated by the number of hours they spent within a set of well-defined parts of the agricultural production line; they were given "points" in return for those hours, which could be used to procure daily commodities. The products of their labour went to the government's purse.

The farmers remained farmers only in the small fraction of communal land in which they were allowed to grow produce as they saw fit and which they used to complement the material basis of their livelihood. Ironically, the production performance of these small communal lands exhibited the farmers' inherent capacity for production. However, this could not alleviate the overall productivity decline seen throughout the early years of the 1960s.

Still, the North pushed for the expansion of *Hop Tac Xa Bac Cao* above the 17th Parallel, undoubtedly motivated by the need to install a socialist mode of production and rule to replace the old one. However, long before a conclusive evaluation of *Hop Tac Xa Bac Cao* could be made, new factors began affecting the applicability of the collective mode of production to the country's faltering productivity: the worsening of the conflict within the South and the Americanization of the war after 1965. The war turned the cooperatives into a device with which to mobilize Vietnamese youth in the North for the war effort.

In the farmers' minds, an important distinction, between agricultural production as a practice of socialist rule and agricultural production as an integral part of the war effort, began to fade. In the North, an estimated 1,000,000 regular soldiers and militia accounted for nearly 20% of the entire adult population, and they were ubiquitous evidence of the war waged south of the 17th Parallel, along the Ho Chi Minh Trail, and even north of the 17th Parallel after the U.S. bombing of the North began in 1964. Any inefficiency in the production efforts had the potential to bring the war that much closer to home. Telling evidence of the widespread sense of crisis was the strong belief in the production for the sake of war overshadowing another that *Hop Tap Xa Bac Cao* was the socialist method of production.

Throughout the post-Geneva Conference period, Hanoi needed to sustain these domestic reforms and war efforts when foreign support was, at best, problematic. The Soviet Union was going through a period of "peaceful coexistence" with the United States, which the Cuban Missile Crisis of 1962 reinforced. This socialist giant's support, though substantial at times, was carefully tailored so as not to invite the United States' countering moves in the South. China was the party that had acquiesced to the division of Vietnam at the Geneva Conference in the first place. It was preoccupied with the need to prevent a strong unified Vietnam from rising in the South and/or keep the North under tight control.[8] Chinese support of the North's efforts to unify Vietnam was much less forthcoming than their ideological proximity would have suggested.[9] In fact, China, welcoming stability on their southern front, was particularly critical of any "adventurist" move – such as an armed unification – by the North or the NLF in the South based on fear of the United States' large-scale involvement in Indochina. China's overly patronizing posture, often exhibited in their warnings for cautious action, remained a sore point between the two socialist neighbours.[10]

The fall of Diem in 1963, the result of his own heavy-handed rule, paved the way towards the beginning of the Americanization of the war within two years. The pressure for more production mounted in the North now that the U.S. forces were deeply intertwined with the operations of the Army of the Republic of Vietnam (ARVN) all the way up to the 17th Parallel and along the Vietnamese side of the Ho Chi Minh Trail. Absorbing the costly Tet uprisings in 1968, which depleted much of the NLF's strength, the conflict became a sort of war of attrition – the North's durability in sustaining the war efforts in the South was severely tested by the highly mechanized and mobile U.S. fighting forces. The bombing of the North by the United States nearly convinced it to negotiate a suspending of its Ho Chi Minh Trail-based support for the NLF.

However, political events far outside of Indochina paved the way for the end of the war. Following the 1968 Tet uprisings, the anti-war movement began to gain momentum in the United States. The increasing intensity of this movement, fuelled by the nightly media coverage of the battles fought, mounting casualties, and the war expenditure incurred by the United States, kept President Johnson from seeking a second term and encouraged his replacement, Richard Nixon to search for a way out of a war that was clearly acceptable to the United States; this effort included the eventual détente with China in 1972. China's hands-off stance allowed the United States to negotiate with the North (and the representatives of the Provisional Revolutionary Government of the South) for the terms of the Vietnamization of the war.

Though 1975 saw the end of the division of Vietnam, it hardly saw the end of anything else for the nation's people. The full-scale Cambodian campaign began late in 1978, following the series of skirmishes with the Khmer Rouge since 1975, and was just an extension of the previous war efforts in a new theatre.[11] From a broader perspective, the campaign was a result of increasing tensions between the two neighbours, where the unification of one (Vietnam) resurrected the suspicion of its regional hegemony in the other (Cambodia). From the unified Vietnam's perspective, the territorial disputes and protection of the ethnic Vietnamese, both of which led to limited exchanges of fire soon after unification, were merely the manifestation of a much deeper concern: the rise of Pol Pot, who exhibited an almost uncritical loyalty to China.

The campaign, which suggested a prolonged engagement from the beginning, deprived the unified Vietnam of the precious manpower and resources needed to reconstruct a war-torn society. The campaign did not win the unified Vietnam international acceptance either. On the contrary, it awakened the dormant tensions between Vietnam and its northern neighbour, China. A self-claimed patron of Vietnam and other socialist countries in Indochina, China sent the People's Army across its border to Vietnam late in 1979. Their purpose, as Deng Shao Pin bluntly put it, was to "teach a lesson" as Vietnam was threatening Democratic Kampuchea, the only unwavering China loyalist in Southeast Asia.

As far as Vietnam was concerned, the border war, so close to its capital, was a reminder that the unification within still fell far short of securing it from internal and external threats. Coupled with the U.S.-led sanctions, launched partly as a penalty against Vietnam's Cambodian campaign, Vietnam's regional entanglements continued to exhaust its resources. All indications were that the country, having withstood the United States' and China's interventions, was not in a position to pursue the steps needed for it to recover from the 30-year war of independence and unification, establishment of socialist rule, and navigation of a less-than-friendly international environment. The need to make compromise crisscrossed nearly all policy goals.

State and society

For both North and South Vietnam, the years following the 1954 Geneva Accords were years when resources and energy were exhausted first and foremost to keep the temporary political framework of a divided country from collapsing. In the North, the socialist state of the Democratic Republic of Vietnam was an odd presence. In its international relations, the state presented itself strongly as the war continued. It began to receive the recognition of nations beyond the group of socialist countries. Internally, however, its ability to extract resources and regulate social relations hinged on the extent to which the populace as a whole agreed that their failure to meet the demands of the war might bring about a collapse of society. The North may have had the look of a society that had been under martial law since late in the 1950s, except that the usual state-society relationship was turned upside down in its case. To borrow Joel Migdal's words, the Democratic Republic of Vietnam was the case of a "weak state".[12]

In the South before 1975, the state, the Republic of Vietnam, had been virtually non-existent, especially after the final years of Ngo Dinh Diem. The United States increased its presence in the government of the South as the total number of military advisors skyrocketed from approximately 1,500 to 35,000; their intervention reached as far as the rural South through what is known as the Strategic Hamlet Program. This involved relocating farmers from their fields and villages and keeping them in artificial compounds during the night, and was supposedly designed to prevent NLF members and their sympathizers from submerging themselves in the masses of the rural population. Instead, the programme planted seeds of discontent among the rural Vietnamese in the South and was abandoned within a few years.

Compliance of the villagers was not evidence of their loyalty to the government in Saigon, but it could be attributed to a threat of violence by the U.S.-backed

ARVN. The fall of Ngo Dinh Diem in 1963 and the ensuing shuffling and reshuffling of the military governments stripped the state of its inherent ability to govern.

The unification brought together two entirely different societies with two different wartime experiences. The establishment of the Socialist Republic of Vietnam was announced in 1976. The removal of the supporters of the old regime in the cities and in the rural South alone, however, did not make the entire society more responsive to the new state. The establishment of the socialist state across all of Vietnam was only the beginning of another round of uncertainties.

There were very few surprises in what the leaders of the new state launched in the South, while the population in the North remained on high alert due to the continuing military campaign in Democratic Kampuchea and the looming threat of China. The ruling Party leaders needed to install an entirely new administrative apparatus in the South, even though the party cadres in it were unfamiliar with civilian administration.[13] Attempts to establish a socialist rule were made as the normative and practical foundation of the unification.

The new leadership, formally installed at the Fourth Party Congress in 1976, tried to reach both urban and rural societies, especially in the South, with the vigorous and often ruthless "re-education" of the supporters of the fallen regime, on the one hand, and a new round of land reforms, on the other, over the course of just a few years.

In addition to the reorientation of the old-regime sympathizers, among the southern cities, Saigon in particular needed to be downsized. Nearly ten years of war in the rural South, where battles of both small and large scale had taken place, had pushed many farmers to seek refuge in the city, turning it into an oversized metropolis. One of the mechanisms through which to enforce both the reorientation of and a reduction of the size of cities was the creation of new economic zones (NEZs).[14] The North had briefly experimented with these when expanding its frontier in the early 1960s. In the South, after 1976, NEZs relocated the urban population to rural areas in the country, filled with war-ravaged fields requiring cultivation, and to remote areas in order to reclaim the land for farming. These efforts, characterized as "Pasturelanding of the South",[15] were met with a certain cynicism in the South, where the anti-North sentiment may have been as strong as, if not stronger than, the anti-communist sentiment, especially among the small shop owners and urban intellectuals in the cities.

These initial efforts are reminiscent of the early 1960s, when the North was caught between the pressures, on the one hand, of preparing for and surviving the precarious division of the nation and those, on the other hand, of establishing socialist rule on a firmer ground. As in the North in its earlier years, the pressure to secure the unified Vietnam was felt across partisan lines among the Vietnamese. A large number of Vietnamese soldiers in Cambodia, and those in the South on garrison duty, deprived the new state of human and material resources just when it needed them most in their efforts to unify and reconstruct the war-torn society. The unstable northern border with China was an additional drain on resources as it occupied a large number of soldiers, who had to be on constant alert.

The burden of meeting the multifaceted task of establishing the socialist rule and protecting its economic foundation from collapsing, again, similar to that in the North in the late 1950s and early 1960s, fell on the agricultural sector. Even with no competing regime in the South, the new leadership first cautiously advanced the collectivization of agriculture in the South by promoting no more than the push for mutual aid among farming households. One reason for this was that the rural South had been the basis for the anti-Diem forces. NLF members, among others, had won the rural support partly because they helped push the redistribution of farmland among tenant farmers and landholders who held small portions of land. The complete elimination of private landownership would have been a severe affront to this recent working relationship between the Party and the farmers.

However, the new leaders quickened the pace of placing the rural South under socialist rule. Collectivization of agriculture was pushed on a larger scale within a few years of the unification. In 1978, together with naturalization of private assets among shop owners in cities, a higher level of collectivization, *Hop Tac Xa Bac Cao*, was enforced on the rural South. Farming households ceased to be the principal production units and were reorganized into production and other brigades of specialized functions in agricultural production.

Evidence indicates that collectivization transitioned smoothly as the number of high-level agricultural cooperatives (*Hop Tac Xa Bac Cao*) increased quickly.[16] However, as early as 1981, the Fifth Party Congress recognized what may have transpired behind the collectivization efforts. Despite the brief increase in agricultural production from 1977 to 1979, the performance of agricultural production stalled and began to decline later on. Weather and other natural calamities may have accounted for this, at least partially. However, the concern of leadership shown in such expressions as "hasty collectivization" signalled that there was something more fundamental: southern farmers' reluctance to observe the norm of the socialist mode of production.[17] The farmers in the South countered the pressure to build *Hop Tac Xa Bac Cao* by abandoning their land and selling their farming tools and water buffaloes. In other words, some of them resisted collectivization (reorganization into functional brigades) by refusing to be "farmers" in name only.

The North, freed from the demands of sustained war efforts, also began to show a decline in agricultural productivity. Increase in the number of production brigades (3,182 in 1977 to 18,041 in 1979) notwithstanding, the farmers began to produce less and less after a brief surge in production. Facing this critical test of the state's authority, the new leaders had no choice but to retreat from the socialist method of agricultural production. In 1981, the Party issued a directive, known as Directive 100, which allowed farming households to remain with, or return to, a somewhat more familiar mode of farming activities – the household as the principal unit of production. The farmers were "contracted" (*khoan*), or assigned, by the state to take care of the entire agricultural production in the allotted land. They were required to provide a certain amount of produce for the state, while leaving the responsibility of procuring agricultural inputs to the *Hop Tac Xa*. Production went up. A brief decline a few years later was taken as a sign that the restoration of households as the principal production unit was incomplete, *not* a sign of the failure of the "contract" farming system.

Doi Moi, literally the renovation, is often believed to be a feat by the leaders of socialist Vietnam as it departed from the socialist mode of production. As shown later, however, it is an extension of the far more interactive processes between the leadership and the population, farmers in particular, where the latter played a weighty role in testing the socialist method of production.

Telling evidence of the farmers' way of navigating the difficult decade following the unification underlies Decision 10 of the Party's politburo in 1988. Through this, farmers regained nearly all responsibilities for production, including the ownership of farming tools and other means of production, plus land-use rights. *Hop Tac Xa*-owned agricultural tools and machinery were often sold to individual farmers. Even the land-use rights were distributed among farming households through competitive bidding or by contract for a period of 10–15 years.[18]

The ensuing land reforms in 1993, 1998, 2001, and 2003 were, in effect, adjustments to the changes in the early 1980s. Although the leaders were compelled to justify this clearly non-socialist ideal of land use, they merely needed to acknowledge the widespread production practices that the farmers were returning to, including those in the North freed from the pressures of war efforts. The practices now clearly reflected the familiar notion that the farming households, not the production brigades or *Hop Tac Xa Bac Cao*, *were* the principal actors of production. The rights to use, exchange, concede, rent out, inherit, and even mortgage farmland were widely and increasingly acknowledged, and received official sanction. The land even emerged as a "market" commodity.

Doi Moi, implemented in 1986, a decade after the unification, is often heralded as Vietnam's move towards a market economy, indicating that it had finally overcome the post-unification confusion and reconstruction. The state, the source of governing authority, at last achieved a degree of legitimacy that the leadership could rely on in implementing policies that deviated from their own political agenda – socialist rule and governance. It is closer to the truth of the matter that the state served more as an agent of adjustments and, in this, sanctioned the manner of the ordinary farmers' efforts to survive the unpredictably winding path. *Doi Moi* is a national adjustment to the local responses along a twisting path towards independence, unification, and reconstruction.

Farmers in "changing" Vietnam

How did this winding path appear to those who were actually treading it? The path was an immensely difficult and costly one, to say the least. As we witnessed in Phu Cat District, Binh Dinh Province, in central coastal Vietnam, it is not rare for parents and children or siblings to have lived separately for over 30 years.

Two brothers might have both participated in the liberation war against the French army as members of Viet Minh, then taken separate paths at the division of the country in 1955 (the younger of the two may have decided to stay in the South, while the older one moved to the North) and reunited only later in the 1980s, or even later, in the unified Vietnam. Such actions were not responses to a singular incentive, such as support for socialist justice. Instead, the brothers examined the merits of one choice – say, joining Viet Minh or staying in the North – against other costs – such as damage to familial integrity, loss of a kin, or even survival.

An obvious and concrete indicator of difficulty is the number of reported war casualties. There seems to be no definite information on the casualties among the Vietnamese and much less on other collateral damages. One Internet source shows that there were four million civilian casualties on "both sides", i.e., the United States and Vietnam.[19] The civilian casualties may not have exceeded a few hundred among the Americans residing in some cities south of the DMZ. That would mean that Vietnam's civilian casualties, including those in North Vietnam at the time of the U.S. bombing after 1965, account for most of that four million, reaching nearly 10% of the entire population. It is not that difficult to imagine that until very recently the path was littered with the ubiquitous and unmistakable signs of war, which are now stored in the minds of many Vietnamese.

The winding path is an especially difficult one to tread on when captured at the ground level, as many farmers did in their villages. It was a series of quick turns of events, constantly confronting the Vietnamese with several alternative courses of action from which to choose. At each turn, many ordinary Vietnamese citizens, especially farmers and small shop owners, would have to speculate on what might await them: whether to stay in the South or the North in and around the years following the Geneva Conference, whether to support the war efforts for a socialist cause or for survival, whether or not to support the NLF at the risk of severe punishment by the ARVN or the U.S. Army, whether to abide by the socialist method of production or by the familiar family-based method when pressured to produce more, or whether to support or refuse the socialist rule following the unification.

The farmers' behaviour more than mirrors the winding path. The constant and quick turn of events meant constant betrayal of their own expectations, either for better or for worse. All these years of war, unification, and reconstruction severely challenged the farmers' ability to endure the unexpected. One of the most popular words, *so phan* (fate), may have been employed, if not originated, in these difficult years as their own explanation of the events over which they had very little control. In the years when uncertainty figured prominently into their contemplation of any action, farmers may have simply acquiesced to the orders and directives coming from above, be they from the ARVN's officers, an NLF officer spearheading the infiltration in the rural South, or party cadres in the North. Such acquiescence was still a choice: a choice to buy time to see how the turn of events might work out to their advantage.

At the root of their behaviour, there was a realistic resignation that many of the promises of a better life remained promises and that the quick turn of events simply did not provide a long enough time for any to come to fruition. What was left for the farmers was their own way of reducing the vulnerability of their life to an unpredictable turn of events. Such is the basic predisposition towards action, shared by the farmers, that this book draws attention to.

More specifically, in the eyes of the farmers, the winding path usually took the form of changes in their relationship with the very foundation of their life – the land and means of generating gains from the land.

The picture of changes in the farmer-land relationship in the South was considerably more complex than it was in the North. Under Diem's rule, half-hearted efforts were made to redistribute the land among the tenant farmers and landholders who held small portions of land. The farmers in the South were, in due course, also exposed to the overtures of the NLF for further land redistribution in return for their support. The heightening war with the United States made it virtually impossible for them to remain disengaged from the battles, especially since the U.S.-backed South adopted "search and destroy" as the principal strategy for containing the NLF forces and the infiltration of the North's Regular Army. The strategy, with its reliance on the ubiquitous U.S. bases throughout the South, and the United States' air mobility, with its immense number of helicopters of various sizes for launching airborne attacks on spotted enemies, turned the rural South into a virtually permanent battleground. Farming seemed like a leisure activity, taking advantage of the unpredictable respite during the "search-and-destroy" operations. Yet it is an activity that the farmers maintained almost unremittingly. It was a sight to behold for many U.S. soldiers who were on their way to and from the ambush sites as often depicted in many autobiographical novels, such as Philip Caputo's *A Rumor of War* or John M. Del Vecchio's *The 13th Valley.*

Unification of Vietnam for the pro-NLF southern farmers did not necessarily mean the multiplication of awards for their support of the NLF. In fact, as the collectivization of agriculture was pushed further following the Fourth Party Congress, even the lands that some of the farmers had acquired were targeted for redistribution.

The changes in the farmer-land relationship may be explained in the following schematic framework. A farmer in the North, most likely a tenant farmer initially, who was given a break – access to farmland – when the Democratic Republic of Vietnam was in power in 1955, would soon learn that his family had been deprived of the right to farm in their newly acquired land just as they had been in the past; the family would then find themselves engaging in the division of agricultural labour, as managed by the officials of the newly established agricultural cooperatives, *Hop Tac Xa*, in 1959 and thereafter; they would then find solace in producing whatever they saw fit only in small sections of land or "household plots", which accounted for around 5% of the land[20] given by the cooperatives and were used to supplement their household economy.

The same farmer may have also learned that in some other communities, the families as production units, a serious deviation from the socialist mode of production, were tolerated by the local party leaders and cadres as sustaining a high level of production was deemed indispensable for the war efforts.

Unification of the nation meant for him freedom from the pressure of production for war purposes. He might not only continue to perform the role given in the division of agricultural labour but also continue to make use of, though not so openly, a small fraction of land allotted for the family to produce extra products as a way of ensuring some supplemental income. This practice began to expand even in the North.

A farmer in the South, by contrast, who had to acquiesce to the virtually unchanged land-farmer relationship, even after the French left Vietnam, would agree, in some cases, to relocate his family's home away from the field under the "strategic hamlet" programme when the war accelerated and decide to risk supporting the NLF's anti-government activities in return for assurance that the land he and his family cultivated was theirs and/or that they could stay put. Following the unification, he would find his land taken away from his family again under, this time, the collectivization programme of the newly established Socialist Republic of Vietnam, which was poised to establish socialist rule and its method of agricultural production. While losing the ownership of a small landholding, he might also learn that family-led farming remained widely practised among his neighbours; thus, he himself would engage in the production of whatever products fit the need to support his family. Nevertheless, under the new socialist rule, he would routinely allocate the bulk of work hours to fulfilling his obligations as a member of the production brigade.

In 1981, Directive 100 released the farmers in the North and the South from the pressure of having to conform to the rules of collective farming. It placed the unwritten custom of family-based production into an officially sanctioned framework. The farmers were *primarily* contracted to produce and contribute a portion of their produce to the state, while a degree of freedom was ensured to help them engage in production that would supplement the family's economy.

For these farmers, a series of land reforms, starting with Decision 10 in 1988, preserved the principal tenet of socialism: the land belonged to the state. However, they were now relieved of most of the duties prescribed by the socialist mode of production in the form of *Hop Tac Xa*. *Hop Tac Xa*'s role, from their perspective, appeared to be complementary, or even secondary, to the family-led agricultural production as it was reduced to a cooperative management of irrigation, plant protection, agricultural tools, and the like.

What is striking about the Vietnamese farmer-land relationship is that for the farmers in the North, in the South, or in unified Vietnam, no single type of relationship had lasted long enough for it to take root in their farmers' life since at least 1955. In light of this, it may be reasonable to suppose that the farmers might not have readily been persuaded to go along with any given type of land relationship sanctioned by higher authorities. Diem's officials, the American promoters of the "strategic hamlet" programmes, and the party cadres in the North offered various reasons for the farmers to abide by their choices of actions. The farmers' response, however, was fully informed by hard evidence: the path they took, as manifest in the land relationship, might not be sufficiently long-lasting to reach its terminus, or its direction could easily be replaced by another. The farmers responded to the merits and costs of a promoted course of action in their own way and not in ways that the promoters saw them.

The problem: farmers' perception of risks

We now look at Vietnamese farmers in light of these parametric changes in life and offer alternative explanations for how they have come to behave. At the core of their behavioural basis is their perception of risks, or uncertainties, of various kinds, which have inspired them to take or not take certain actions. Equally important is the sense of *efficacy* of their own action, without which no one is in a position to perform an action even if the utility of the action may have been guaranteed, promoted, and pushed by somebody else in a position of authority. A constantly changing living environment does not offer hard and empirical evidence that any action one takes will lead to expected consequences. A result may make perfect sense in that, instead of the action's expected effect, one is likely to respond to the cost of the steps taken towards it. It is a reaction that gives a real-life example of Kahneman's loss aversion, a reaction based on the estimated loss of what one already possesses.[21]

A resulting lack of receptivity on the part of the farmers to what appears to be a reasonable, or even obvious, incentive for action – be it socialist justice, an efficient use of division of labour in agricultural production, or the use of fertilizers for higher productivity and the like – underscores the frustration of those who promote the goals of the farmers.

This lack of receptivity is often a source of frustration, or even ridicule, for development specialists towards farmers not only in Vietnam but also more broadly in developing societies. International organizations such as the World Bank often make a plea for the improvement of the performance of the agricultural sector as key to promoting the country's economic development.[22] When the plea falls on the farmers' deaf ears, or so it appears, the frustration transforms itself into a sweeping characterization of farmers as irrational, ignorant, or even "idiotic".[23] Medical and health specialists offer a similar but more sub-textual message when they often repeat that farmers need to be "educated".

Before considering Vietnamese farmers as captured in the economic development context, we should consider the context provided by two leading studies: James Scott's *Moral Economy* and Samuel Popkin's *Rational Peasants.*[24] Both of these tap into colonial Vietnamese villages for their imaginative observations on the farmers' behaviour. Setting aside the relevance of the colonial period for the present-day Vietnamese farmers, the studies also draw attention to the basis of farmers' behaviour under the strain of confronting alternative courses of action: rebellion against authorities, acquiescence to the settings, or seizure of opportunities for communal and/or personal gains.

They differ from each other in one aspect. In Scott's villages, the farmers (peasants) are found to be bound by a common factor, the right to subsistence that survived the test of time. For Scott's farmers, the ultimate value of life lies in protecting that right and, when it is tested, the reciprocal efforts to mitigate the problem or survive the test. The downside to Scott's conceptualization of the farmers (peasants) is that the threat to subsistence may be neither persistent nor constant, raising the question of how the farmers behave when they are not confronted with a threat to their subsistence. Scott's portrayal of the "communal" behaviour of the farmers may be derived from too unusual a situation. The reconstruction of a "moral community" through observation of the colonial Vietnamese villages, especially in the 1930s, may be an instance of what Polly Hill calls the "misuse of averages".[25]

Popkin, on the other hand, focusses on the margin of freedom by which the farmers may place their self-interest ahead of communal insurance against the threat to subsistence. As he puts it, "there are still many occasions when peasants do have some surplus and do make risky investments".[26] However, what remains unexplained in Popkin's farmers' behaviour is how they develop a sense of what may constitute *risky* investment in action. Furthermore, he also fails to recognize that, risky or not, the investments may be distributed among many types of personal gains. Farmers may be concerned at times with their own welfare and at other times with their rapport with the larger community of which they are a part. Why shouldn't the farmers, especially when given "some surplus", be making a little compromise, even to their communal obligations? Here, Popkin's shortcomings echo those of a development economist.

A closer look from development economists and planners reveals that farmers in developing societies are at fault in one area. The following observation by the development economist Theodore Schultz may represent the dominant thinking of the majority of agricultural development specialists in their preoccupation with how to increase agricultural productivity *and* fault farmers for not realizing its merits.

> The man who farms as his forefathers did cannot produce much food no matter how rich the land or how hard he works. The farmer who has access to and knows how to use what science knows about soils, plants, animals, and machines can produce an abundance of food though the land be poor. Nor need he work nearly so hard and long. *He can produce so much that his brothers and some of his neighbors will move to town to earn their living. Enough farm products can be produced without them.*[27] (Italics added)

A more straightforward plea to make use of the agricultural sector's potential (including abundant labour) for economic development may be found in Arthur Lewis's study[28] and those that have followed.[29] Known as the dual-economy model of development, Lewis's argument draws attention to the "surplus labour" – that is, a pool of cheap labour – that can be released from the agricultural sector by raising its productivity. The industrial sector is thus assured of a labour supply without the pressure of rising cost, and the food supply is ensured so as not to allocate precious foreign reserves for its import.[30] Lewis is a little more direct than Schultz in suggesting what may be preventing the farmers from realizing their contribution to economic development. He sees the catalyst for raising agricultural productivity in a group of men "who [can] think in terms of investing capital productively".[31] In other words, the majority of the farmers are held to be irresponsive to the rational course of action taken in a dual-economy model. How such investment-minded men can be raised is not part of Lewis's concern.[32]

Provided that Schultz's concern was with "the production behavior of farmers"[33] and Lewis's idea of efficient capital investment, would it still not be more sensible to take into account the fact that the farmers are not singularly consumed by the question of how to increase their financial gains? Equally important for the farmers may be the price that the change in their behaviour, a deviation from past practices, may demand of them. Having their relatives and neighbours move to cities may not only incur costs but also give rise to a high degree of uncertainty concerning the job security in big cities of the "brothers and neighbours" who contributed to the "surplus" labour at home.[34] Neither of these costs are within the purview of development economists.

The lack of receptivity to development economists' and planners' pleas for change cannot be attributed simply to the farmers' inability to recognize the merits of the reformative actions these professionals promised to bring about. The lack of receptivity, if anything, may merely reflect the farmers' well-founded cautiousness, wrought in their exposure to shifting policies in the recent past. It may well be indicative of the farmers' cautious efforts to contextualize the implications of what others may project as a desirable course of action against their own familiar life. Schultz may lament that "changing farmers is the hardest art to master".[35] Hardest for a development economist or planner is the art of viewing the farmers as more than a group of individuals who are consumed by agricultural productivity.[36]

Throughout the second half of the 1990s and 2000s, Vietnam showed signs of successful economic development, such as increasing contributions to industrial output from the private sectors and a high rate of annual GDP (Gross Domestic Product) growth, consistently in the region of 5% and 9%, as well as emergence as the world's leading agricultural (rice, sugar, and cashew nuts) exporter, doubling its agricultural production.[37] Given that less than ten years ago Vietnam was still under the excruciating strains of U.S.-led trade and other embargoes, and the collapse of its long-time supporter, the Soviet Union, the nation's macroeconomic performance since the mid-1990s has been truly remarkable.

However, the farmers have ample evidence of costs that may offset these national economic achievements. Vietnam's macroeconomic performance largely increased the income gap between the urban and rural workforce (Table 1.1, below). The "surplus labour", supplied from rural Vietnam, is not the beneficiary of better-performing cities. Early in our research, one of our informants, the eldest son of a farm household in Phu Cat in central Vietnam, made the following statement:

> Oh no, my mother [who had moved to and lived in Ho Chi Minh City until recently] does not send us money. She is busy supporting herself. We are just as happy if and when she comes home for the Tet.

Table 1.1 National/Rural Widening Income Disparity in Lower Mekong Region for the Decade of Rapid Economic Development

	1994/1996	*2001*	*2005*	*2007*
Cambodia	1.61	1.91	2.3	2.51
Lao PDR	1.59	1.47	1.72	1.81
Myanmar	x	x	x	x
Thailand	6.36	5.45	5.69	5.62
Vietnam	2.51	2.75	3.16	3.42

Source: Vu Le Thao Chi, "Farmers in a developing country: An inquiry into human insecurity of the many", *Journal of Human Security Studies*, Vol. 1, No. 2, 2012, pp. 94–108.

Perhaps the absence of a decline in the agricultural workforce (which remains at around the neighbourhood of 50%) in contrast to the sharp decline in agriculture's contribution to the national income (from 40% to 20%) may be a testimony to the farmers' judicious calculation of the cost and benefits of a head-on plunge into making their productivity higher and more efficient.

The following evidence may also offer the farmers a basis for second thoughts. In 2006, the World Bank reported that the cost of chemical-induced ill health and other damages in Vietnam surpassed one billion U.S. dollars a year, accounting for nearly 2% of Vietnam's GDP (2006) or $57 billion. This total is estimated from medical costs and losses from the foregone markets of contaminated agricultural products.[38] This evidence is a testimony, as discussed later, to the increasingly wide circulation of toxic agrochemicals in the marketplace; it is also a basis for the caution in alerting the farmers that the choice of higher productivity may come with unacceptable collateral damage.

These preceding observations prepare us to follow a reversed recipe for observing the farmers' action. The value or utility of a given action cannot be determined solely by those who promote it and is largely determined by whoever decides to take it. It is the farmers who decide what is good for them. Having thus reversed the usual recipe, we draw attention to factors that may be considered extra-economic or financial.

The farmers in Vietnam have been subject to constantly shifting macro-policies sanctioned by higher authorities in their recent past. First of all, they were more accustomed to the declaration of changes for the collective well-being of agricultural cooperatives, and less so to the results of these changes since pronounced changes and the corresponding prescriptions for action rarely reached completion. Their action's efficacy test is thus limited to a narrower sphere of action – the well-being of their households, the primacy of which the *Doi Moi* reforms restored. Even their communal obligations find their routes in this primacy. Second, and consequently, it is the farmers who examine and contextualize those towering policy goals offered by the higher authority against their daily lives. Given these experiences in their recent past, the farmers would be quick to calculate the gains and losses accompanying any action that may threaten to alter something that, in their perspective, should be the least susceptible to constant changes – their daily life, in which they are occupied by many concerns, such as familial and communal relationships.

The fact that they have many concerns in life suggests that: (1) gains in one area of concern may well be losses in other areas of concern; (2) losses may be easier to recognize than gains depending on the risks, or uncertainties, involved and on the resources for livelihood; and (3) the need to maintain a certain consistency among different actions cannot be taken too lightly.

One hint for sustaining this reversed recipe for observing the farmers' action comes from the more human assumption of Herbert Simon and others that men are not fully informed of all possibilities of the alternatives available to them and that they have severely limited key resources, such as time, in completing a reasonable computation of the consequences of each and every alternative. Such an assumption, the bounded rationality, draws attention to factors other than their ability (reinforced through education) to act rationally or according to the "utility" of a chosen course of action. This assumption brings in the perspective that men may try to maximize *their efforts* to gain and can still satisfy themselves with results that fall short of the maximum gains.[39]

Amartya Sen's capability analysis[40] also offers a paradigmatic shift in our understanding of Vietnamese farmers' behaviour. Sen recognizes men as independent agents of their own will, determining the utility of a given commodity. Sen's capability is variable with regard to education, gender relations, and other factors of social positions, and the resources at the disposal of men. Yet the key point about this shift remains that men are free from the dictatorship of a commodity's producers' definition of its utility.

A group of behavioural economists are also willing to compromise on the characterization of human behaviour, and they offer a similar perspective on it, which is dictated by "reasonability". Daniel Kahneman and Amos Tversky draw attention to the conditions under which a decision-maker calculates the gains and losses accompanying a course of action by bringing in the notion of a "reference point", the starting point against which the gains and losses are measured. The decision-maker is neither perfectly rational, as a model of an economic man is supposed to be, nor irrational, as one who ignores the weight of utility of the choices before him. He is a dynamic calculator of what his needs are given where he is and what he possesses, of the "reference point", against which he calculates the utility of his actions.[41] We will make use of some of these theoretical and conceptual devices, and ideas in reconstructing the behaviour of Vietnamese farmers.

Another important notion that underlies our observation and analysis of the farmers is the "individualization", in the manner of Ulrich Beck, of farmers in perceiving, calculating, and acting in the face of various risks (or uncertainties) they are confronted with.[42] It is explained in detail later that the farmers have been pressured and counselled by various experts, ranging from party cadres, development planners, and economists to medical and other scientists. But recently, the farmers in Vietnam have been through the processes by which they (and their families) have become their own agents. Released from the agricultural cooperatives, from the collective mode of production, the recent development in rural Vietnam has placed the responsibility of managing life squarely on the shoulders of individual farmers.

One last point of note in this reversed recipe for observation is derived from how we usually manage our everyday life.[43] We allocate the bulk of our time and resources to expanding, establishing, and stabilizing the sphere of routinized decision-making, i.e., the sphere of action that requires no distinct effort to decide alternative courses of action. Given this approach, our initial response to the changes that may disrupt daily routine is to view them as, and/or make them look, "unproblematic", and not prepare for them or contemplate ways of removing them. Vietnamese farmers are no exception in the management of everyday life.

Throughout our research, we have used this reversed framework to examine and recapture the behaviour of Vietnamese farmers. First and foremost, before they are "agricultural producers" they are practitioners of everyday life; likewise, the families of disabled children who stand out among Vietnamese farmers due to their obvious misfortunes are also primarily practitioners of everyday life.

Notes

1 Francis Fukuyama, "The End of History?", *The National Interest*, Summer 1989, pp. 3–18.

2 Of all the histories of war in Indochina, Marilyn Young's *The Vietnam Wars: 1945–1990*, New York, Harper Collins, 1991, stands out as it places the war with the United States in a much broader perspective, embracing all wars that Vietnam has fought after the Second World War. Although the book's coverage of the domestic conditions in Vietnam throughout the war years is limited, it gives a distinct feeling of how exhausting these tumultuous war years were to the Vietnamese, well into the 1980s. See also Mark Philip Bradley and Marilyn Young, eds., *Making Sense of the Vietnam Wars*, New York, Oxford University Press, 2008, which covers the wars in detail from the local perspective. On the wars from the U.S. perspective, scores of studies stand out for their well-documented, yet imaginative interpretation. Nevertheless, the focus is usually on the war between the United States and Vietnam. Among these, George C. Herring's *America's Longest War: The United States and Vietnam, 1945–1975* (4th edn), New York, McGraw-Hill, 2001, gives the most succinct account of the war. For a unique perspective that also gives a raw sense of the war see Al Santoli's collection of witness accounts, *To Bear Any Burden: The Vietnam War and Its Aftermath in the Words of Americans and Southeast Asians*, Bloomington, Indiana University Press, 1999.

3 Laos, Vietnam, and Cambodia were independent before 1954. However, they were essentially the front prepared by the French, who granted independence in exchange for their staying within the French Union.

4 There is no definitive account of land redistribution in the South under Diem. One account puts the figure at 244,000 hectares for the redistributed land for the period 1958–1961. Considering that the Delta region alone had nearly 2,000,000 hectares under cultivation, the figure shows how limited the land reform was. See Douglas C. Dacy, *Foreign Aid, War and Economic Development: South Vietnam, 1955–1975*, Cambridge, Cambridge University Press, 1986, pp. 111–13. See also Nancy Wiegersma, *Vietnam: Peasant Land, Peasant Revolution: Patriarchy and Collectivity in the Rural Economy*, New York, St. Martin's Press, 1988.

5 William J. Duiker, *The Communist Road to Power in Vietnam*, Boulder, CO, Westview Press, 1981, p. 177. Also Wiegersma, *op. cit.*, Chapter 8.
6 Duiker, *ibid.*, pp. 177–9.
7 Martin Ravallion and Dominique van de Walle, *Land in Transition: Reform and Poverty in Rural Vietnam*, Washington, DC, The World Bank and Palgrave, 2008, especially Chapter 2.
8 See, for example, Donald Zagoria, *Vietnam Triangle: Moscow-Pekin-Hanoi*, New York, Pegasus, 1967.
9 Perhaps the best account of the complex interaction between Vietnam and China is Nayan Chanda's *Brother Enemy: The War after the War*, New York, Harcourt, 1986. Chapters 7–10 give a detailed account of how the war unfolded between the two neighbouring Asian communist countries. See also Duiker, *op. cit.*, Chapter 13.
10 See, for example, Young, *op. cit.*, Chapters 12 and 13. Chanda, *ibid.*, Chapter 10 and Alexander Woodside, "Nationalism and Poverty in the Breakdown of Sino-Vietnamese Relations", *Pacific Affairs*, Vol. 52, No. 3, Autumn 1979, pp. 381–3.
11 Stephen J. Morris, *Why Vietnam Invaded Cambodia: Political Culture and the Causes of War*, Palo Alto, CA, Stanford University Press, 1999.
12 The notion of the extractive and regulatory capabilities' being integral to the presence of the state is articulated in Joel S. Migdal, *Strong Societies and Weak States: State-Society Relations and State Capabilities in the Third World*, Princeton, NJ, Princeton University Press, 1988, especially pp. 5–7.
13 This is a period that produced much discontent, even among the ranks of communist supporters and sympathizers in the South. See, for example, the case of Truong Nhu Tang, from a notable family in the South, who rose to become minister of justice in the provisional revolutionary government and fled Vietnam in 1978. *Vietcong Memoir*, New York, Harcourt Brace Janovich, 1985.
14 New economic zones were also conceived to displace a large number of the southerners from the cities in order to enable close to a million northerners to migrate to the South. See Trung Dang, *Vietnam's Post-1975 Agrarian Reforms*, Canberra, Australian National University Press, 2018, especially Chapters 3 and 4, for occasional witness accounts of how the southerners viewed the NEZs.
15 Douglas Pike, "Vietnam during 1976: Economics in Command", *Asian Survey*, Vol. 17, No. 1, 1976, p. 39.
16 One source puts the rate of collectivization in the South at 36% of all farm households. Vu Tuan Anh, *Vietnam's Economic Reform: Results and Problems*, Hanoi, Social Science Publishing House, 1994, p. 140. See also Nguyen Sinh Cuc, *Agriculture of Vietnam, 1945–1995*, Hanoi, Statistical Publishing House, 1995.
17 Edmund McWilliams, "Vietnam in 1982: Onward into the Quagmire", *Asian Survey*, Vol. 23, No. 1, January 1983, pp. 62–72, Trung Dang, *op., cit.*
18 Dwayne Benjamin and Loren Brandt, "Agriculture and income distribution in rural Vietnam under economic reforms: A tale of two regions", *William Davidson Working Paper Number 519*, March 2002, pp. 3–6.
19 See www.statisticbrain.com. Of the casualties, listed as 58,220 from the United States, 55,661 died in South Vietnam. www.archives.gov/research/ military/ vietnam-war/ casualty-statistics.html#category. It is virtually impossible to estimate the number of Vietnamese civilian casualties. However, Marilyn Young quotes over 160,000 "for each year of Nixon's presidency" alone. Young, *op. cit.*, 1991, p. 280. This does not include casualties in the North, in Laos, or in Cambodia.
20 In Vietnamese, it is called *dat nam phan tram*, a "five per cent" land. See Benedict J. Tria Kerkvliet, *The Power of Everyday Politics: How Vietnamese Peasants Transformed National Policy*, New York, Cornell University Press, 2005, pp. 76–7.
21 See Kahneman, 2011, Chapter 8 on "How Judgements Happen".
22 The best example is the World Bank, *World Development Report, 1982*, Washington, DC, World Bank; New York, Oxford University Press, 1982, especially Chapter 1 and part II.

23 In a review of Samuel L. Popkin's *The Rational Peasant: The Political Economy of Rural Society in Vietnam*, Berkeley, University of California Press, 1979, Donald McCloskey refers to this expression as often circulated among development specialists in organizations such as the World Bank. *Journal of Political Economy*, Vol. 89, August 1981, p. 837.

24 James C. Scott, *The Moral Economy of the Peasant: Rebellion and Subsistence in Southeast Asia*, New Haven, CT, Yale University Press, 1977 and Popkin, *op. cit.* About 10 years later, Wiegersma, *op. cit.*, especially Chapters 2–4, provided an account of Vietnamese rural life somewhat in line with Scott's view.

25 Polly Hill, *Development Economics on Trial: The Anthropological Case for a Prosecution*, Cambridge, Cambridge University Press, 1986 (1995), p. 21.

26 Popkin, *op. cit.*, p. 18.

27 Theodore Schultz, *Transforming Traditional Agriculture*, New Haven, CT, Yale University Press, 1964, p. 3.

28 W. Arthur Lewis, "Economic development with unlimited supplies of labour", *The Manchester School*, Vol. 22, No. 2, 1954, pp. 139–91.

29 See especially Mark Figueroa, "W. Arthur Lewis versus the Lewis Model: Agricultural or industrial development?", *The Manchester School*, Vol. 72, No. 6, 2004, pp. 736–50.

30 This is a summary of Lewis's 1954 essay and the revisions he has added since. The particular attention to agriculture that may provide the surplus labour comes from the now famous realization that Lewis had while walking down a Bangkok street. He realized then that one neo-classicist assumption of a fixed labour supply had been blinding him to the dynamic production factor – labour – abundant in both nineteenth-century Britain and developing nations (Lewis, "Autobiographical Notes", *Social and Economic Studies*, 1980, Vol. 29, No. 4, pp. 1–4). Lewis only later argues that

> the model is intended to work equally well whether the capitalists are agriculturalists or industrialists. ... In its first version ... the model presupposes that the capitalist sector is self-sufficient and contains every kind of economic activity. This explanation may serve to refute the charge that the model identifies economic growth with industrialization.

He produced a similar argument a little earlier:

> In the model, the non-capitalist sector serves *for a time as a reservoir from which the capitalist sector draws labor.* The original [1954] paper makes it clear that this labor does not all come from agriculture—a fact which has escaped the attention of many subsequent writers.
>
> (Lewis, "Reflections on Unlimited Labor", in L. DiMarco, ed., International Economics and Development, NY, Academic Press, 1972, p. 76, italics added)

31 Lewis, *op. cit.*, 1954, p. 160.

32 Gerald M. Meier, *Biography of a Subject: An Evolution of Development Economics*, New York, Oxford University Press, 2005, p. 153.

33 *Ibid.*, p. 24.

34 See Clifford Geertz's involution as a testimony to the Bali farmers' calculation of gains and losses, which includes the protection of communal ties over economic gains. *Agricultural Involution: The Processes of Ecological Change in Indonesia*, Berkeley and Los Angeles, University of California Press, 1963.

35 Schultz, *op. cit.*, p. vii.

36 For a brief discussion see Vu Le Thao Chi, "Farmers in a developing country: An inquiry into human insecurity of the many", *Journal of Human Security Studies*, Vol. 1, No. 2, 2012, pp. 94–108.

37 See, for example, the Asian Development Bank, *Statistical Database System*, https://sdbs.adb.org/sdbs/index.jsp.

38 World Bank, "Vietnam Food Safety and Agricultural Health Action Plan", *Document of World Bank*, 2006, Report no. 35231 VN, p. xii. Also Food and Agriculture Organization, *FAO Statistical Year Book*, 2004 and 2010. Income disparity is arrived at by dividing GDP per capita by GDP per economically active person in agriculture.
39 See Endnote 7 in the Introduction.
40 Amartya Sen, *Commodities and Capabilities*, New York, Oxford University Press, 1999 (1987), and *Development as Freedom*, New York, Knopf, 1999, especially Chapters 2 and 4.
41 Daniel Kahneman and Amos Tversky, "Prospect theory: An analysis of decision under risk", *Econometrica*, Vol. 47, No. 2, 1979, pp. 263–92.
42 Ulrich Beck, *Risk Society, Towards a New Modernity*, London, Sage Publications, 1992.
43 Berger and Luckmann, 1966, *op. cit.*, Chapter 1.

2 Development, agriculture, and farmers

Vietnam's economic development broadly defines the perimeter within which farmers faced the pressure of having to make decisions about rebuilding after the war. A broad outline of the country's economic development is in order, followed by a closer look at the period in which our informants acted as representatives of these farmers.

Role of agriculture in Vietnam's economic development

In 2004, ten years after the United States lifted its embargo on Vietnam, a team of development economists and planners from the United States, the United Kingdom, Canada, and Vietnam put together a seminal work on Vietnam's economic development during the 1990s. They called it "nothing short of amazing".[1] One of the editors, Paul Glewwe, offers a convenient point to start this chapter (Table 2.1).

Doi Moi, which was initiated in 1986, marked a key turning point in the history of Vietnamese farmers as Vietnam's national economy continued to grow. Between 2001 and 2005, the rate of annual growth remained high (5–7%).

Table 2.1 Macroeconomic Performance of Post-*Doi Moi* Vietnam

	Annual Growth Rates (%)		
	1985–1988	1988–1994	1994–2000
GDP	4.2	6.9	7.4
Agriculture	1.8	3.9	4.4
Industry	8.1	7.5	11.1
Services	3.6	8.5	6.4
Population	2.1	1.8	1.5 (77.64 million)
GDP/capita	2.0	5.0	5.7
Exports	13.4	33.1	23.6
Imports	16.1	24.5	17.9

Source: Paul Glewwe, "An overview of Economic Growth and Household Welfare in Vietnam in the 1990s", in Paul Glewwe, Nisha Agrawal, and David Dollar, eds., op. cit., p. 5.

An increase in the size of the national economy and a corresponding reduction in poverty, as indicated by household income, were observed. The IMF reported a sharp decline of 17% in the poor household ratio in 2001.[2]

Additional evidence, though less remarkable, of Vietnam's improving economy and its accompanying consequences may be the leaps that the country was making in their human development performance. Between 2004 and 2007, it moved from the 113rd to the 108th place among the 177 countries listed, up by five places, which is a huge leap compared with the members of the Association of Southeast Asian Nations. Vietnam's Human Development Index, which indicates the combined effects of per capita income, education rates, school enrolment, and literacy rates, increased constantly from 0.583 in 1985 to 0.691 in 2004 and reached 0.704 in 2007. The country's life expectancy increased from 68.6 in 2003 to 69 in 2004 and to 70.5 in 2007, while its per capita income rose from $2,300 in 2004 to $2,490 in 2005.[3]

Given that the population nearly doubled, reaching over 90 million, between the unification in 1976 and 2010, ranking it the 13th largest in the world, the agricultural sector that still absorbs the largest portion of the working population has been playing an important role in Vietnam's sustained economic development. The basic data on Vietnam's agricultural sector confirm this (Table 2.2).

Vietnam has been steady in terms of agricultural improvement. In 2000, the agricultural sector accounted for 13% of export revenue, mostly from the cultivation of rice in the Red River and Mekong River Deltas. The share of agricultural exports in Vietnam is higher than the total of the other countries in the Southeast Asian region and three times the average of the world. Rice was the main food crop, accounting for 85% of the total cultivated land and 43% of the total output value as of 2000. Vietnam had become the second-largest producer of rice worldwide by 2005. It not only could produce enough to meet the domestic demand but was also one of the world's leading exporters of rice.[4]

The decline (from 70% to 54%) in employment in the agricultural sector was not as steep as that in the agricultural contribution to the increasing national

Table 2.2 Agricultural Sector in Vietnam: Basic Data

	1987	*2010*
Agricultural land	20.7%	33.1% (2009)
Arable land	17.1%	20.3% (2009)
Employment in the total employment	70% (1995)	53.9%
Contribution to GDP	41% (46%, 1988)	20.6%
Agriculture value (current $)	10 billion	22 billion

Source: Data collected for the 25 years following *Doi Moi* in 1986 and summarized from *World Bank Databank Source* at http://data.worldbank.org/indicator/NV.AGR.TOTL.ZS?page=4

income (from nearly 40% to 20%). This may explain why the growth rate of the agricultural sector, although high, was nowhere near that of the industrial sector (see Table 2.1). Vietnam does not have an advantageous physical landscape, with 6,600,000 ha of arable land, accounting for a little over 21%, ranking it 34th among all countries in terms of arable land. As such, the rise in agricultural productivity appears to be *less important* than that in other sectors in sustaining economic development.

Therefore, it can be argued that the agricultural sector carries a burden that is not so readily translatable into the performance of the national economy. With the rapid increase in population, the contribution of Vietnam's agriculture moderates the impact of high economic growth on the population. Agriculture, as a slower-development sector in the economy, sustains a much larger workforce than its contribution to the national income suggests.

In 1982, before Vietnam's sustained growth began, the *World Development Report* indicated a rapid economic growth in virtually all countries where agricultural development had been strong. Faster agricultural growth in low-income countries was also expected to reduce rural poverty since over 90% of the absolute poor were rural people.[5] The *World Bank Report*, 25 years later, in 2007, still drew attention to the significant role of the agricultural sector in the country's economic development. However, the plea for attention to the role of agriculture in economic development this time had a distinctly different undertone, a pessimism developed over the previous 25 years in which the problem of poverty had remained unsolved:

> Three out of every four poor people in developing countries live in rural areas – 2.1 billion living on less than $2 a day and 880 million on less than $1 a day – and most depend on agriculture for their livelihoods. Given where they are and *what they do best*, promoting agriculture is imperative for meeting the Millennium Development Goal of halving poverty and hunger by 2015 and continuing to reduce poverty and hunger for several decades thereafter (italics added).[6]

For Vietnam and most other developing countries, changes in agriculture matter in a sense much broader than its contribution to increasing the national income.

Post-*Doi Moi* development

Doi Moi*: changing policies*

The landmark policy changes, *Doi Moi*, the "renovation", began while Vietnam was still in the midst and under the immense strain of the Cambodian campaign on its human and other resources. The key components of these changes are summarized below, with the distinct message that the Vietnamese economy increasingly relied on the private sector for economic growth.[7]

1 Decentralization of the management of state-owned enterprises (SOEs) in decisions relating to production, distribution, and financing;
2 Introduction of market-oriented monetary policies to control inflation;
3 Adjustments in Vietnam's external economic relations through the adoption of a realistic exchange rate and a liberal foreign investment law, among others;
4 Adoption of agricultural policies that allowed for long-term usufruct rights and greater freedom in marketing products; and
5 Adoption of measures to promote the private sector as the engine of economic growth.

Not long after these sweeping efforts were launched, an observer speculated as to whether Vietnam was to follow the forerunners of the East Asian economic miracle such as South Korea and Taiwan.[8] *Doi Moi* had a far-reaching impact on just about every aspect of the country, including the agricultural sector. From "one of the poorest countries in the world with an estimated seven out of every ten Vietnamese living in poverty",[9] Vietnam was to make steady improvements and become one of the leading rice exporters in the world.

Because of the drastic changes in all areas since 1986, *Doi Moi* monopolized the attention of those interested in, and has become the foundation for, examining all sectors of development in Vietnam. For that reason, it has been a part of the Vietnamese identity for the over 30 years since its inception. *Doi Moi* reform is, however, not the beginning, of a longer and winding path.

The night before Doi Moi

Statements like the one below, made by Truong Chinh, party secretary general, in 1986, may have the effect of overdramatizing *Doi Moi*:

> ...we have made mistakes due to "leftist infantilism", idealism, and to the contravention of the objective laws of socio-economic development. These mistakes were manifested in the...[emphasis given to] developing heavy industry on a large scale beyond our practical capacity...[maintaining] the bureaucratically centralized mechanism of economic management based on state subsidies with a huge superstructure which overburdens the infrastructure. As a result, we relied mostly on foreign aid for our subsistence.[10]

However, this surprisingly forthright admission and criticism of Vietnam's recent past since the unification reflects both its dire need for changing its course of action and the recognition by many of that need even before 1986. The period before *Doi Moi* is known as "the night before *Doi Moi*" to imply the darker years the country was subjected to, despite the end of the war in 1975. The need for a reform of such a sweeping effect was deeply and widely felt when Vietnam plunged into a quagmire, from which it found it almost impossible to extricate itself, with the ongoing Cambodian military campaign. Struggles between the old (promoters of a socialist, planned economy) and the new (reform advocates) emerged constantly at all levels.

In 1976, the Party Central Committee declared that the nation's economy had entered a period of transition to socialism. "After decades of struggle, members of the Vietnamese Communist Party were understandably *in a rush* to implement socialism throughout the country" (italics added).[11] However, from the very beginning, national reconstruction faced thorny issues, including a sudden drop in foreign aid, a sharp fall in domestic production, and accompanying social disruptions and political instability.

One of the major obstacles to the reconstruction process was the gap in the production systems between the North and the South, which were brought into one system of rule after the reunification. In the North, the economic development policy was mainly based on collective agriculture and an emphasis on developing heavy industries. However, the pressure of, and the consensus support for, sustaining the war efforts had begun to lose its tight hold on the populace once the fall of the South became a foregone conclusion soon after the 1973 Paris Peace Accord. The South, on the other hand, had sustained a more liberal-capitalist facade where the core of the economy consisted of private, small-scale agriculture, small- and medium-sized, consumer-oriented light industries, and the service sector.[12] The unification meant fusing these two vastly different parts into one whole.

An urgent issue following the unification was the budget deficit. For a country largely dependent on foreign aid (almost half of its revenues),[13] the reduction in foreign aid added up to a great deal of difficulty for both North and South Vietnam. The United States stopped the aid soon after they withdrew Americans from South Vietnam, China terminated its aid in 1978 when Vietnam started sending troops to Pol Pot's Cambodia, and the Soviet Union terminated its trade preferences and switched from gratis to non-gratis aid (the Soviet Union gradually cut down on and had finally stopped its assistance by the middle of the 1980s).

The unified Vietnam was in no position to support and finance its efforts to install a unified planned economy. The production cooperatives-based planned economy was on the verge of bankruptcy. This led to the poor performance of the national economy in the first five years after 1975, during which it fell far behind the planned targets (Table 2.3).

Table 2.3 Growth of Output: Planned and Actual Results, Vietnam, 1976–1980 (Annual % Increase)

	Planned	*Actual*
National income	13–14	0.4
Agricultural production	8–10	1.9
Industrial production	16–18	0.6

Source: Adam Fforde and Stefan de Vylder, "Part Three: Vietnam", in: Pradumna B. Rana and Naved Hamid, eds., *From Centrally Planned to Market Economies: The Asian Approach, Vol. 3: Lao PDR, Myanmar and Vietnam*, Hong Kong; Oxford; New York, Oxford University Press, 1996, p. 342.

The actual increase in national income was only 0.4%, virtually stalling, while the planned increase was projected at 13–14%. Industrial production was staggering with an increase of a meagre 0.6%, i.e., less than 4% of the projected plan was achieved. Agricultural production was only slightly better, compared with industrial production, with about 20% of the expected projection achieved, thanks probably to the brief period of strengthened collectivization in both North and South soon after the end of the war.

There are two main reasons for the poor performance of the national economy as a whole: the imbalance in investment with an overly favoured focus on heavy industries and the increasing disharmony between the socialist mode of agricultural production and the farmers. The excessive concentration of investment in the heavy industries sector accounted for 60–80% of the total throughout the first decade after the end of the war.[14] Meanwhile the agricultural sector did not meet the immediate need of the population – food. Coupled with harsh weather conditions, regional disparities in rice production, and inefficient inter-regional transport networks in the latter half of the 1970s, which locally contained the agricultural gains, food shortage became a major issue in Vietnam (Table 2.4).

The promotion of agricultural collectivization, especially in the southern part of the country, did not help the situation. Instead, it plunged the country even deeper into crisis. In the North, the collectivization of agriculture took place as early as in the late 1950s and picked up its pace during the 1960s and the first half of the 1970s. During the war years before 1975, the production cooperatives may have been successful, at least on the surface, just as the socialist leaders had expected. They did work equally because the national threat had escalated to personal threats as the war progressed and lingered on, pushing the farmers in the North to rally around the cooperatives. In other words, the production cooperatives were not only "production" units, but they were also popular vehicles that helped recruit and mobilize local youth for the front line.[15]

Following the unification in 1975, the whole country, both North and South, was placed under a single system of large-scale socialist production. But

Table 2.4 Regional Disparities in Rice Production, 1988

Region	*Total Production (million tons)*	*Population (million persons)*	*Per Capita Production (kg/person)*
North mountains and midlands	1.77	19.07	93
Red River Delta	3.45	13.57	254
Central coast of North	1.48	8.57	173
Central coast of South	1.54	6.66	231
Central Highland	0.35	2.49	141
North-east of South	0.80	7.81	102
Mekong River Delta	7.60	14.20	535
Total	17.00	64.41	264

Source: Mya Than and Joseph L. H. Tan, *Vietnam's Dilemmas and Options: The Challenge of Economic Transition in the 1990s*, Singapore: Institute of Southeast Asian Studies, 1993, p. 151.

the system was no longer as workable. It lost the extra incentive – the ongoing war in the homeland – for the farmers to push themselves to achieve efficient production.

After either the initial fear of reprisal by the new socialist regime wore off, or the paralyzing costs of reconstruction and continued war in Cambodia set in, the farmers in the South began resisting the socialist mode of agricultural production. As observed, "most of these cooperatives and production groups [in the South] had disintegrated, and the rest existed only *pro forma*, not as real productive units".[16] The form emptied of the contents was in place for a little longer, perhaps because of the explicit and implicit coercion from higher authorities. Not surprisingly, rice production decreased sharply. Accompanied by the population increase, Vietnam suffered an acute food shortage, leading to rice imports of about half a million tons a year on average until 1989.[17]

In the late 1970s, decisions made by the Party leaders to send Vietnamese soldiers to Cambodia only deepened the economic quagmire, among others, for Vietnam, even if they may have been politically justifiable or necessary. By 1977, China had ended nearly all economic aid to unified Vietnam; at the same time, it expanded military aid to the Khmer Rouge, encouraging the latter to increase activities around the Vietnamese border provinces. Vietnam responded by sending troops to Cambodia via Laos and through the westernmost province of Tay Ninh in late December 1976. Beijing retaliated by invading Vietnam in mid-February 1979, opening up a new front for Vietnam in the North. The six northern provinces of Vietnam were nearly destroyed by China, forcing Vietnam to station a large number of war-weary soldiers there. The conflict with China and Cambodia diverted a large portion of the Vietnamese population from productive development activities to non-productive military affairs as well as displacing a large number of Vietnamese civilians.

Finally, in response to the invasion of Cambodia and the resulting pressure from the U.S. government, the U.S. allies cut off virtually all economic assistance to Vietnam. The loss of both Chinese and Western aid was disastrous for a country heavily dependent on foreign resources. In the end, the total cost of the Vietnamese invasion and occupation of Cambodia remained difficult to quantify; however, it served to severely regress Vietnamese economic development.

The sustained war, the sharp drop in foreign aid, the demand for non-productive (military) goods, and the inability to procure goods, as exemplified by rice production, all cumulatively and quickly increased inflation. On the eve of the Sixth Party Congress in 1986, Vietnam was experiencing a hyperinflation of well over 700%.[18]

The search for a way out

In light of these economic developments, several points need to be noted. First, *Doi Moi* was a response to the cumulative changes that presented the leaders with few alternatives. How did it come about? Hanoi leaders were open to improvement. Under worsening economic conditions, the idea of breaking "with the traditional model of socialist management" began to influence the leaders in Hanoi.[19] Yet the second five-year economic plan (1981–1985) after the unification fell short of arresting the worsening economic conditions. The plan aimed at increasing the production of food and other daily necessities, with the central government providing greater autonomy to local governments and production units as regards production management. It also aimed to make better use of the more liberal-capitalist mode of business, especially in the southern part of Vietnam, and to bring prices and wages more in line with market prices. All of these measures were incremental compromises on the socialist principle of a planned economy.[20]

However, these efforts were disrupted from the very beginning by an ungrounded assumption of massive foreign assistance, despite Vietnam experiencing an abrupt decrease in foreign aid. The planners were also blissfully negligent of the weak infrastructure isolating productive from unproductive regions; the loss of management skills in both agriculture and business sectors (including that of the economically active ethnic Chinese), especially in the South; and the highly centralized and rigid style of management.[21]

The coming of *Doi Moi* was certainly the making of the realization that these incremental compromises of socialist principles – the centrally planned economy – were not nearly sufficient. Truong Chinh, cited above, may blame the predicament on the "contravention of the objective laws of socio-economic development" and claim that the move towards *Doi Moi* was the feat of the leaders.

However, it was the farmers, among others, who first recognized the negative consequences of ignoring the "objective laws of socio-economic development" through the usual conduct of daily life. The farmers were quick to see the limited purchasing power of "points", which they earned through the cooperatives, in the volatile marketplaces racked by high inflation. Their work in the cooperatives did not secure them enough "points" to support their families. The realization, in turn, pushed them to invest their productive hours in the "household plot", that old "five-per cent (*dat nam phan tram*)" land, even more.

The final crossing to *Doi Moi*, the need to move out of the dominant official – socialist – thinking, would require practical evidence that a more fundamental departure from the socialist mode of production was needed. The evidence was there in the behaviour of the farmers. However, the question of drawing the attention of the leaders to what had been sown at the ground level – in the efforts to protect the well-being of households – remained unanswered.

That role of the protector was performed by Nguyen Van Linh and conceivably scores of men like him. Nguyen Van Linh, a northerner, stayed in the South following the 1954 division of the country and was actively involved in the liberation of the South; he was appointed a politburo member in 1976 at the Party's Fourth Congress.

The difficult times in the South before the unification did not seem to turn him into a blind ideologist for a socialist revolution. Instead, they trained him in pragmatic thinking, especially later in moderating the impact on the South of the second five-year plan following the Fourth Party Congress. This move may have cost him a politburo seat temporarily, yet he quickly reacquired an important position, that of chairman of the People's Committee in Ho Chi Minh City. His quick return to political prominence suggests that he had retained a group of supporters in the Party. He became party secretary at the Sixth Party Congress, succeeding Truong Chinh, and is often identified as the key figure in launching *Doi Moi*.[22]

Nguyen Van Linh was a popular critic of the social ills under the centrally planned economy before *Doi Moi*, writing in the daily People Newspaper (*Nhân Dân*) under the pen name N.V.L. These initials not only represent his name but are also interpreted as *Nói và Làm*, meaning *words and action*, to describe his personality or signify his dream of much-needed political leadership.

Having been active in the South since 1954, and having served as the head of the socialist re-education camp in the South (*Ban Cải Tạo Công Thương Nghiệp*) after 1975 until 1978, Nguyen Van Linh developed a profound understanding of the need for small-business owners and farmers to be liberated from the state control. He personally saw to it that the idea of a "product contract-based salary" (*lương khoán sản phẩm*) was put into practice in Ho Chi Minh City early in 1980 as the secretary of the city's People's Committee. This model gave small shop owners a degree of autonomy in managing their business, which soon gained popularity, and began to lead to some successful cases, such as the Thanh Cong Textile Enterprise, Mien Nam Washing Powder Enterprise, 2–9 Pharmaceutical Enterprise, and Beer Saigon Enterprise, among others. The practice quickly spread across the southern regions.[23]

With Nguyen Van Linh regaining a higher position in the Party hierarchy quickly, some of the changes began to deviate from the socialist principle. The development towards a multi-sector economy where the private sector coexisted with the state-run business and cooperatives found itself a legal basis eventually in 1987 when Resolution 217-HDB was issued.[24] Through these changes, even SOEs acquired a degree of autonomy at the operational level in the right to determine what and how much to produce, for instance. This made the foundation for the emerging market economy firmer, even though the socialist orientation still remained operational in securing a certain degree of social equality.

In the agricultural sector, to be discussed in greater detail later, two decisions prompted what amounted to a radical departure from the socialist mode of production: Directive 100 in 1981 and Decision 10 in 1988. The former found a fuller version in the latter.[25] Both of these placed farming households as the principal agricultural production units. By so doing, the cumulative effects of these measures liberated individual farmers from the vertical division of agricultural labour along with the raising of the seedlings, planting, weeding, and tending of the paddies, and harvesting.

In Directive 100, the farming households were contracted (*khoán hộ*) by the state – thus "contract farming" – to produce a predetermined quantity of grain and deliver it to the state using the cooperatives' lands. Its fuller version, Decision 10, liberated the farming households from the obligation to provide their collective labour to the state. Through Decision 10 and related land reforms, the farming households pushed this liberation even further.

Farmers, short of claiming private ownership of the land, were free to acquire and choose the means of production, and to sell their products either to the state or to private buyers at market rates. Also, the cooperatives did not simply disappear but remained a de facto framework for mobilizing labour from one paddy to another during especially labour-intensive phases of production such as harvesting. In effect, Decision 10 transformed the division of agricultural labour from the vertical one in *Hop Tac Xa Bac Cao* into a more spatially division-based, or horizontally division-based, reciprocal labour exchange system. Under Decision 10 and another set of changes (see below), farming households as units began moving among the paddies where their services were needed. The new arrangement was reminiscent of a system of labour exchange, *to doi cong*, among the families that North Vietnam installed prior to the full-fledged *Hop Tac Xa Bac Cao* in the late 1950s.

A series of land reforms accelerated changes in 1988, facilitating Decision 10's effects. The farming households were provided with leases that lasted for 15 years or more for the plots of land they received. In the early 1990s, the government increased property rights for farming households and, more generally, reduced restrictions on agricultural markets. Decree Number 5 of 1993 (Land Law 1993) granted more rights and security. Tenure lengths were extended to 20 years for annual cropland and 50 years for perennial cropland.[26]

In line with these changes turning farming households into independent agents of action, a new constitution was passed in April 1992, amending the 1980 constitution.[27] It ratified the six-year economic programme and allowed private citizens to engage freely in business, and own the means of production. The right of citizens to do business and make profits was now codified into law, and the idea of a market economy was made permanent and deemed politically correct.[28]

With the spirit of "Reinforce peace for economic development" (*Giữ vững hòa bình phát triển kinh tế*), Vietnam's politburo, under the guidance of Nguyen Van Linh, announced Resolution 13 in May 1988.[29] The Resolution was a breakthrough in Vietnam's diplomacy due to its role in mending the tension-filled relationship between Vietnam and other countries. The four major points of the Resolution were: withdrawal from Cambodia; normalization of the relationship with China; mending ties with ASEAN countries; and gradual normalization of the relationship with the United States. With the adoption of Resolution 13, Vietnam began making the international environment friendlier towards its more market-oriented economy and open society.

In 1989, Vietnam withdrew troops from Cambodia, paving the way for the Chengdu conference in the process of normalization with China. In 1995, Vietnam became a full member of ASEAN, signed a Framework Agreement on cooperation with the EU, and officially normalized the relationship with the United States with the visit by President Bill Clinton. Later, in 2005, Vietnam became the 150th member of the World Trade Organization.

Vietnam's leaders joined with others in an euphoria, which was best expressed in such a statement on *Doi Moi* as the one provided by Nguyen Van Giap, vice-chairman of the Council of Ministers of the Socialist Republic of Vietnam: "Vietnam has marked a new development in our thinking on economic theory, and in our socio-economic policies in a renewal process full of difficulties and complexities".[30] Others also tended to view *Doi Moi* and the accompanying changes as transforming the overall environment for motivating the farmers (and small businesses) to produce more.[31]

In the euphoria of transformation without violence, however, one important point may have gone unnoticed: through *Doi Moi*, the signs of which there were already hints in the late 1970s, the farming households reinstated themselves as the dominant agent of their own action; and agricultural production is only a part of their actions to protect and promote their well-being.

Doi Moi *and beyond*

Doi Moi brought a new face to Vietnam by changing social relations domestically and by ending international isolation. The macroeconomic performance in the following decades was, to repeat, "nothing short of amazing". Vietnam's controlling the hyperinflation prior to *Doi Moi* and reducing the rate to under 10% may top the list of its economic achievements.

More goods and services through trade, production, and investments also contributed to sustaining the annual GDP growth rate in the region of 5–8% in the following decade and beyond. Given the semi-international isolation into the early 1990s, it is not surprising that the export growth rate was double that of the import growth rate, in which the rising production of rice and its exports played a dominant role.[32] In the early 1990s, Vietnam was the world's second-largest exporter of rice.

Vietnam's economic expansion is also reflected in the change in trade partners. Up to the early 1980s, the socialist countries accounted for 75% and 80% of Vietnam's export and import, respectively. The changes in the latter half of the 1980s greatly reduced the presence of the socialist countries in Vietnam's export and import, accounting for about 13% and 5%, respectively.[33] Vietnam began to diversify its export strategies to include as trade partners both neighbouring countries *and* capitalist countries after the political tensions began to subside. A mutually reinforcing relationship may have also worked between the liberalization of its trade practices and the farming households' freedom to procure means of production: the flow of fertilizers, a key agricultural input, across the border, on the one hand, and the widening market for fertilizers combined together led to a sharp drop in fertilizer prices.[34] The overall achievement may be best summarized by the data prepared by the World Bank. It shows an astonishing jump in the size of the economy where a little over $6.3 billion (current US$) in 1989 reached $224 billion in 2017. For the same period, per capita income increased from $94 to $2340.[35]

On the international interface, the Vietnamese economy's achievement is remarkable. In addition to the sheer increase in volume of both export and

Table 2.5 Development Indicators of Vietnam

	Vietnam
Population (2011)	90 million
GDP growth rate (2010)	6.8%
GDP (2010) (official exchange rate)	$103.6 billion
GDP per capita $	1,300
Export (2010)	$72.3 billion
Import (2010)	$80 billion
HDI ranking	128
Health: life expectancy	75.2
Expenditure on health, public	2.8%
Public expenditure on education	5.3% GDP
Adult literacy (2009)	94%
Population living below $1.25 (PPP USD) per day	13.1%

Source: Summarized from the three websites http://hdr.undp.org/en/data/profiles/, www.economywatch.com/, and www.indexmundi.com/

import, Vietnam diversified exportable goods, such as crude oil, textiles and garments, rice, coffee, rubber, coal, aquaculture products, and processed forest products. Following the lifting of the U.S. embargo, foreign investors quickly increased their role in diversification as their companies contributed 36% of the total imports in 2009, while the remaining 64% was provided by local companies. Diversification of imported goods paralleled that of exports: petroleum, steel, fertilizers, electronics, and machinery. Vietnam also diversified its major trading partners to include Japan, Singapore, Hong Kong, Korea, and European Union (EU). Its trade with the Asian economies reached about 80% of its total trade.[36]

The most remarkable improvement is the constant drop in Vietnam's poverty rate. An observer declared, "Vietnam no longer an underdeveloped country" in 2004, with a table showing that the poverty rate in 1993 was a little below 60% and a fraction less than 20% in 2004.[37] The overall picture of Vietnam at this stage – the mid-point of our research – is summarized in the table above (Table 2.5).

Agriculture in Vietnam: a closer look

The *Doi Moi* of 1986 marked an important turning point in the transformation of Vietnam in general and agriculture in particular. As one observer puts it, "reform and change in Vietnam [... are] part and parcel of the internal processes of Doi Moi".[38] However, this characterization may need to be reversed: *Doi Moi* has been a part of the changes and disruption in the country far beyond the decade in which it was implemented.

Vietnamese farmers had lived with, survived, and embraced the impact of these changes and disruptions. Even before the collective period (1959–1988), they had already gone through ebbs and flows in well-being, given the period of constant disruption since the middle of the nineteenth century. Before 1945, the majority of farmers in rural Vietnam were tenant farmers. The almost 100-year-long presence of French colonialists and their penetration into even the smallest unit of the Vietnamese social structure – villages – placed millions of Vietnamese farmers under the immense strain of colonial exploitation.[39]

Among the causes of the strain, perhaps the severest may have been a series of taxes – head tax and land tax, among others – imposed upon the villagers. Farmers, from one generation to another, were constantly caught in debt and in dire need of securing the minimum base for living. James C. Scott, in his *The Moral Economy of the Peasant* (1976), draws attention to the presence of a community-based economic behaviour revolving around a sort of asymmetrical symbiosis between the patron (landowners) and clients (the tenant farmers) in earlier Vietnam, where they were bound by the need to secure the subsistence of the latter. Seemingly taking the opposite stance to Scott, Samuel Popkin in *The Rational Peasants* (1979), which also deals with pre-independence rural Vietnam, draws attention to the rural Vietnamese preoccupation with personal (household) gains in choosing crops, in soliciting support from others, and even in allocating labour.

The common point about the farmers for these earlier observers is that the rural Vietnamese were not merely passive onlookers of incidents that interfered with their lives – they were conscious of their behavioural basis firmly rooted either in their community or in their household. An observer's brief description of the management of "communal land" in traditional Vietnamese villages (before the 1945 Revolution) draws attention to the remarkable consistency in the maintenance and production of communal land throughout the eras of royal and French colonial rule, regardless of the changes in specific institutional definitions of the land. This astonishing stability is sustained by the stability in farming households as units of action and their relationship with others.[40]

Farmers in Vietnam were thrown into rounds of eventful and disruptive changes following independence in 1945. Part of North Vietnam was entirely ravaged by a famine, caused by a misallocation and excessive procurement of rice by Japan's imperial army due to war exigencies, costing an estimated several hundred thousand lives. Major battles against the French colonial army took place in the North. In 1954, the country was divided into the North and South under the Geneva Accord. The North came under the Labour Party's rule, and the South under Ngo Dinh Diem, a nationalist with a definite liberal-capitalist political outlook. The division remained intact until 1975, when what the North had experienced was to be imposed on the South. These drastic changes – the independence, and the division and reunification of the country – broadly defined the parameters of rural life and those of the farmers.

Collectivization of agriculture before 1975 – socialist or wartime demands?

Collectivization was one of the key tenets of socialist production. This model was widespread in socialist groups, especially during the Cold War period. Vietnam was not an exception. However, because of its special situation – the prolonged war of unification, the Vietnam War – the features of collective agriculture cannot be evaluated solely on the merits and demerits of agricultural cooperatives.

Initially even in the North, efforts to liberate the tenant farmers from their landless status were much less than absolute. When they were reorganized under earlier forms of cooperatives, first "groups for exchanging labour" (*to doi cong*) and "lower-level cooperatives" (*Hop Tac Xa Bac Thap*), the farmers retained their households as the distinctive units of production activity in the lands that now belonged to the cooperatives. Their field was their familiar lands that they, mostly as tenant farmers, had always cultivated.

The specific catalysts for bringing this earlier form of cooperatives to a higher level, *Hop Tac Xa Bac Cao*, were not obvious. However, a realistic view among the leaders that unification could not be achieved overnight may have led them to concentrate on socialist reforms within the North first and reinforced the view among them that an "industry develops only to the extent that agriculture itself develops".[41]

Higher agricultural productivity through division of labour rather than through profit incentives, and socialist justice in terms of equal access to land among the farmers paved the way towards a higher form of agricultural production system. The farmers, now released from their households, were mobilized and assigned to engage in discrete parts of the whole agricultural production process.

Initial confusion among the farmers resulted in a dip in the level of their reorganization into cooperatives, as can be seen in Tables 2.6-1 and 2.6-2.[42] The rise in the number of cooperatives and decline in that of labour exchange groups should match as the former took over the function of the latter.

There were signs of confusion or even outright resistance among some of the farmers. However, that did not deter the leaders. The plea for emancipating the farmers from the control of the landowners, or even from their traditional loyalty to them, may have alerted the leaders to the acute need to push for a higher level of collectivization. Moreover, the North had a more obvious need to meet: preparation for the *eventual* unification. The question remained as to how to

Table 2.6-1 Labour Exchange Groups in Northern Vietnam, 1955–1960

Year	*Number of Groups*	*Average Number of Households per Group*
End 1955	153,000	7.1
End 1956	190,200	7.1
Mid 1957	72,000	N/A
End 1957	100,900	5.9
End 1958	244,400	7.3
April 1959	249,025	N/A
End 1959	97,600	10.6
End 1960	12,971	9.8

Table 2.6-2 Agricultural Cooperatives in Northern Vietnam, 1955–1960

	Number	*Percentage of Agricultural Households*	*Percentage of Cultivated Land*	*Average size*	
				Households	*Hectares*
End 1955	10				
End 1956	42				
Mid 1957	33			13	10
Mid 1958	134				
End 1958	4,729	5	5	26	17
Mid 1959	16,150	22		35	
End 1959	28,840	45	41	43	25
End 1960	40,420	86	68	59	34

procure heavy machinery and equipment, and how to secure the industrial basis for the procurement.

The North's ability to procure industrial products domestically was woefully limited. Vietnam's reliance on the Soviet Union for these goods for the first ten years after the Geneva Conference exceeded well over 50% of its export value. An estimate in 1965 put the number of middle- and technical-level workers at fewer than 124,000 and the number of skilled workers at fewer than 100,000.[43] A sizeable trade deficit with the Soviet Union and the Eastern Bloc countries was expected to worsen, with the equally disturbing possibility of increasingly heavier reliance on foreign assistance. The notion that "industry develops only to the extent that agriculture itself develops" was all the more pressing.

The first five-year plan (1961–1965) emerged from this background. The realization of the efforts to make the plan workable weighed heavier than the cost of overcoming the initial confusion accompanying the push towards a higher level of agricultural cooperatives, *Hop Tac Xa Bac Cao.*

The earlier form of cooperation among the farmers, the labour exchange groups, *to doi cong*, may have retained their basic function while transforming into "brigades" consisting of 40–100 farmers. Under the higher cooperatives, the division of labour was pushed further – the farmers or the members of the brigades became more like factory workers on an assembly line. Within this framework, the farmers pooled their resources, mainly labour and equipment, and were expected to perform their parts of the production process.[44] Despite this transformation, irrespective of the work efficiency: the brigades' – or their members' – contributions to production could not become the basis of disparity in wealth.[45]

In January 1959, at the 16th Labour Party's Central Conference, the Decision on "cooperation in agriculture" was issued, making the introduction of the higher-level cooperative, *Hop Tac Xa Bac Cao*, official after a few years of experimentation. A key component of this collectivization – aimed both at higher productivity and a prevention of income disparity – was the use of "work points" (*công điểm*). A member of a brigade earned a certain number of points, which usually equalled one workday (*ngày công*). The value of each workday within a brigade was arrived at by the amount of produce earmarked for distribution to its members, which was divided by the total number of workdays used for production. Not all brigade members could earn the same number of points even if the work hours were the same, depending on the types of work and age, among other things. A complex calculation was adopted to determine the work-work point conversion.[46]

The points that the brigade members earned served as a "currency", which allowed them to acquire daily necessities from the state-run shops. As long as the North was suffering from a perpetual shortage of goods, the brigade members were susceptible to the lure of extra earnings from the "household plot", the 5% of land within the cooperative's land or face a threat to their subsistence.[47]

Furthermore, whether or not the allocation of the work points was managed on a fair basis became critical in keeping the brigade members honest. However, the points based on "fair evaluation" could be widely dispersed throughout the entire process of the production line, stretching from preparing, pulling, and carrying seedlings to ploughing, harrowing, and weeding; from carrying and spreading the manure to ploughing and planting; and from carrying water to irrigation canals. Mismanagement of "fairness" could easily spread among the officers of the cooperatives, which might also lead to laxness on the part of the brigade members in performing the given tasks in the production process. Fairness was an immensely difficult rule to observe.

Although the extent is difficult to determine, outright deviations from the intent of collectivization were spotted in the North. The work of the production brigade, with all the internal division of labour intact, was delegated back to the household with the explicit and implicit consent of the brigade's officials. Usually, the households offered some of the produce and kept the remainder. Kerkvliet reports one such case in Vinh Phuc where the practice of the household-based production continued with the full consent of the Party secretary Kim Ngoc. References to the provincial Party leaders' admonition elsewhere, around the same time, are a testimony to the fact that the practice went unnoticed fairly extensively.[48]

Nguyen van Ton, head of the agricultural department in Vinh Phuc Province, reported accordingly:

> [T]he situation of farming collectively, benefiting collectively, prolonging the work, and inflating the points caused corruption, and especially wasted a lot of public assets. Farmers were not attached to their farms, just going after work points. They only went to the fields at the call of the brigade leader and the bell. They didn't initiate work. Cheating, working carelessly, refusing to work etc. were popular phenomena in any of the cooperatives.[49]

Earlier in the establishment of *Hop Tac Xa Bac Cao*, the farmers were confused and acted like "ants crawling around the rim of a basket, not sure whether inside or outside was better for their livelihood".[50] The spreading of the cooperatives among the farmers was also a process by which they lost the sense of involvement with their farm work. "Prolonging the work, inflating the points" (*dong cong phong diem*) began to spread. The farmers might just show up without doing much in the rice paddies and leave soon after the bell rang signalling the end of the day's work. The meetings among the brigade members became the stage for protesting against each other's work points. As recalled by one farmer: "The neighbourhood was cosy before [...] Now people do not even want to see each other's face. How come?"[51]

One additional development pushed this demoralization even further. For one reason or another, the cooperative style of farmers' life impacted several areas beyond that of agricultural production. It began to run primary schools, day-care centres, and health clinics, as well as to manage funds available for future investments and social welfare.[52] These at once multiplied the evaluation points for the work points and, by the same token, devalued the individual work points. From the farmers' perspective, the production cooperative, through its infiltration into many phases of rural life, left very little opportunity for the farmers to act as farmers.

The United Nations Development Programme rightly points out:[53]

> Cooperatives in the North developed from a pure production unit into a social, economic, and quasi-political entity. During wartime, they were turned into strategic units and took upon themselves many non-economic functions. *[Especially] when the cooperative coincided with the area of a village*, the distinction between economic and politico-administrative management virtually disappeared even though legally they remained two separate entities (italics added).

Ironically, it was this loss of the distinctness of the production cooperatives that also prevented their disintegration. Soon after the first five-year plan was announced, it became clear that the confrontation in the South between the pro-North Liberation Front and Diem's troops could easily engage the North in a massive operation in support of the former. After 1965, following the landing of U.S. Marines in Da Nang, the North's direct and indirect involvement became irreversible. Given the limited ability to procure war material domestically, *Hop Tac Xa Bac Cao* became both the leverage point for increasing the pressure for more production *and*, through its expanded presence in village life, a vehicle for recruiting and sending young people to the front.[54]

As they farmed the collective fields, often at night and in the early hours of the morning to avoid U.S. bombers, after 1965, the villagers were not just mindful of the nation's struggle in abstract terms. They were thinking of their children, siblings, relatives, and friends fighting on the front line. Sixty per cent of the families in Vinh Phuc and Phu Tho Provinces, for example, had husbands, sons, brothers, or sisters who were directly involved in the war effort; many of them were in the army treading the Ho Chi Minh Trail. Meanwhile, for the people on the front line, the cooperatives were the assurance that their families back home would have something to eat precisely because the produce was divided not only in line with one's ability to work but also based on their needs.[55] This intimate bonding between people working in the cooperatives and people fighting on the front line kept the former afloat. They were the vehicle for "fighting the US and saving the country" (*chống Mỹ cứu nước*).

Before 1975, northern village life was overwhelmed by the presence of production cooperatives. Ironically, as seen above, the cooperatives survived not so much as part of a socialist economy as part of a wartime economy. It was the war that provided a *raison d'être* for the agricultural cooperatives to survive.

Collectivization in Vietnam after 1975: continuation and resistance

Vietnam witnessed a transformation within the collectivization process after 1975. The country was transitioning from a wartime economy to a massive reconstruction economy. The agricultural cooperatives, though transformed as seen above, continued to operate at the core of the economy. Now, with the immediate threat of war, or foreign intervention, having largely dissipated, motivating farmers to work within the cooperatives became a real challenge for Hanoi. With this uncertainty, Hanoi needed to expand this socialist model of production to the South – an area totally new to the model.

In addition, Vietnam also needed to exhibit its enthusiasm for, and commitment to, the socialist road to win support from other socialist countries after the renewed tension with China over the rise of Democratic Kampuchea. The efforts, at least in the North, were met with the farmers' decision to stay within the framework of the cooperative (Table 2.7).

The size of an average cooperative in 1979 was also expanded to cover 378 households (five to six times bigger than in 1960) and 202 ha of cultivated land (6.1 times larger than in 1960).

The responses to the introduction of *Hop Tac Xa Bac Cao* were different in the South, where some tenant farmers and/or small land holders had supported the National Liberation Front in exchange for the latter's help to liberate the former from the large land owners (Table 2.8).

The collectivization was most successful in the central coastal areas, where one of our research communities is located, and in the central highlands. The

Table 2.7 Proportion of Northern Vietnam Farming Households (%) in the Agricultural Cooperatives, 1976–1981

	1976	*1977*	*1978*	*1979*	*1980*	*1981*
Entire North	93	93	95	97	97	96

Source: Tran Thi Que, "Land and Agricultural Land Management in Vietnam", in Ha Huy Thanh and Shozo Sakata, eds., *Impact of Socio-economic changes on the Livelihoods of People Living in Poverty in Vietnam,* IDE ASEDP Series, 2005, No. 71, pp. 175–96, p. 22.

Table 2.8 Collectivization of Agriculture in the South (%), 1978–1980

Areas	*1978*	*1979*	*1980*
South (total)	3.2	21.1	24.5
Central coastal area	8.6	66.5	83.8
Central highlands	7.2	26.5	30.2
South-East	1.6	5.5	4.5
Mekong Delta	0.2	1.8	1.7

Source: Tran Thi Que, "Land and Agricultural Land Management in Vietnam", in Ha Huy Thanh and Shozo Sakata, eds., *Impact of Socio-economic changes on the Livelihoods of People Living in Poverty in Vietnam,* IDE ASEDP Series, 2005, No. 71, pp. 175–96, p. 25.

former multiplied by tenfold the level of collectivization between 1978 and 1980, whereas in the central highlands, 30% of agricultural households joined the agricultural cooperatives, four times the percentage, 7.2%, in 1978.

The picture, on the other hand, was quite dismal further south. In 1978, in the South-East, only 1.6% joined the collectivization. Despite the new regime's efforts, the modest increase to 5.5% in 1979 immediately dropped to 4.5% in 1980. The situation was not much brighter in the Mekong Delta area, with only 1.7% of all agricultural households in the cooperatives. The poor performance in the South in the initial phase of collectivization can be attributed to the following: (1) a series of land reforms between 1956 and 1974, albeit modest, had allowed South Vietnam to successfully overcome the problems of skewed land distribution and high land rents; (2) consequently, South Vietnam's agriculture had already been relatively mechanized; and (3) a division of labour among the producers; intermediaries, such as procurers of agricultural input and buyers of produce; and produce distributors had been relatively developed.[56] These developments were predicated upon the farming households being freed from the colonial and large land owners' control throughout the preceding decades of post-Second World War development. All this may suggest that there may have been only limited room for *Hop Tap Xa Bac Cao* to intervene with its claim to secure productivity.

One more ironic factor is that the war ravaging through the rural South emptied it of a large proportion of the farming population. This is ironic as it had the effect of increasing the average size of farming plots, enabling the remaining farmers to exploit the "economy of scale", which, in turn, made them especially resistant to the intrusion of the agricultural cooperatives.

Given these conditions in the South, the liberation from the pressure of the war alone could not simply induce its population to share the norms and practices of collectivization. The new regime was still adherent to the model of agricultural cooperatives practised in the North to secure food production for the entire population and to support heavy industries for the continued war in Kampuchea first and then with China. The farmers in the South saw something else: agricultural collectivization deprived them of the autonomy of the farming households and the cooperatives had all sorts of loopholes, which could be exploited for personal gains.

To all of these, one critical factor – the absolute shortage of goods – must be added. Whether distributed fairly and effectively or not, the work points that the farmers in the unfamiliar cooperatives earned were virtually no help in securing the well-being of the household. Although no data are available, the southerners in the unfamiliar cooperatives may also have sought means to supplement their meagre income by making the fullest use of the "household plots", or the production brigades' leaders may have deviated from the norm, as in the case of Vinh Phuc and elsewhere in the wartime North. Black markets in place since the war offered convenient outlets for the surplus produce.

A shift from the cooperatives to the farming household

Directive 100 was introduced as early as January 1981. It indicated that the merits of *Hop Tap Xa Bac Cao* alone could not sustain it as the foundation of the new socialist Vietnam, even in the eyes of the Communist Party leaders. Farming households were contracted by the state to produce using the cooperatives' land. They were allowed to sell their products in free markets provided they fulfilled their production contracts with the cooperatives. Thus, the emphasis on the farming households as the key units of production virtually discredited the core component of *Hop Tap Xa Bac Cao*, the division of agricultural labour among the individual members of the production brigades.

Farming households still did not receive complete concessions. There were areas of activities in which the cooperatives retained their own work in a manner similar to the earlier "labour exchange" (*to doi cong*) groups, such as harrowing, ploughing, irrigation and drainage, and pest control. The households were "contracted" to take care of the rest of the production – planting, weeding, and harvesting – to secure the produce to be delivered to the cooperatives. The cooperatives also retained the prerogative of planning the household-based agricultural production. They lost, however, the tight control over the sale of products.

What stopped the farmers short of becoming entirely independent of the cooperatives was the residual role that the cooperatives played in controlling the greater portions of procuring the agricultural input such as machinery, fertilizers, and land. The restoration of the farming household in its rightful place followed a series of twists and turns in a short period following the early 1980s.

The complex interactions of the factors that contributed to the farmers' awakening to the merits of the household-based production pushed their disregard for the boundary set by Directive 100. An agronomist, Vo Tong Xuan, lists those factors:[57]

1 Top-down planning on land use and crop choice without consideration of the farmers' preferences and local market conditions;
2 The government's frequent inability to secure all contracted production at harvest time;

3 Seasonal surpluses at the farm gate led to a crash in private rice prices in several regions, which, while benefiting the urban poor, had severe negative effects on farmers;
4 The persistence of centralized input supplies resulted in inadequate and untimely provision of input to farmers;
5 A lack of security of land tenure resulting in inadequate farm-level investments for maintaining long-term land productivity.

An additional factor is no less important. In the euphoria of the nation's unification, some zealous party cadets may have pushed the practice of *Hop Tap Xa Bac Cao* to the neglect of its adverse effect on the farmers' will. Setting the production quota too high, which led to factor 2 above, for example, only furthered the decline in the popularity of Directive 100.

Resolution No. 10, popularly known as Decision 10, was introduced in 1988 in the wake of the *Doi Moi* announcement, effectively terminating the agricultural cooperatives-based production throughout Vietnam. There were several components in this drastic shift in the Party's agricultural policy.

In farmers-state economic transactions, the price was set at the free market level, though it was subject to mutual agreement. Farmers no longer needed to sell their produce to the state (via the cooperatives or state enterprises) at low prices. Their obligations were now fulfilled by paying agricultural taxes based on the yield of the land they received from the cooperatives. Moreover, beyond the confines of the contract, the farmers were free to sell their produce on the free market.

The excess of official (Party's and cooperative's) interference did not go unnoticed. It was tamed by the cooperatives' budget cut or by the greatly reduced number of cooperative officers, reinforcing a sense of spontaneous cooperation among the farming families.

An additional push for the farming household as the primary actor came from the distribution of farmland on the basis of the size and farming capacity of each, even though some of the cooperatives still claimed the *de facto* ownership of the land, consistent with the *de jure* state ownership of the land. In some cooperatives, 40–50% of the land was even distributed on a per capita basis among households. The cooperatives were left with supplemental jobs, especially in the labour-intensive phase of the production process, such as irrigation, where their role was to coordinate with the farming households and ensure cooperation.

The most important component of all was that these measures of ensuring the farming households' autonomy were predicated on the requirement that the agricultural cooperatives were legally *obliged* to "contract" their land to the farming households for 15 years for annual crops and 40 years for perennial crops.[58]

What had been dormant even in North Vietnam before the unification finally came to its fruition. Through these twists and turns in the land-farmers relationship, it began to surface.

The preceding discussions on the restoration of farming households as the principal production units should not reduce the significance of the fact that the farmers' negative response to *Hop Tac Xa Bao Cao* had *not* been limited to the latter's interference in the production process alone. The ideal of cooperative-based production did not appeal to the farmers due to the questionable management practices of the cooperatives' officials. Besides, more importantly, the farmers' were sceptical of the cooperatives' extensive interference in rural life, in general. When the farming households were restored, *so was the broader management of their own life.*

The return of the independent farming household would still need one more step to become complete. The expansion of the rights of the farming household over the land or the Land Law of 1993.

Confusion over who could claim the right to produce using the contracted lands had followed Directive 100, and it was pronounced in the South, where the past practices of independent cultivation were widespread, and the mobility of the residents during the war was high. The past practices and the wartime mobility, among others, made it difficult to identify who had a legitimate claim to contract farming.[59]

Moreover, Decision 10 of 1988 had put a ceiling on the size of the contracted land: for annual crops, the limit was 2 ha in the central and northern provinces and 3 ha in the southern provinces, and for perennials, the limit on land holdings was 10 ha.[60] Consequently, the value of the land did not change noticeably since the right of the farming household to cultivate was perceived as being strictly confined within the contracted land as defined in Decision 10.

The land reform of 1993 was an attempt to clear up such confusion and deficiencies, and more.[61] The law extended the land-use rights to 20 years for annual crops and 50 years for perennial crops. More importantly, it explicitly granted five rights to the farming households: transfer, exchange, inheritance, rent, and mortgage. The issuance of the land certificate formalized these rights.

The institutionalization of the household-based use of land left room for disparities between the law and its practice. Local variations in physical conditions as well as recent history were both potential and actual sources of dispute and conflict. "Different solutions by localities"[62] seem to have been in place.

We interviewed a group of farmers in Phu Cat in 2010, who revealed that considerable variations existed not only in the right to the land under the 1993 law but also in the variations' description in the vernacular (see Table 2.9 below).

Among a dozen farmers who were interviewed, some responded with a fairly accurate grasp of the contracted (allocated) land. More details on the farmers are presented in Chapter 4. From the extensive interviews, we managed to reconstruct the following points, including the local regulations as stated by them:

1 *Allocated farmland*: This is the obvious consequence of the 1993 Land Law and ensuing afforestation programmes. Every family has at least 1,000 m^2 for rice cultivation, more widely known as "contracted land" (*ruộng khoán*). Under Instruction 64-CP, each member (born before 1993) is qualified to claim one "*sao*" (500 m^2 in this central coastal area, equal to 360 m^2 in the North and 1,000 m^2 in the South).
2 *Auction farmland*: There are four families in the list who have "auction land" (*ruộng đấu giá* or *ruộng công ích* – land for public use). *Ruộng đấu*

Table 2.9 Land-Use Rights and Size of Landholding among Selected Farmers with the Cashew Nut Growing Operation

	Total	*Allocated Farmland*	*Auctioned Farmland*	*Allocated Forestland*	*Others*
*No. 1	N/A	N/A			
**No. 2	2.1 ha	1500 m^2	0	2 ha	N/A
**No. 6					
No. 3	3.2 ha	2000 m^2	1 ha	2 ha	N/A
No. 4	8.5 ha	5000 m^2	0	8 ha	N/A
No. 5	1.6 ha	1000 m^2	3000 m^2	1.2 ha	N/A
No. 7	2.85 ha	2000 m^2	1000 m^2	2.4 ha	1500 m^2 for house
No. 8	2.25 ha	2500 m^2	0	2 ha	N/A
No. 9	1 ha	2000 m^2	3000 m^2	0.5 ha	N/A

* No. 1 is the "middleman" in the cashew nut deal.

** No. 2 and No. 6 are wife and husband, respectively. The figures here and below represent the combined total.

giá belongs to the community, managed by the local Commune's People's Committee. It is meant for those who have the need to produce extra rice for the purpose of household consumption. Usually they are considered unproductive, ranked 4, 5, 6, or 7 (out of seven ranks) and good for only one crop annually. Every four years, *ruộng đấu giá* needs to be returned and auctioned again. Usually, however, the farmers keep the same plot of land so that their cultivation is not disrupted. They pay rent in kind of about 30 kg/*sao* of the produce – in their case, cashew nuts.

3 *Allocated forestland*: Each of these families also has a piece of forestland (located in the Nui Ba mountains) under Programme 327–1992 and the Five Million Hectare Reforestation Programme to grow perennial trees.[63]

Although many farmers whom we interviewed had been granted the right to use these plots of land, their responses indicated their conviction that they *owned* the plots. In two years, according to the law, they would have to return the land (for annual crops) after 20 years of use. However, they were also aware of the 2004 amendment to the law that if farmers continued cultivation on the same plots of land, they would be allowed to extend the contract for another 20 years. At least the knowledge of the amendment was the rationale behind their conviction. The case of the farmers in Phu Cat is noteworthy due to the presence of local variations in the actual application of the 1993 law and the unshakeable belief that they practically owned the land, together with their families.

Mixed blessings: commercialization of agriculture

As Vietnamese farmers regained their rightful and normal rural lives, after decades of collective farming and the war that they had fought in their backyards had constantly disrupted peace, the process of de-collectivization was, most of all, one in which the farming households restored themselves as the primary agents of action in establishing a life free of disruption.

Our observations span the period following, and at least partially covering, those trying years. A singular value of economic gain (or performing its "role" in the division of the agricultural production sector for "work points") did not consume the farmers; they were equally concerned with a broader view of what may constitute a life worth pursuing. They engaged in production activities and communal obligations, and looked after their families' well-being, while also performing many other mundane activities. Their responsibility, as they saw it, was far more diverse than that of economists, health specialists, or the officials of the cooperatives, who were in a position to characterize the basis of the farmers' behaviour and their actions in the event of commercialization of agriculture.

The government's role in the development of agriculture as business was not limited to officially sanctioning the changes in the farmer-land relationship that had been taking place. Their efforts were also aimed at keeping the new "landed class", the farming households, above the subsistence level. They began with a resolution on an agricultural tax exemption in 1990, "Agricultural Land Use Tax Exemption to the testimony of Ho Chi Minh", wherein the farmers were exempted from 50% of the agricultural tax during 1990 and 1991.[64] In 1993, this resolution was replaced by the Agricultural Land Tax,[65] but the intent remained intact. In 2003, in keeping up with the government's support for the United Nations Millennium Development Goals, Decision 129/2003-CP continued the exemption from 2003 to 2010, authorizing 100% exemption for poor households or households located in faraway mountainous areas. Within eight years, 11.2 million households were estimated to have enjoyed the tax exemption on 5.5 million ha. Furthermore, acting on these accomplishments, the government extended, in 2010, under resolution 55/2010/QH12, the agricultural tax exemption for another ten years (2011–2020).[66]

Along with these, the government's increasing realization of the need to sustain harmonious international relations inevitably deepened. As mentioned earlier, Vietnam, under the reformist Nguyen Van Linh, embarked on earnest efforts to improve its relationship with its neighbours, including ASEAN countries and China, with Resolution 13 in 1988. As the resolution was prefaced with the slogan "Reinforce peace for economic development" (*Giữ vững hòa bình phát triển kinh tế*), the government took upon itself, in particular, the tasks over which the farmers had little or no control.

One of the tasks was to adjust Vietnam's economic performance within a broader international economic environment, in which the improvement of its status within the ASEAN framework regionally and the international trade regime of WTO globally figured prominently. Through a series of reforms covering the years of the *Doi Moi*, the state's role in setting the commodity price was terminated. The efforts were partially to eliminate excessive government interference with market forces, which were increasingly dominating both the regional and the global economy.

Included in these efforts was the removal or reduction of government subsidies to agricultural inputs such as seeds, fertilizers, pesticides, electricity, and even various forms of agricultural loans. The pace of these efforts to synchronize Vietnamese macroeconomic performance with the free trade regime improved further as Vietnam joined ASEAN in 1995[67] and the WTO in 2007. In 2001, Vietnam removed rice export quotas except in emergencies and at the same time lowered the average tariff rate on agricultural imports, especially input commodities for agricultural and industrial production. Vietnam also reduced export tax on agricultural products from 1987. The export taxes on rice, peanuts, cashew nuts, coffee, tea, and rubber were gradually cut down from an average of 10–5% for rice; 4% for rubber; and 3% for cashew nuts, tea, coffee, and pepper. Currently, most exportable agricultural commodities are free, or close to being free of such taxes, and all of it is a part of the package to provide production incentives for farmers.

It is worth noting that these efforts to adjust to international trade practices were carefully balanced, at least initially, by the efforts to moderate the impact of the sudden exposure of Vietnam's agriculture, in particular, to international competition. One such measure was the establishment of the Price Stabilization Fund in 1993. By using various forms of surcharges on trade activities, the Fund was to finance the stockpiling of crucial commodities such as important crops and key agricultural inputs. It also aimed to protect the contributors to the Fund against sharp domestic and international price fluctuations.[68]

As pointed out earlier in this chapter, the government's efforts to synchronize Vietnam's economic performance with free trade practices have been amply rewarded with the expanding national economy. However, the blessings are mixed, especially from the perspective of the farmers, who are supposed to be the direct beneficiaries of the government's efforts. The government may have fallen short of fully extending its efforts to cover the areas of shortfall that directly touch upon the lives of the farmers. The problem here is the rapid increase in the use of one key agricultural input, namely pesticides, herbicides, and other agrochemicals, and the failure of the government to address its consequences.

The opening up of Vietnam to international trade inevitably opened the floodgates to some unwelcome goods. The use of agrochemicals such as DDT was nothing new to the Vietnamese farmers since the cooperative farming era when the Soviet Union and China were the principal suppliers. DDT was extensively employed as a key pesticide to protect azolla, a kind of water fern, which was widely used in China and Southeast Asia as an organic fertilizer long before the modern era. It is not surprising, then, that North Vietnam, especially under pressure to achieve higher agriculture production as the war worsened in the 1960s, relied heavily on DDT.[69]

The sudden surge in the import and use of agrochemicals such as pesticides is, nonetheless, staggering. Statistical records show an increasing trend of pesticides and herbicides being imported into Vietnam, from around 15,000 tons in 1990 to more than 36,000 tons in 2002. The figures do not include illegally imported pesticides (accounting roughly for 30% of all pesticides used). Pesticide use increased rapidly within a few years between 1991 and 1998, from 21,200 to 41,411 tons. From 1990 to 1998, the amount of, and expenditure on, pesticides used per cultivated land increased 2.17 and 22.8 times, respectively. Also, the use of herbicides and fungicides increased in terms of both ratio and amount. The records also show the regional concentration in the rice-producing Red River and Mekong River Deltas (Table 2.10).

Of the pesticides sprayed, over 90% were insecticides. About half of these contained organophosphorus, including restricted or banned varieties, falling under the World Health Organization's categories I and II, which are classified as extremely to moderately hazardous to health, respectively.[70] Before 1990, the government seemed to be preoccupied with procuring the chemicals at a lower cost as they were imported and distributed to the farmers by state agencies with government subsidies. One estimate shows that on average, the annual pesticide use across the whole country was between 13,000 and 15,000 tons. These chemicals included highly hazardous varieties (World Health Organization's categories I and II), such as DDT, heptachlor, and others.[71]

Throughout the years of *Doi Moi* and after, the government increasingly tightened its control over the distribution and use of agrochemicals. However, their efforts did not begin in earnest until after 1991. In 1991, the Ministry of Agriculture and Rural Development (MARD) listed 77 types of active ingredients that were legally permitted for import, production, distribution, and use in Vietnam. In 1992, MARD issued a list of pesticides classified into three categories: (1) pesticides permitted for use; (2) pesticides restricted for use; and (3) pesticides banned from use.

Table 2.10 Statistical Data on the Chemicals used in Different Regions of Vietnam (1999)

Region		*Insecticide*		*Fungicide*		*Herbicide*		*Total*	*%*
		%	*metric ton*	*%*	*metric ton*	*%*	*metric ton*	*%*	
1	Red River Delta	2846	13.2	1315	11.4	297	4.3	4438	22.7
2	North-East	2334	10.8	1315	6.9	155	2.3	3504	10.0
3	North-West	364	1.6	10	0.3	0	0	464	1.0
4	North Central	1432	6.6	551	3.2	85	1.2	2068	5.5
5	Central Coast	1525	7.1	385	2.2	350	5.2	2252	5.9
6	Highland	873	4.0	249	0.4	185	2.6	1307	3.5
7	South-East	2354	11.0	1230	3.3	597	8.7	4181	11.2
8	Mekong River Delta	9878	45.7	4427	40.0	5189	75.7	19404	51.2

Source: Nguyen Thi Ha and Nguyen Manh Khai, "A case study of pesticide use and its effect on health and environment", in Peter Kunstadter, ed., *Pesticides in Southeast Asia: Environmental, Biomedical, and Economic Uses and Effects*, p. 140. Nguyen M. Quang, "An evaluation of the chemical pollution in Vietnam", *MekongInfo*, September 2001, www.mekonginfo.or./mrc en/docilib.nsf/ 0/1D952C500BE72DC587256-B74000703C8/$FILE/ FULLTEXT.pdf

In 1993, the government issued a decree that marked the first comprehensive legal framework in Vietnam for pesticide use and management. It made explicit the requirements for pesticide production, packaging, distribution, and use; the responsibility and right of relevant state agencies in monitoring and inspecting all activities related to pesticides; and the establishment of a plant protection system from the central to the district level. The decree also stipulated that pesticides of the second category in the WHO's hazardous list were not allowed to be advertised. In 1995, MARD reinforced the control of the second-category pesticides by limiting their use to the wood industry, disinfection, and the health-care system.

In 1999, in a somewhat delayed response, the Ministry of Health (MOH) stipulated that all organizations and individuals need to declare, register, and be certified for the use of the second-category pesticides identified by MARD. Since 2001, through state regulations, pesticides have been considered "special goods with strict limitations on trade", which means that pesticides are traded under specific conditions. To comply with these regulations, all activities related to pesticides, such as registration, import, production, export, storage, transport, trade, and use, took place under state management.[72]

However, it is one thing that the government tried to install a system of chemical watch and control, and entirely another that such a system was put into practice as intended. Ironically, the shift towards a market economy resulted in the rampant rise of profit-seekers among small-shop owners, who seized the opportunities generated by the national campaign for higher agricultural productivity. Nguyen Huu Huan and Dao Trong Anh reported that 24% of over 10,000 pesticide shops inspected by the Department of Plant Protection in 2000 did not have a permit from any appropriate authorities, 87% of the shop owners had no pesticide-handling certificates, and 50% of the shops had no adequate pesticide storage facilities. If the illegally imported or manufactured agrochemicals were to be added to the current situation, then the picture would become even worse. Illegal pesticide trading (mainly highly toxic pesticides) was far from marginal. A nationwide inspection in 2000 detected 2,500 kg of banned pesticides, and 4,753 litres and 5,645 kg of illegally imported pesticides.[73]

That leaves the farmers with the sole responsibility of respecting the government's intention, and the consequences of a failure to do so would have to fall squarely on them. Individual farmers often appear to be casual consumers of chemicals. Although not necessarily limited to Vietnamese farmers, there are many reports that farmers ignore the caution instructions on the chemicals' labels: they use a higher density than suggested, use the chemicals more frequently than instructed, and don't use gloves, among other things.[74]

In Vietnam, in addition to these instances of neglect of precautions, the average volume of pesticides used per hectare of agricultural crops increased by more than 100% in the 1990s alone. Farmers in many areas were believed to have sprayed 20–30 times more than the recommended per cabbage crop. In the South, about 96.6% farmers used pesticides more intensely than instructed, and 95% dumped leftover pesticides into a source of water for irrigation later. Most of these pesticides contained DDT.[75] Furthermore, there was an ironic development in agriculture concerning the use of pesticides and other chemicals. There may have been a stronger pressure against the use of chemicals, especially for rice production, but the farmers began to shift their activities to producing more cash crops such as vegetables and fruits, where they applied cheaper and more hazardous chemicals. Apparently, vegetables tend to have the highest pesticide exposure.[76] There is a sad joke about people not eating clean-looking vegetables or fruits in Vietnam. The neglect by the farmers was met with gains in agricultural productivity. They were also faced with losses that may well have offset the gains. In 1993–1994, there were about 600 cases of pesticide poisoning caused by contaminated vegetables. The trend of food poisoning seemed to continue unabated. In 1998, out of 23,000 people with food poisoning, 6,500 were related to pesticides. In 2002, in 37 out of the 61 provinces, more than 7,000 cases (including 7,647 people) of food poisoning due to pesticide residues were reported, resulting in 277 deaths. The situation seems to be getting worse as it was recently revealed by one medical official:

> the rate of acute food poisoning in Vietnam is 80/100,000 inhabitants. Every year, about 66,000 cases of food poisoning are reported and it is believed that there are 50 cases unreported for every reported case. Beyond these numbers representing the situation, there are also reports, albeit sporadic, that the abuse and/or mismanagement in storing chemicals turn some rural communities into "cancer villages".[77]

In 2006, the World Bank reported that the costs of chemical-induced ill health and other damages in Vietnam surpassed $1 billion a year, accounting for 2% of total GDP ($57 billion, 2006).[78]

In sum, there were signs in the macroeconomic trends showing that Vietnam was benefiting from its shift towards a market economy. Market opportunities for their products and access to necessary agricultural inputs such as agrochemicals were now available. There were also signs that the benefits of a market economy came with costs. The costs included damaged health and lost markets for the contaminated agricultural products, both of which affected the farmers directly. They also included the surplus of "labour" in agriculture that the shift towards commercialized-agriculture-cum-more-efficient-agricultural-production generated. Employment seekers from rural Vietnam account for a large portion of the "informal sector" in urban Vietnam.

Nonetheless, development economists and planners still evaluate Vietnamese farmers almost exclusively in light of their willingness to seize these opportunities. Whether or not the same farmers are in a position to bear those costs does not concern them. The characterization of those farmers who fail to see market opportunities as irrational or ignorant reveals another group of farmers who fail to observe instructions and advice on the use of agrochemicals. Therefore, in addition to development economists and planners, health officials and medical specialists characterize these farmers as irrational, ignorant, or in need of "education".

This attention to individual farmers' willingness and ability to go along with specialists' counsel, however, glosses over the one crucial facet of the changes the farmers have been facing as individuals in the rural order, a challenge of an unfamiliar kind.

This view of the farmers captures them in another critical perspective. The role of specialists (development economists and planners, health specialists, or the collective's officials) may be delineated along with their expertise, and their responsibility may end when they deliver the most unequivocal message as to what and what not to do. The farmers, on the other hand, would have to be the ultimate calculators of the risks, i.e., uncertainties that cut across many dimensions of their life. The farmers in Vietnam, and perhaps in other developing societies too, face what Beck and others call the "individualization" of responsibility by confronting a risk- and uncertainty-ridden life head-on.[79] This attention to individualized responsibility may open up the almost impossible task of grasping how the farmers choose the basis of their decision-making behaviour. Nonetheless, it remains close to our observations.

Notes

1 Paul Glewwe, Nisha Agrawal, and David Dollar, eds., *Economic Growth, Poverty, and Household Welfare in Vietnam*, Washington, DC, The World Bank, 2004, p. vii.

2 IMF, "Vietnam: Poverty reduction strategy paper", *IMF Country Report*, No. 06/70, February 2006, p. 9.

3 *Human Development Report*, 2005 and 2008, New York, United Nations Development Program, 2005 and 2008. These per capita income figures represent purchasing power parity.

4 Hoa Nguyen, Ulrike Grote, Agricultural policies in Vietnam: Producer support estimates 1986–2003, MTID Discussion Paper No. 79, International Food Policy Research Institute, 2004, p. 21.

5 John W. Mellor and Mohinder S. Mudahar, "Agriculture in economic development: Theories, findings, and challenges in the Asian context", in Lee R. Martin, ed., *A Survey of Agricultural Economics Literature, Vol. 4, Agriculture in Economic Development, 1940s to 1990s*, Minneapolis, University of Minnesota Press, 1992, p. 340.

6 *World Bank Report, 2008*, Washington, DC, World Bank and Oxford University Press, 2007, p. 1.

7 Mya Than and Joseph L. H. Tan, *Vietnam's Dilemmas and Options: The Challenge of Economic Transition in the 1990s*, Institute of Southeast Asian Studies, 1993, p. 240 and Paul Glewwe, "An overview of economic growth and household welfare in Vietnam in the 1990s", *op. cit.*

8 David Dapice, "Vietnam at the starting point: Just another successful Asian economy?" in Borje Ljunggren, ed., *The Challenge of Reform in Indochina*, Cambridge, MA, Harvard University Press, 1993, pp. 167–81.

9 Paul Glewwe, Michele Gragnolati, and Hassan Zamanet, "Who gained from the Vietnam's booms in the 1990s?" *Journal of Economic Development and Cultural Change*, Vol. 50, No. 4, 2002, pp. 773–92.

10 Truong Chinh, then the Party Secretary-General, 1986, *In Preparation for the Sixth Party Congress*, Foreign Languages Publishing House, Hanoi, quoted in Brian Van Arkadie and Raymond Mallon, *Vietnam: A Transition Tiger?* Canberra, ANU E Press, The Australian National University, 2003, p. 65.

11 Ronald Bruce St John, *Revolution, Reform and Regionalism in Southeast Asia: Cambodia, Laos and Vietnam*, London and New York, Routledge, 2006, p. 25.
12 Than and Tan, *op. cit.*, pp. 238–9.
13 Vo Nhan Tri, *Vietnamese Economic Policy Since 1975*, Singapore, Institute of Southeast Asian Studies, 1990, p. 101.
14 Ngoc Q. Pham, Bui Trinh, and Thanh Duc Nguyen, "Economic performance of Vietnam, 1976–2000" *DEPOCEN* (Development and Policies Research Center) *Working Paper Series*, 2007/2013, p. 7.
15 Kerkvliet, *op. cit.*, see especially p. 86 and p. 149.
16 Peter Boothroyd and Pham Xuan Nam, *Socioeconomic Renovation in Vietnam: The Origin, Evolution and Impact of Doi Moi*, Singapore, Institute of Southeast Asian Studies, 2000, p. 14.
17 Pham, Trinh, and Nguyen, *op. cit.*, p. 10.
18 *Ibid.*, p. 9.
19 Than and Tan, *op. cit.*, p. 211.
20 *Ibid.*, p. 211.
21 *Ibid.*, p. 239.
22 The life of Nguyen Van Linh is succinctly presented in *Nguyen Van Linh: Tong Bi thu thoi dao doi moi*, Hanoi, VNA Publishing House, 2009.
23 *Phap Luat News*, retrieved at http://phapluattp.vn/20100630112827794p0c1013 / nguyen-vanlinh-nguoi-cua-thoi-doi-moi.htm
24 Library of Laws, retrieved at www.thuvienluat.com/chitiet.asp?id=30658.
25 For a succinct description of this development, see Michael Kirk and Nguyen Do Anh Tuan, "Land-tenure policy reforms: Decollectivization and the Doi Moi system in Vietnam", *IFPRI Discussion Paper* 00927, International Food Policy Research Institute, November 2009, pp. 2–13.
26 Glewwe, *op. cit.*, p. 3.
27 For the English version of these constitutions and amendments, see *The Constitutions of Vietnam: 1946–1959–1980–1992*, Hanoi, The Gioi Publishers, 2003.
28 Than and Tan, *op. cit.*, p. 253 and Kirk and Anh Tuan, *op. cit.*, pp. 5–8.
29 Communist Party Website, retrieved at http://dangcongsan.vn/cpv/Modules/News/NewsDetail.aspx?co_id=28340641&cn_id=424457.
30 Than and Tan, *op. cit.*, p. 208.
31 Examples are Wim P. M. Vijverberg and Jonathan Haughton, "Household enterprises in Vietnam", in Glewwe et al., eds., *op. cit.*, pp. 95–132 and Michael Kirk and Anh Tuan, *op. cit.*
32 Than and Tan, *op. cit.*, p. 232 and Melanie Beresford and Dang Phong, *Economic Transition in Vietnam: Trade and Aid in the Demise of a Centrally Planned Economy*, Cheltenham; Northampton, MA, Edward Elgar, 2000, especially pp. 69–72.
33 Than and Tan, *op. cit.*, p. 232.
34 Dwayne Benjamin and Loren Brandt, "Agriculture and income distribution in rural Vietnam under economic reforms: A tale of two regions", *William Davidson Working Paper*, No. 519, March 2002, p. 133.
35 http://data.worldbank.org./country/vietnam.
36 Beresford and Phong, *op. cit.* Also "Vietnam trade, exports and imports", Economy Watch, www.economywatch.com/world_economy/vietnam/export-import.html.
37 Jane Le Skaife, "Vietnam no longer an underdeveloped country", *Newgeography*, 2011 www.newgeography.com/content/002154-vietnam-no-longer-underdeveloped-country.
38 St John, *op. cit.*, p. 50.
39 Wiegersma, *op. cit.*, Chapters 3 and 4.
40 To Lan, "On communal land in the traditional Viet village", in Phan Huy Le et al., eds., *The Traditional Village in Vietnam*, Hanoi, The GIOI Publishers, 1993, pp. 156–94.

41 See Jan S. Prybyla, "Soviet and Chinese economic aid to North Vietnam", *The China Quarterly* No. 27 (July–September, 1966), pp. 84–100.

42 Taken from Kerkvliet, *op. cit.*, p. 248.

43 Prybyla, *op. cit.*, p. 87.

44 Tran Thi Que, *Vietnam's Agriculture: The Challenges and Achievements*, Singapore, Institute of Southeast Asian Studies, 1998, pp. 12–13.

45 Kerkvliet, *op. cit.*, p. 256.

46 See *ibid.*, Appendix 2, for a succinct summary of this work point system.

47 *Ibid.*, p. 77.

48 *Ibid.*, pp. 100–103.

49 Dang Phong, *Pha rao trong kinh te vao dem truoc Doi Moi* (Breaking economic barriers before the night of Doi Moi), Nha xuat ban Tri thuc, 2009, p. 3710.

50 Kerkvliet, *op. cit.*, p. 74.

51 Van Thao, *Bí Thư Tỉnh Uỷ- Từ Cuộc Đời "Cha Đẻ Khoán Hộ" Kim Ngọc*, Hanoi, Tre Publishers, 2010, p. 230.

52 Kerkvliet, *op. cit.*, p. 255.

53 United Nations Development Programme, *Report on the Economy of Vietnam*, December 1990, p. 86.

54 Kerkvliet, *op. cit.*, p. 86.

55 *Ibid.*

56 *Ibid.*, p. 26. See also Dang, *op. cit.*, Chapter 7.

57 St John, *op. cit.*, p. 47.

58 See United Nations Development Programme, *Report on the Economy of Vietnam*, December 1990, p. 88. For a succinct summary of the resolution, Kirk and Anh Toan, *op. cit.*

59 See, for example, Tran Thi Que, "Land and agricultural land management in Vietnam", in Ha Huy Thanh and Shozo Sakata, eds., *Impact of Socio-economic Changes on the Livelihoods of People Living in Poverty in Vietnam*, IDE ASEDP Series, 2005, No. 71, p. 181.

60 *Ibid.*

61 *Ibid.*, especially pp. 178–80.

62 *Ibid.*, p. 184.

63 For 1992, "On a number of guidelines and policies to use vacant land, hills, forests, alluvial and coastal water", www.moj.gov.vn/vbpq/Lists/ Vn%20bn%20php%20 lut/View_Detail.aspx?ItemID=11124 and for the Five Million Hectare Programme, "Regarding goals, tasks, policies and implementation of the Project on Planting 5 Million Hectares of Forest", www.moj.gov.vn/vbpq/ Lists/Vn%20bn%20php%20 lut/View_Detail.aspx?ItemID=26199

64 The resolution was passed at the seventh plenary session of the Eighth Party Congress on June 30, 1990. Hereafter, unless otherwise noted, all legal documents are accessed at Thư Viện Pháp Luật (Library of Legal Documents), http://thuvienphapluat.vn/

65 *Financial Magazine* at www.tapchitaichinh.vn/Nghien-cuu-trao-doi/Chinh-sach-thue-voi-tam-nong-Co-so-ly-luan-va-thuc-tien-o-Viet-Nam/10917.tctc

66 www.tiengiang.gov.vn/xemtin.asp?idcha=9662&cap=3&id=16012

67 An insightful examination of Vietnam's efforts to join ASEAN with its emphasis on the internal process reaching the decision is Nguyen Vu Tung, "Vietnam's membership of ASEAN: A constructivist interpretation", in *Contemporary Southeast Asia*, Vol. 29, No. 3, December 2007, pp. 483–505. The year 1995 was also the year when Vietnam sent in its application for membership of the WTO.

68 Hoa Nguyen and Ulrike Grote, "Agricultural policies in Vietnam: Producer support estimates, 1986–2002", *MTID Discussion Paper No. 79*, Center for Development Research (ZEF) Discussion Paper No. 93, December 2004, p. 25 and p. 28. www.zef.de/fileadmin/ webfiles/downloads/zef dp/zef_dp93.pdf

69 Apparently, it is reported that in the 1960s DDT was widely used to protect azolla, which was utilized as both green manure and fertilizer for rice, in China and Southeast

Asia. Thomas A. Lumpkin and Donald L. Plucknett, "Azolla: Botany, physiology and use as green manure", *Economic Botany*, Vol. 34, No. 2, April–June 1980, pp. 130–40.

70 Thi Ha and Nguyen Manh Khai, *op. cit.*, p. 140.

71 *Ibid.*, p. 140.

72 The above account relies on Tran Duc Vien and Pham Van Hoi, "Pesticide dependence in agriculture: Policy for productivity and policy for security in Vietnam", in Umegaki et al., eds., *Human Insecurity in East Asia*, Tokyo; New York, United Nations University Press, 2009, pp. 191–210.

73 *Ibid.*, p. 198.

74 Kunstadter, *op. cit.*

75 Thi Ha and Manh Khai, *op. cit.*, p. 141.

76 P. Van Mele, Nguyen Thi Thu Cuc, and A. van Huis, "Farmers' knowledge, perception and practices in mango pest management in the Mekong Delta, Vietnam", *International Journal of Pest Management*, Vol. 47, 2001, pp. 7–16 and Pham Binh Quyen, Duc Dang Nhan, and Nguyen Van San, "Environmental pollution in Vietnam: Analytical estimation and environmental priorities", *Trends in Analytical Chemistry*, Vol. 14, No. 1, 1995, pp. 383–7, quoted in Tran Duc Vien and Pham Van Hoi, "Pesticide uses in agriculture: Food and water contamination and health impacts in Vietnam", unpublished paper presented at *4th workshop for Human Security at East Asia*, February 25–27, Keio University, Japan, 2007.

77 See, for example, *Thanh Nien News*, September 7, 2004.

78 World Bank, "Vietnam food safety and agricultural health action plan", *Document of World Bank*, 2006, Report no. 35231 VN, p. xii.

79 Beck, *op. cit*, 1992 (1986); also see Ulrich Beck, Anthony Giddens, and Scott Lash, *Reflexive Modernization. Politics, Tradition and Aesthetics in the Modern Social Order*, Palo Alto, CA, Stanford University Press, 1994.

3 Agent Orange and its impact on Vietnamese farmers

A distant legacy

Rural Vietnam, the war, and Agent Orange

Our examination of the farmers' behaviour begins with that of a group of farmers who embrace the evidence of health risks that have materialized before their eyes. The members of the group are distinguished by having one or more family members physically and/or mentally disabled by direct and indirect exposure to the use of toxic herbicides like Agent Orange (AO) during wartime. These disabled family members include not only the war generations but also those who were born after the war.

Many in this group of farmers also exhibit behaviour that at least appears unaffected by having their members negatively affected by exposure to AO. They were persistent in living lives full of all demands so that they offset the effect of living with AO victims within their households. In other words, AO victims' families (hereafter we refer to them as "AO families") represent ordinary farmers *because of*, and not *despite*, the evidence of misfortune among the family members.

The story of AO families goes far beyond that of personal agony and courage. It includes the ways in which they survive and embrace difficulties whose roots are traceable back to the wartime exigencies. However, AO victims are not merely the result of the wartime use of toxic chemicals. They are also the victims of an immensely strenuous and time-consuming process: AO's wartime use by the United States and the government of the South was preceded and paralleled by a seemingly endless exchange between scientific findings supporting or discrediting the claim of toxicity of the chemicals, partisan manipulations of the findings, problematic self-constraints exercised by scientific experts on the use of chemicals, and political interferences.

The toxicity of certain chemicals and substances that threaten human health continues to interest many scientists (experts). At issue are the implications of its use: not all toxic chemicals have a clear "threshold for harm",[1] below which a small dose may even be beneficial. What is the responsibility of scientific experts – how strong would the evidence have to be for them to insist on banning the chemicals or even pressure users into taking extra caution in using them? More importantly, what may be their responsibility, with all the scientific knowledge, while their findings remain inconclusive?

The story does not end when the families encounter unexpected misfortune. It begins only when the AO families and their community struggle to respond to this legacy of a bygone war. Ordinary people live with unimaginably clear evidence and threat of disruption. There is a distance, or even conflict, between the dictates of expert knowledge and of that which the ordinary people have developed and preserved in continually facing the threat of disruption.

The AO victims and their families are, in other words, a metaphor of the problem attendant upon anyone's life. They are evidence of the "individualized responsibility" in practice for better or worse. They raise a series of questions: whether or not one should base one's well-being upon what a scientific community may offer; whether or not one should put one's life on hold while scientific experts engage in an endless debate on their findings; and what life may be like when one is left solely to one's own discretion.

The story of AO victims and their families is also one of failure, although not the result of their own, to generate a broader and more responsive mass among their fellow farmers. To ordinary farmers, the AO families' plight is a story with a fairy-tale quality that has its origins in a remote past or too unusual a life for anyone else to draw lessons from. Here, too, the life of AO victims and their families is a metaphor for general conduct of life, where one tends to gloss over rare events, or "cases" too outlying to be relevant.

War and Agent Orange

It was not a coincidence that AO first caught the attention of medical specialists in the North Vietnamese Regular Army. A high-ranking health official in Hanoi recalled his wartime experience when he was a soldier in a medical unit assigned to the Ho Chi Minh Trail, and his unit's special assignment was to collect blood samples from soldiers who exhibited unusual symptoms soon after their exposure to the white mist. The efforts to transport the blood samples preoccupied him as he also witnessed the sudden death of some soldiers on the Trail following their being sprayed by a U.S. aircraft. Only later did he learn that the white mist was that of a dioxin-yielding herbicide, known as Agent Orange because the toxic chemical was stored in 200-litre cans that were painted orange.[2]

Dr Le Kao Dai, the health official's superior, detailed his initial encounters with the mist and his subsequent efforts to understand its role in the unexpected ailments and eventual death of the soldiers on the front line in his *Memoirs of War: The Central Highlands*.[3] Both the official and Dr Le Kao Dai extended their efforts beyond the end of the war and became critical role players in publicizing and addressing the issue of dioxin-yielding AO in Vietnam. It was through two of their close associates, the late Dr Trinh Van Bao and Dr Tran Duc Phan, that the research sites for this study were selected: Phu Cat in a coastal province in central Vietnam; Thanh Khe in Da Nang next to a major airbase; and Kim Bang some 50 km south-east of Hanoi in the north, with a heavy concentration of the North Vietnamese Regular Army.

Phu Cat District (pop. 210,000) in Bin Dinh Province represents rural Vietnam in many ways. The district's Ngo May section, which offers government and other services, stretches along the north-south Highway One. Some 300 km north of the District is Da Nang. A hundred m off the highway, and away from the Ngo May section, we find ourselves already in the middle of rice fields of various sizes. The rice fields, in turn, are usually hedged by small but thick bushes of short and tall tropical trees, including 20-m-tall coconut trees. Small groups of brick houses are tucked in among these bushes. Narrow winding paths snake through the rice paddies and the bushes, blocking a clear view at any one spot of the whole landscape.

The lowland around Phu Cat District gradually rises towards the west until it merges with the foot of the Chuonson Mountains (Annamite Range) in the central highlands separating Vietnam from Laos and Cambodia further to the west. Running closely to the border on the Laos and Cambodian side, the Ho Chi Minh Trail served as an artery, pumping goods and personnel from the North to the South during the war. An untold number of small paths sprang from the Trail and reached everywhere in the lowland, including Phu Cat and Da Nang. The villagers, protected by the maze of numerous paths running through the rice fields and bushes and the canopy of tropical trees, made frequent trips between their villages and the Ho Chi Min Trail carrying food, ammunition, medicine, and other supplies to and from the Trail.

The National Liberation Front (NLF) fighters took advantage of this rural landscape of Vietnam. They moved along the branches of the Trail undetected and managed to transport and store ammunition and food supplies in the villages. The NLF soldiers and the NLF sympathizers from the villages, who called themselves *du kich* (militia or guerrillas), were often almost interchangeable in what they did; in what they perceived themselves to be; and, indeed, in what they were.

Yet another factor effectively erased the boundary between the front and the rear. While the NLF's (and the North Vietnamese Regulars') aim was to infiltrate and turn the villagers against the Republic of Vietnam, the United States' strategy, known as "search and destroy", was to spot the infiltration and eliminate the seeds of pro-revolutionaries. The war, in other words, was a series of incessant and unpredictable encounters between these two on constantly shifting battlegrounds, not quite like more conventional frontal and sustained confrontations between division-size adversaries. Any place at any time could easily turn into a battle. At the same time, for the villagers, there was plenty of time and even space to sustain life *as usual*, albeit with an immensely heightened sense of danger.[4]

Given this overall landscape of rural South Vietnam, Phu Cat differed in one feature. Phu Cat had an airport, which turned an otherwise ordinary rural district into a strategic stronghold for the United States and the Republic of Vietnam. The airport, located 15 km south-west of the Ngo May section of Phu Cat, sits in a red soil surrounded by thick bushes. The airport and its surrounding area no longer have the look of what they used to be even in the early 2000s after the recent years of renovation and expansion. It is still easy to imagine that the personnel manning the airport during the war had a sense of constant surveillance by the enemy as if they were at the forefront of the battle.

It was against this background as literally and figuratively represented by Phu Cat that the United States pushed the use of toxic herbicides: the intention was to transform the landscape by removing the thick bushes and ever-present green canopy of the tropical jungles and expose the approaching enemy. The use of herbicide had found an opportune "precedent" for its effectiveness in the successful British campaign against the communist insurgents in the Malay tropical forest in the late 1950s.[5]

Vietnamese soldiers from the North and NLF fighters were the first to encounter the deadly chemicals sprayed by the United States, which, ironically, also turned U.S. soldiers into collateral damage. After all, in the "search and destroy" missions, the U.S. soldiers' role was to walk right into areas that the U.S. and South Vietnamese soldiers suspected the NLF soldiers and North Vietnamese regulars had infiltrated, or those they considered vulnerable to infiltration, thereby warranting the use of the herbicides. There were also numerous villagers and non-combatants who became part of the collateral damage as they witnessed the descending white mist (or yellow rain, depending on whom you talk to) at close range. The spraying was not restricted to the airport area alone.

Outsiders got a first glimpse of what AO and other herbicides were capable of as the spraying operation was at its peak around 1967–1969. Arthur Westing, an American botanist, visited the South several times between 1969 and 1973 and uncovered massive ecological damages inflicted by the war. The use of herbicide was still listed merely among many "means" of war when his report was published in 1976. The purpose of Westing's visits was to broadly evaluate the ecological consequences of the war.[6] He witnessed a vast wasteland and bare mountains left by the heavy use of bulldozers and other machinery employed in constructing airbases, roads for the military to transport weapons and goods, and more, in addition to the use of the herbicides.

One decade later, Westing and his associates' efforts obtained a sharper focus on the impact of the herbicides, and the sharper focus also found itself a broader audience. Most of the over two and a half million U.S. soldiers who served in Vietnam had been left in the dark as to why the herbicides and their deadly impact on human bodies mattered until one U.S. TV network made and aired a documentary programme on AO in 1978, sending shock waves through their ranks. This shock picked up more momentum before culminating in a massive class action suit in 1980 and an eventual out-of-court settlement between the representatives of the AO victims among the U.S. soldiers and the manufacturers of the herbicides, including Dow Chemicals, Monsanto, and five other chemical companies in the United States in 1984.[7]

A Vietnamese encounter with AO, as mentioned at the beginning of this chapter, took place at the chaotic front on the Ho Chi Minh Trail. However, the unification efforts and the ensuing Cambodian campaign gave very little time, if any, for anyone in the government or the military to launch a systematic examination of the wide-ranging damages and implications of AO and other herbicides. Although there is no way of documenting the connection, the Vietnamese government monitored closely what had been transpiring in the United States, especially legal actions taken by U.S. veterans of the war, and established the national 10-80 Committee in October 1980 to oversee all activities concerning the damages done by AO and other chemicals used during war.[8]

The substance AO comprises dioxin-yielding chemical compounds. A 50–50 mixture of the powerful phenoxy herbicides 2,4,-D and 2,4,5-T, AO was found to contain the most toxic chemical known to men, 2,3,7,8-T (tetrachlorodibenzo-para-dioxin, or TCDD).[9] Eighty grams of dioxin, if poured into the water system of New York, is claimed to be capable of annihilating the entire population of the city.[10]

Under the code name Operation Ranch Hand, the United States sprayed 21 million gallons of herbicide between 1962 and 1972, which is estimated to have yielded 170 kg of dioxin.[11] However, as was discovered later, it is not only the *sprayed* herbicides that could produce dioxin. The leaked AO and other chemicals from storage, and those abandoned are believed to continue to produce dioxin. The adjusted estimate of the dioxin emitted in Vietnam is believed to be over 600 kg.[12]

The damages to the environment and humans were extensive. Destruction of the tropical forest in the mountains alone could trigger a chain of damages beyond the areas of spraying. With the destruction of trees, the surface soil could easily slide into the rivers, raising their beds and contributing to constant flooding. The mountains would no longer be able to retain rainwater, making water reservoirs an absolute necessity. The rainwater running through the AO-sprayed surfaces would easily reach the rivers, contaminating the water bodies, which were often valuable food resources for the residents living near the rivers and lakes, or it could seep into the soil and contaminate well water.

The sprayed AO and the dispersed dioxin had many ways of reaching human bodies – through drinking water or the food chain, and through those, especially mothers, who ate and drank the contaminated food and water. As such, they could also reach several generations after the war.

In official documents in the United States, the language describing the cause-effect relationship between the exposure to AO and other herbicides and health hazards is, however, at best indirect. The language may perhaps reflect the caution on the part of medical and chemical experts about making a direct link, or it may suggest political prudence in such a potentially divisive (for the Americans) implication. However, the point is unmistakable. Researchers conclude "with a very high degree of confidence" or feel "comfortable to conclude"[13] that the exposure induced a wide range of often terminal or debilitating ailments, such as prostate and other kinds of cancer, Hodgkin's disease or multiple myeloma, or spina bifida, often found among the second-generation children of Vietnam War veterans. These are also found among the second and third generations of Vietnamese residents in the sprayed areas as well as among war veterans.

Various researchers have arrived at differing estimates of the total number of victims of AO, but anything remotely approaching a ballpark figure seems impossible. The question of unravelling who was exposed to AO/dioxin, and when, is a formidable task since the sprayed areas were immense and, more importantly, since the United States sprayed the chemicals on extremely mobile people. Moreover, the food chain as a carrier of the contaminant further complicates the calculation because, again, a food chain could be almost infinite when it includes breast milk. One of the more recent estimates, by a Columbia University Public Health group, sets the total number of Vietnamese victims at somewhere between 2.1 and 4.8 million. While they were mainly in the South, there were also AO victims in the North, among those who were active on the Ho Chi Minh Trail during the war.

Agent Orange after the war

After the war, the Vietnamese in the North and those in the South resumed their daily lives with more hope for the future. However, many of them did not know that something had changed in their living environment, especially in the South, and even in their bodies. Dioxin contaminants continue to reside in the soil, water sources, and human bodies. This residue is a powerful reminder that even though nearly 35 years (as of the beginning of our research) had passed since its end, the brutality of the war remains close to home.

The three sites of our research in Vietnam illustrate this incongruity between life as usual and the potential for its disruption. The presence of one or more members in the family with AO/dioxin-induced deficiencies makes the daily preoccupation with a livelihood that much more difficult.

Of the three chosen sites, Thanh Khe and Phu Cat, both to the south of the 17th Parallel, are the two "hot spots" in Vietnam because of the high dioxin contamination in the living environment due to the wartime exposure to AO. The last of the three, Kim Bang in Nam Ha Province, is a rural district, 50 km south-east of Hanoi, that was spared the AO spray. However, the town is one of the areas in the North where there is a heavy concentration of former North Vietnamese Regular Army soldiers who participated in the war. These soldiers are believed to have been exposed to AO and other herbicides while fighting and moving along the Ho Chi Minh Trail.

Thanh Khe is a district right in the middle of the city of Da Nang while Phu Cat and Kim Bang are rural districts, whose primary source of livelihood is agriculture. Thanh Khe is located right next to the former U.S. military airbase, one of the most severely AO-contaminated areas, but the number of certified victims in this site was only 147 in 2006. One of the reasons may be the stricter medical examination of the residents in determining the "victims". Another is the greater technical difficulty that some of these residents' involvement with (or contributions to) the war of revolution and unification posed, which is almost impossible to document since their roles were those of *du kich* or the militia.

Table 3.1 Basic Statistics of the Three Research Sites as of 2006

	Population	*Certified Victims*	*Suspected Victims*
Thanh Khe	160,000	147	NA
Phu Cat	210,000	1857	NA
Kim Bang	130,000	4233	3625

Source: Obtained from Health Centres in Thank Khe, Kim Bang, and Phu Cat, and General Statistics Office, 2006.

Although Thanh Khe is in a commercially dynamic city, many residents in this district still rely on farming for their livelihood and consume fish from the nearby Sen Lake, which was found to be heavily contaminated with AO, even during the initial phase of our research.[14]

Kim Bang also has a heavy concentration of former North Vietnamese Regular Army soldiers. Unlike the residents in Thanh Khe and Phu Cat, the documentation of their participation in the "revolutionary" war is relatively easy and readily available for identifying the "victims" of the AO contamination and providing government compensation (AO pension), which explains a large number of the certified victims of AO in this site (Table 3.1).

Phu Cat in Binh Dinh Province combines two of the characteristics of Thanh Khe and Kim Bang. It is a large rural and agricultural area, embracing both the Nui Ba Mountains and the strategic Phu Cat Airport. Both were the targets of heavy herbicide spraying during the war. The residents mainly rely on farming – rice, cassava, peanuts, and recently commercial products like cashew nuts – and have thus been in direct contact with the contaminated environment not only during the war but also since. The majority of the victims in this area are civilians or former local militia or *du kich.* They were directly exposed to the spraying of AO and indirectly exposed to AO-contaminated rivers and well-water, and through the food chain after the war's end. Again, very much like the residents of Thanh Khe, their participation in the revolutionary war is not so easily documented. Furthermore, some of the residents fought against the NLF and the North Vietnamese Regular Army. This, partially at least, may account for the difficulty in identifying the AO victims as shown by the use of "not applicable (NA)" for the category of "suspected victims".

Families of Agent Orange victims

Due to the reasons mentioned above, it is not an easy task to locate and identify families with at least one victim in their second or third generations. We needed to rely on Hanoi Medical University's initial research conducted by Dr Trinh Van Bao and others in 2001–2002 for locating the AO families.

The unusually large number of disabled children per household is the common denominator. On average, each household has 1.27 disabled children. The number is exceptionally high, at 1.8, in the case of Kim Bang, where there is a high concentration of former NLF soldiers. It is 1.16 for Phu Cat and 1.26 for Thanh Khe, respectively. This high rate of instances of disabled children, especially among the families of the former regular soldiers, may have prompted the famous statement made by Madame Nguyen Thi Binh, foreign minister of the Provisional Revolutionary Government of the Republic of South Vietnam, who later became vice-president of the unified Vietnam:

> All of our returning veterans had a burning desire for children to repopulate our devastated country. When the first child was born with a birth defect, they tried again and again. So many families now have four or five disabled children, raising them without any hope.[15]

Having many children (including disabled ones) seems to be a feature of the families in rural Phu Cat. In Phu Cat and Kim Bang, the size of families is generally large (Table 3.2). One main reason for this is that in rural areas, the need for labour resources is much higher. The other reason is that even though the government put a family planning policy into effect in 1988, the intention of the policy was understood best at the level of local party organizations such as the People's Committee,[16] which also has the ultimate responsibility for its enforcement. A penalty of a couple of kilograms of grain rice for giving birth to one extra child after the first two may have been only a limited deterrent. It was just a "fee", which they sometimes conveniently "forgot" to pay.

During our initial phase of research, of the 48 AO families we interviewed in Phu Cat, there were still nine, with only three or four members (including parents). The young parents may explain the concentration of the small-size households in the younger generation, as the heads may well be better informed of the chances of unwelcome births. There were up to 12 heads of AO families under 40 years old (Table 3.3). However, it is equally likely that these families would add more members later, as we witnessed in more than one case where the families added more members after our initial contact with them. That undermines the claim that the younger Vietnamese may be better informed, or more fearful, of the unwelcome consequences. By contrast, all parents in Kim Bang were over 50 years old. These relatively older parents reflected the simple fact that they were former members of the regular North Vietnamese army and

Table 3.2 Size of the Agent Orange Victims' Families

	3–4 Members	*5–6 Members*	*7–8 Members*	*9+ Members*	*NA*
Thanh Khe	5	6	4	0	0
Phu Cat	9	18	18	1	2
Kim Bang	0	13	14	2	1

Source: Tables 3.2 and 3.3 are from Michio Umegaki, Vu Le Thao Chi, and Tran Duc Phan, "Embracing Human Insecurity: Agent Orange and the Legacies of the War in Viet Nam," in Michio Umegaki, et al., eds., *Human Insecurity in East Asia*, Tokyo and New York: United Nations University Press, 2009, p. 33.

Table 3.3 Average Age of AO Families' Head

	*1**	*2**	*3**	*4**	*5**	*6**
Thanh Khe	5	0	4	4	2	0
Phu Cat	1	2	9	17	12	2
Kim Bang	2	11	16	0	0	0

* Birth year: 1* before 1935; 2* 1936–1945; 3* 1946–1955; 4* 1956–1965; 5* 1966–1975; 6* after 1976.

were exhibiting behaviour closer to that which Madame Ngyuen Thih Binh had observed.

Thanh Khe's AO families exhibited a somewhat different pattern. As shown in Table 3.2, the size of each AO family was relatively small compared to those in Phu Cat and Kim Bang. Many of the household heads were also younger, under 50 years old. This relatively smaller size may partially show the effectiveness of the 1988 family planning policy,[17] which was rigorously enforced, especially on the party members or state enterprise workers ***in the urban area*** as it entailed wage reduction and demotion, among other things, as the penalty for failing to comply. In the four larger-sized families (seven or eight members), the parents were older, and they had had children either before the family planning policy became stricter in the later years of reinforcement or during the early 1990s, the early phase of the family planning campaign.

Livelihood

Among the indicators illuminating AO families' lives, income may be an obvious primary and reliable choice. However, for reasons explained below, income can be a misleading indicator, except to get a general picture of the three sites from high (Thanh Khe) to low (Phu Cat) income. This is based on the overall economical location and set-up of the AO families that enables them to procure their daily necessities: Thanh Khe, in the middle of a major city, requires the families to sustain a relatively high income if they are to prevent their household economies from collapsing, whereas, in Phu Cat, where street-side mini-markets often serve as sites for exchanging goods, a higher income may not be so critical a need.

Another reason is the dubious figures that the interviewees often cited when asked about their monthly or yearly income. The answers, often given very quickly, were usually in perfectly round figures such as "200,000" VND (roughly $15) per month or "300,000" VND ($20). Perhaps cash income was not as meaningful to them as it is to us, and as such, they were not able to recall the figures at will. Yet another reason was the portion of "debt" owed to their relatives or local financial institutions, such as the Rural and Agricultural Development Bank. In their minds, especially those of Phu Cat families, the debt was (and still is) often an integral part of their "income", as indicated in their responses such as "I'll borrow money from the bank to pay the debt [to another]" or "I know the official [of the bank], and he'll wait".

There are also significant differences between the AO-dioxin families in the three sites in terms of the sources of income, in which some of the families in Phu Cat were in a more disadvantaged position as they relied on irregular menial work or run a small convenience store where the sales were small and the earnings utterly unpredictable. At least, however, nearly all were still above the national poverty line ($11–12) and the international poverty line ($25),[18] as of our initial inquiry.

In Thanh Khe, an urban district, the majority of the victims' parents were or used to be, state workers. For some of the older parents, their former status as soldiers in the North Vietnamese Regular Army helped them find stable jobs in state-run companies or offices after the war. For the younger parents, thanks to the better access to education, they were able to find employment in stable jobs such as in medical offices and banks, among others. Therefore, the primary sources of income were from their regular salary, and sometimes also their pensions (Table 3.4).

Moreover, if fathers or mothers who used to be former soldiers and were injured during the war, they qualified for war pensions, including the pension for invalid soldiers or the pension for soldiers who had lost their working ability, depending on the seriousness of their injury or health problems. Their experiences in the war and proven exposure to AO would also help their affected children receive financial support monthly from 180,000 VND to 300,000 VND (as of 2004).[19] Thanh Khe's income level was higher than that of the international poverty line and reflected stable sources of income.

In contrast, the income level of those victims' families in Phu Cat has been much lower. There were a few whose income level was bordering on, or lower than, the national rural poverty line. One reason was that the people here had to rely mainly on farming, which is sometimes unstable and generates much

Table 3.4 Sources of Income (in order of relative weight)

Thanh Khe	*Phu Cat*	*Kim Bang*
1 Salary: – Salary from stable jobs 2 Pension (state support): – Invalid soldier pension – Lost working ability pension – "Contributors to revolution" pension – Agent Orange victim pension 3 Others: – Extra income from menial work	1 Farming: Rice, vegetables, animal husbandry 2 Menial work: House and other construction works, and other small-wage labour 3 Others: Manual work in other cities like Quy Nhon (the principal city of the province) or Ho Chi Minh City (shoe factory and other labour-intensive, small-sized factories)	1 Farming: Rice, vegetables, husbandry 2 Pension: – Invalid soldier pension – Lost working ability pension – "Contributors to revolution" pension – Agent Orange victim pension 3 Others: Menial work or low-income jobs in Hanoi (bread making)

smaller surpluses. There were a few cases in Phu Cat where the father might be unemployed and the mother was making barely enough to make up for it as a regular employee (midwife, earning about the equivalent of $70 a month) at the District Health Centre or a local Commune Clinic. We needed to bear in mind that, even when the income was higher, it was still precarious. The incomes of midwives varied depending on the need for their services. Such instability has been ongoing. It is against this or a similar background that many families sent some of their members to bigger cities, either to earn a little more and send the money back home, to downsize the family, or to remove one "mouth to feed". Apparently, even those who moved to cities often could not afford to send part of their income back home.[20]

Similar to the Phu Cat families, many of the AO families in Kim Bang rely on farming for a living. However, what makes the overall income level of these families higher, even higher than that of the families in Thanh Khe, is the greater variety of pension sources. As mentioned before, the majority of the parents of the AO victims in Kim Bang are former soldiers of the North Vietnamese Regular Army. Therefore, they are qualified to receive all war-related pensions, such as pensions for invalid soldiers, for those who lost the ability to work, and AO pensions for their affected children. What struck us as odd was that so many families received all these pensions at the same time, and the pensions alone have become one of the major sources for their living in addition to farming. Their income is not only higher than that of others in Phu Cat and Thanh Khe, but also very stable. In sum, generally speaking, the AO-dioxin victims and their families in Kim Bang have been living under relatively more fortunate conditions than those in Thanh Khe, who are still better off than those in Phu Cat.

Where they live matters

However, what makes up sources of livelihood, such as cash income, only makes sense when certain other factors, such as the physical size of the community or the population density, are taken into consideration, particularly since they directly influence the accessibility of certain services, such as medical services, which are essential to AO families.

Table 3.5 presents the basic profiles of the three research sites. Thanh Khe is the most densely populated among the three, with a population of more than 160,000 within a small area in Da Nang. Both Phu Cat and Kim Bang are located in large rural areas and are more sparsely populated, even though their population sizes are roughly the same as that of Thanh Khe. The population density of Phu Cat is only 286 per km^2, about a third of that of Kim Bang and an eighth of that of Thanh Khe.

Taken as an isolated indicator, the number of medical doctors per population in Vietnam is a modest figure for a developing country.[21] However, a closer look reveals that the total number of medical staff for the three districts is 133, 190, and 188 for Thanh Khe, Phu Cat, and Kim Bang, respectively. Adding the size of the population, the difference in the burden per medical worker is 1,207

Table 3.5 Basic Profiles of the Three Areas and Medical Services

	Thanh Khe	*Phu Cat*	*Kim Bang*
Number of communes/wards	8	18	19
Size of area	9.3 km^2	679 km^2	184.9 km^2
Total population	160,582	194,100	129,541
Population density per km^2	17,267	286	701
Number of health units	11	24	24
Medical staff	133	190	188
– Doctors and higher degree	51	45	45
– *Assistant physicians*	51	81	57
– Nurses	15	48	NA
– Midwives	16	16	NA
Pharmaceutical staff	9	7	48
– High-degree pharmacist	1	2	6
– Middle-degree pharmacist	4	3	6
– Assistant pharmacist	4	2	36

Source: Acquired from Health Centres in Thank Khe, Kim Bang, and Phu Cat, and General Statistics Office, 2006.

people in Thanh Khe, 1,021 people in Phu Cat, and 689 people in Kim Bang (Table 3.5). From the perspective of those who need medical services, Kim Bang residents are much better off than those in Phu Cat and Thanh Khe.

Adding the physical size of the areas, yet another result is obtained. In Phu Cat, which is the largest district in terms of size, medical workers must cover all residents, who are scattered within this large district. For example, some Communes are a 30- or 40-minute drive from Ngo May in Phu Cat, where the District Health Centre is located, or close to about an hour and a half from Qui Nhon, where there is a major provincial hospital. In Thanh Khe, people can walk from one commune to another, or to the District Health Centre, in much less time. From the residents' perspective too, the distance is a barrier to their utilization of medical services. Dr Truong Quang Dat, former director of Phu Cat District Health Centre and a member of the Keio-Hanoi Medical University research team reported that the distance between the residents and medical service establishments such as district or provincial hospitals makes a big difference to the residents' utilization of, and reliance on, the full medical services.[22]

There is also something else in the aggregate data, as shown in Table 3.5. Thanh Khe, Kim Bang, and Phu Cat have 8, 19, and 18 communes, respectively.[23] Having a clinic in each of these Communes may help maintain the presence of medical services throughout each district. Or so it appears. However, that presence may be empty of corresponding contents. For one thing, many of the medical doctors (with a degree in medicine) are scattered thinly and widely among the clinics in nearly 20 communes in Phu Cat and in Kim Bang. "Uh, I am a generalist" is the usual answer to the question concerning the doctors' specialties. We wondered then and now what the initial contacts with the patients entail, beyond a perfunctory diagnosis.

Another factor needs to be computed into this. In Phu Cat and Kim Bang, the majority of the medical workers are "assistant physicians", a category of medical professionals somewhere between physicians and nurses. They typically have three years of basic medical training after high school in what may be tantamount to medical vocational school. Their presence in the communes is ubiquitous as they man the commune clinics and even help the residents in many of their community and household affairs.

Yet their *professional* qualifications limit them to administering prescription drugs, measuring blood pressure, or arranging a full medical examination in a major hospital. In other words, the fact that a commune has a sufficient *number* of medical workers does not mean that it offers sufficient medical services. Moreover, we witnessed on more than a few occasions that these assistant physicians, not out of ill intention but out of pure sympathy, often made conclusive, and unwarranted, remarks to members of the AO families concerning the finality of the AO-induced ailments, such as "[There's] no cure for this". The fact that the qualified medical doctors are spread thinly throughout the area makes the presence of these assistant physicians far more prominent.

We also noticed that the number of available medical staff is lesser than indicated by the statistics in Table 3.5, and the distance to the established medical facilities is even greater. Sometimes, clinic heads are assistant physicians and not medical doctors, or they may be preoccupied with something else. In one of our visits to Cat Khanh Commune Clinic in Phu Cat District, for the first time, in May 2005, the clinic head – an assistant physician – was absent as he was studying at Hue Medical University to acquire a medical degree for the status of a full "doctor", leaving one nurse tending the clinic. On the same day, we stopped by another commune clinic in Cat Lam Commune and had a talk with the clinic head, Nguyen V. L. He is a 50-year-old assistant physician, not a medical doctor.

These medical workers at commune clinics may not be fully or exclusively engaged in providing medical services. Because of the stable and higher income (a difference of about 200,000 VND-\$10 – to 400,000 VND-\$20 – in monthly income in the case of doctors, compared with the other two sites), the medical workers in Thanh Khe can commit their time more fully to both the work and social activities within the framework of the medical centre or commune clinics. Their part-time activities, if any, after their official work time are also medically relevant, such as running a pharmacy or home medical consulting room. By contrast, the medical staff in Kim Bang and Phu Cat engage themselves in farming and see this as a no less important source of livelihood. When interviewing Nguyen V. L., as mentioned above, we happened to notice his hands. Contrary to the common image of a medical professional with soft, clean, and white hands, his were typical of a farmer's hands – tanned, brawny, and with bulging tendons, and the tips of his fingers were covered with dirt. It came as no surprise when he told us that he also had to go harvesting rice after a day's work at the Commune Clinic. The same finding was noted when we met with the vice-director of Kim Bang Health Centre, Mrs Xn, in early May 2006. Even though she had a more "medical-doctor-like" look, she was laughing as she said she was very good at cultivating rice, which helped her earn a little extra income to raise her two children.

The irony is that the physical distance alone is deceptive. For those who seek *medical* services, the distance between their location and district or provincial hospitals matters, not that between themselves and Commune Clinics. In fact, the presence of Commune Clinics may make the distance between the medical services and the villagers seem larger than the physical distance may suggest.

Agent Orange "victims" as they see themselves

Despite some of the differences in the surrounding conditions, AO victims and their families share a set of troubles that make their life more difficult, even when their income is above the poverty line. The difficulty, as they see it, seems far more complex than what conventional understanding of the hardship associated with having permanently disabled children may suggest.

Perhaps the most important "given" for all the AO families is the fact that the disabled child(ren) *is (are)* part of their "normal" life. Their life has already been reconstructed to see having disabled children as "normal". Everything is built on this "normalcy". There were more opportunities to observe this in AO families in Phu Cat since we made frequent visits over a much longer span of time than we did to the other two research sites.

Like everyone else, the parents of the disabled children need to face their unpredictable, though not always so serious, illnesses, such as colds or stomach aches. For everyone, these unpredictable illnesses may constitute a health "crisis" as they need to purchase extra medicine and reallocate work to care for their sick children. For everyone else, the pressure of dealing with the "crisis" ends when the children recover from the illness. However, for the AO families, the relief from the "crisis" merely means a return to that "normal" life that has already embraced the presence of children with permanent or near-permanent physical and/or mental disabilities.

There are variations among the AO families, of course. One group of AO families consists of those with children predisposed to disruptive behaviours and incidents or unpredictable seizures of one kind or another, while another group consists of those who suffer from chronic but not necessarily disruptive incidents.

The former clearly sees the disabled children as a constant reminder of how taxing their life is. The disabilities common to the children in this group include brittle bone disease (osteogenesis imperfecta), epilepsy, cerebral palsy, and serious cases of mental disorder, among others. These children are incapable of taking care of themselves. They rely on the family members for just about every basic need. A few of them are living a vegetable-like existence. Their conditions do not improve and remain critical or even deteriorate. None of these victims usually receives regular treatment or medical check-ups, however. The initial diagnosis by medical doctors and clinic workers, "Agent Orange, no cure", has led the parents not to invest in improving the health conditions of the children.

Instead, by staying on high alert, they respond to unpredictable situations: convulsions, fits of madness, or breaking bones. If and when any of these happens, they may rush their children to the District Health Centre (from a few minutes to a 30- or 40-minute drive) or to a provincial hospital (a one- to two-hour drive) because only those institutions can handle such serious ailments. These actions are virtually a conditioned response to the incidents rather than a projection of hope for better health in the future.

Some of the families even put their children in a cage (a wooden cage or isolated and locked room) to stop them from destroying furniture in the house or hurting themselves or others. There always has to be someone who can keep an eye on them, just in case these children need to be rushed to major hospitals. Usually, such rounds of treatment make a huge dent in their purses or leave them in debt.

For the latter category of AO families, the ailments are milder, and embracing the disabled children is easier. They are cases of Down's syndrome, mild cases of mental disorder, mild cases of cerebral palsy, speech, and other physical movement impediments. Like every other AO family with a disabled child, they felt shocked and then disappointed when they learned of the child's birth defect(s). Unlike the first category, though disabled, these children are in more stable medical conditions and less likely to disrupt their families' lives. If anything, they may become hyperactive under certain conditions, such as sudden shifts in the weather or exposure to strangers. This relative stability of the disabled children helps their parents and other family members come to terms with their existence, however "unusual" they may be. These family members do not see the need to take the disabled children for regular medical check-up or treatment. They are not indifferent to any signs threatening the children's undisruptive presence. Even then, they are ready to let it pass. At least, to them, that is what coming to terms with entails.

Across nearly all AO families, there is one common choice of action: shying away from any medical treatment of physical and mental defects of the children on a regular basis. If it is only for the sake of their children "getting better", they may just give some cheap supplements and nutrients to their children. Or they may occasionally ask some of the good-natured Commune Clinic staff to provide simple physical therapy for very minor cases of physical disability. These choices of action are not aimed at recovering the "losses" at birth. Having disabled children is an integral part of their "normal" life.

Financing disabled children

Given that the families of AO victims must live with the fact that the children's disabilities stay with them as long as they live, it is obvious that financial problems are the most constant risks that the families have to face. The presence of disabled children alone may not throw them into debt, but, at the very least, it worsens their already difficult financial situations.

In the early phase when a child may be or has been born with certain defects or contracts them shortly after birth, the parents are terrified and look for every possible means, almost at any financial cost, even if they have to run around and borrow money, in the hope that the child will become normal. However, once it has been concluded that the child has been affected by AO, the parents, in most cases, give up, take the child back home, and accept the situation, after the initial shock subsides.

A few may still look for ways to help their children, such as buying them supplements, herbal medicines, or acupuncture treatments. This was the case with Dao T. N. in Cat Thanh Commune, Phu Cat District (July 2005). She was 15 years old then, mentally challenged, and had weak legs. Her parents took her to the Institute of Traditional Medicine in Quy Nhon, one and a half hours away, for acupuncture and physical therapy. According to the parents, her legs had improved a little. However, using traditional or herbal medicine for a prolonged time is not cheap. Consequently, they either borrowed money or made the treatment less frequent, and eventually, they gave it up altogether.

Like other normal families, the families of the victims also want to save money to prepare for any potential health "crises" faced by the disabled children. However, families with a low income and many mouths to feed in the first place cannot afford to build such an emergency fund. The families in Phu Cat, who have a much less regular cash income, are no exceptions. They just wait until the health "crisis" occurs and then start running around trying to borrow money to take their children to hospitals, without considering whether they can pay the debts back or not. These expenses are simply added to the regular expenditure of taking care of their handicapped children throughout their whole life. Consequently, being indebted is a common feature among the families in all three sites. The size of the debt often exceeds that of their annual earnings (Table 3.6).

They borrow money from banks, friends, and relatives, and, in a few cases, local moneylenders at very high interest rates. Many of them are reluctant to borrow money from a bank or private moneylenders because they are afraid they won't be able to pay them back. Friends and relatives are still the most common sources that these families turn to in times of crisis. In the case of Phu Cat, 15 out of the 48 families were indebted to banks. Some of these families went to banks where they had "friends".

Table 3.6 Debt Situation (number of families)

	Debt 1	*Debt 2*	*Debt 3*	*NA*	*Total*
Thanh Khe	1	6	1	2	10/15
Phu Cat	15	8	5	5	33/48
Kim Bang	4	7	1	4	16/29

Debt 1: Creditors are commercial and semi-government banks for the poor.
Debt 2: Creditors are banks *and* relatives and friends.
Debt 3: Creditors are relatives and friends.
Source: Michio Umegaki, Vu Le Thao Chi, and Tran Duc Phan, "Embracing Human Insecurity: Agent Orange and the Legacies of the War in Viet Nam," in Michio Umegaki, et al., eds., ***Human Insecurity in East Asia***, Tokyo and New York: United Nations University Press, 2009, p. 35.

Time as a scarce and unstable resource

Having a disabled child in a family means not only lost labour. There must be someone in the family who has to keep an eye on him or her almost 24 hours a day in many cases. Time is not demand-elastic and its allocation is a difficult task for these families. Every member, including the father, mother, and any of the healthy siblings in the family, always has to take the presence of the disabled child(ren) into consideration in whatever they plan to do. As a rule, it appears that those who earn less income spend more time with disabled children and work in businesses that will not take them away from home. Raising pigs or cows, growing vegetables in the backyard, making simple tools like sun masks, or keeping a small grocery shop right in front of their houses are some in the to-do list. This role usually falls to the mother in the family.

A case in point is the family of Le Dich, a farmer from Cat Trinh Commune, Phu Cat. The pattern has not changed over 15 years of our observation. He has two sons. The first son is AO-affected and has a soft skull and brittle bones. His wife stays home and makes dust-protective face masks. Besides earning just around 10,000 VND (55 cents) a day from making masks, the wife raises two pigs. She invests a great deal of time (a year) in animal husbandry and borrows money to raise them before she sells them at a price of about 1,000,000 VND ($50) each.

In Thanh Khe, some of the parents are older and retired, so they have more time to take care of the victims. Among the younger parents, the pattern is the same as for the Phu Cat parents. One of them, usually the mother, decides to do some work near the house like running a small convenient store or a small beauty salon (for the low-income group), subcontracting a tailor shop, or selling rice soup in the morning so that they can always make sure the victims are within their reach.

Giving up a child for adoption is not out of the question either, especially when the arrangement can be made within an extended family. A case in point is that of Nguyen Thi P. Y. and her husband, Tran K., in Xuan Ha Commune, Thanh Khe District, Da Nang, whom we interviewed the first time in December 2005. They had three sons. The first two sons were identified as being AO-affected. The first son, Tran N. K., who was born in 1987, usually looked calm but was mentally challenged and easily excited, and often beat his mother. The second son, Tran K. D., born in 1989, did not develop any signs of mental disorder until the age of four. Unlike his brother, he was always hyper, laughing for no reason. Between 1995 and 1998, he suffered about 20 epileptic seizures a day. On the recommendation of, and pushed by, the Hanoi Medical University team, he was in the care of a mental hospital in Da Nang.

The father was working at the Department of Market Management in Quang Nam, south of Da Nang. The mother had had to give up her job on the District People's Committee in Hien District in 1993 because of her first two sons. She had opened up a grocery shop in front of her house since then. She also processed parts for a bag company at home to earn about 10,000 VND a day

($5). The third son, Tran K. D., born in 1997, was fortunately normal and was a good student at school. Because the father was not working near home and the mother was so preoccupied with the two older disabled sons, they chose to take an action that made us pose for a second. They asked the mother's brother, whose children were all grown up, to adopt the youngest son.

Another case is the family of Truong V. K. in the North (May 2006). He had three sons and one daughter. His brother was an Air Force colonel, living in Hanoi. Mr Truong V. K. sent his last son, Truong V. H., who was born in 1983 with a congenital heart problem, to live with his brother and asked him to take care of his son.

These couples were fortunate to have a close relative in the position of taking in one of their children. Short of that luck, however, the AO families have very few choices other than giving up a steady job. None of the families ever thought of sending the disabled child(ren) away to the care of unfamiliar organizations such as a special school for the disabled with dorms. They had little time to investigate those schools. Finding out the qualifications for admissions, the monthly or annual fees, the living conditions in the dorm, among others, was a time-consuming chore. Furthermore, there was the uncharted terrain of negotiation for their children's admissions without the assurance of the successful result. All in all, entrusting the children with the organizations of unknown characters never crossed the parents' minds.

In Phu Cat, even though parents may not be present with their affected children at all times, their time, especially the mother's, is always split up in order to pay for extra care for the victims. Both parents usually have to engage in farming to earn enough to feed their families. But the mothers spend less time in the rice field in order to spend more time on housework and on taking care of both normal and disabled children. Parents could ask siblings to take care of the disabled, but they usually just provide company and are not really caregivers to the victims. If disabled children can still sustain a certain level of activity, such as running around in the neighbourhood or eating, the parents just let them do so in the community.

Sometimes they would spend hours looking for a child who had gotten lost, as in the case of Nguyen V. T. of Cat Trinh Commune, Phu Cat District, whom we met the first time in October 2004. He and his wife were both full-time farmers. Out of six children, N.T. H. Liem (born in 1993) was suspected of having AO-induced Down's syndrome. Liem was, and still is, a hyperactive child who kept running around everywhere in the Commune. The parents, relatively old as both were born late in the 1940s, could not keep an eye on her all the time because they were also preoccupied with taking care of the rice and other produce. On many occasions, they had to spend hours looking for Liem with the help of their neighbours. Liem even ran to the major thoroughfare of the country, Route 1, a few kilometres from her home. The children often test their parents' ability to keep them within their arm's reach.

During emergencies with regard to health or times of "crisis", the parents must leave all farming work behind to take the child to a nearby District Health

Centre or even to a major hospital in the province (a journey of one to two hours, depending on the means of transportation available), which also costs a considerable amount of time and money.

Here is the case of a Phu Cat family. Dao V. T. and his wife (Chanh Thang Village, Cat Thanh Commune, Phu Cat District, July 2005) had four children, two sons and two daughters. The second daughter, Cam, suffered from schizophrenia. The third daughter was mentally disabled. Whenever Cam exhibited worsening signs of sickness, the parents were in a difficult situation: the mother had to stay with her at a major mental hospital in Quy Nhon, an hour and a half away from their home. The stay might extend over a month, forcing the father to raise enough money for the expense. They even turned to rice buyers and borrowed five to six million VND ($300) in advance, which they were going to pay back by selling "young rice grains" (*lua non*). Taking care of the victim was consuming everything they had, including time and the resources for living.

If the head of the family was a single parent with no other family members, the situation appeared almost unsalvageable. A single parent has to be the breadwinner and special caregiver to the victim(s), both at the same time. Obviously, he or she cannot do these two things at the same time and therefore would have to ask for help from relatives or neighbours to keep an eye on the child(ren). Giving full-time care would have to wait until the end of the day.

Tran T. H., who we mentioned in the Introduction, is another case in point. Her case is extreme, although not necessarily exceptional. She had two out-of-wedlock daughters by different fathers. Both were affected by AO-dioxin contamination. She gave her older daughter away after she was born and found to have mental and physical disabilities. Now she lives with a younger daughter, Mai, who was born in 1998 with some brain damage and a crooked body. When we met for the first time, the mother and the younger daughter lived in a small 4 m × 6 m cubicle with brick walls, a wooden door, and windows. There was nothing inside except a small cupboard and a TV. In addition to farming, the mother also did, as she does now, a lot of menial work to earn extra cash. While she was out working, she had to leave Mai with her brother and his children, who lived nearby, to take care of her and keep her company. Not much has changed since except for better roofing and walls for their small house. Although her case may be extreme, the burden of having a disabled child on her and her extended family is no different from that of other families.

Mothers spend most of their time caring for disabled children, and therefore fathers take on the responsibility of "earning bread". They have to increase their income in some way, either by increasing their productivity or looking for additional job opportunities. Some look for better-paid jobs in big cities. Usually, however, that alternative has not panned out as one that was supposed to supplement the reduced income at home. Dao T. T. (Cat Trinh Commune, Phu Cat District) could not do much else because it was a handful taking care of the two children from her husband's previous marriage and her AO-affected son, Vo V. V., who was born in 1999. Her husband left for Ho Chi Minh City in 2003 and had been working as a carpenter there ever since. The amount of money that her husband sent back home was very little: just about 300,000 VND ($15). And that was only once every three to four months.

Time is one of the important factors in making every AO family's life easier or more difficult. Good time planning helps share the work among family members to sustain and then improve the quality of family life as a coherent unit. For the families of AO victims, time planning is a very difficult task because of the unpredictability or the seriousness of the victims' ailments. Having a disabled child in the family means that at least one of the members must be fully engaged in caring for the child while the others have to spend that much more time working to earn more. Having a child with AO-induced disability in the family also means that the parents have to spend extra time on the victim and less on the other "healthy" children. The goal of the family then becomes as modest as merely sustaining their life as it is on a daily basis.

Social stigma

In Vietnam, as in many other countries, HIV patients can easily become the target of discrimination and isolated from the rest of the community. Unlike HIV patients, AO-dioxin victims and their families are not so readily subjected to biases or prejudices. Perhaps the subtler stigma attached to them is often self-imposed, and they are often subject to other forms of discrimination. The aforementioned isolation of the AO families *from each other* plays a role in this dimension of the AO families' lives.

For one, AO-induced birth defects may trigger a chain reaction in the community that may not be entirely the making of the AO issue. For example, the presence of a child who is handicapped (not necessarily related to AO) would make people around, especially the father's family, strongly suspect that there is something wrong with the *mother* of the child for not being able to produce a healthy and therefore normal child. If more than one child is born with physical and mental problems, this blame becomes absolute, and the husband's family becomes firmly convinced that the mother is the source of the problem. Whether or not the child's disability is AO-induced becomes a secondary issue.

The case of Tran T. H., whom we referred to earlier, is such an example where the mother was blamed for everything. Her socially deviant behaviour (premarital sexual encounters) only aggravated the role that the AO issue played in making her life extremely difficult. She had her first daughter, Binh, out of wedlock. She was born in 1988, a time when the issue of AO contamination was shared exclusively among the top medical professionals in the nation and a time when the conventional norms of the community were much less tolerant of any deviant social behaviour than they are now. As one of the Commune Clinic staff casually confirmed, there was "no better excuse" than the birth of the disabled child for her boyfriend's family to deny their marriage, and force their son to leave her and get married to another woman in the commune. Tran T. H.'s family was no more tolerant of the situation. They asked her to leave the baby for someone else who might want to adopt her because the family considered it a shame that she had had an "illegitimate" child. She gave up her first child to another unmarried woman in the same Commune in a different neighbourhood.

Tran T. H. had another daughter ten years later. Mai (born in 1998) was born with birth defects. She has a learning disability and speech impediment, and can walk only with the support of a cane. Mai is also an illegitimate child. The father did not accept her. The mother decided to keep Mai and tried to work alone to support Mai with the help of her family.[24]

If social stigmas are attached to AO victims, the targets are usually female, reflecting something other than the presence of permanent disability. The status of women is still lower than that of men in rural Vietnam. The case of AO victims is no exception. It is hard for AO female victims to get married because not many of them can work to support a family. It is also feared that they might not be able to produce children or their children might be born with the same, or similar, defects as their parents.

Kim Bang, where relatively many of the victims are married, confirms this pattern. In the ten families we interviewed (in two phases in May 2006), there were 18 certified AO victims. Of the 18, 12 were men, and 6 were women. Out of the six women, only one was married: Dinh T. T., the daughter of Dinh D. T., a former soldier in the North Vietnamese Regular Army. She married and bore two daughters. But she did not fit the profile of an AO victim. Even though she was receiving the largest amount of financial support allowed then for AO victims from the government, her health symptoms were very simple, such as a chronic headache, and she could still work in a chestnut-processing company in Bien Hoa near Ho Chi Minh City. In fact, she did not even need that supporting pension and left it for her father instead.

By contrast, among the 12 men, there were 7 with serious disabilities who had married and had children. It was the parents of these 7 disabled children who had arranged their marriages. One example is the case of a brother of Dao T. N., in Kim Bang (May 2006), who was born mentally challenged in 1973. He could not do anything but look after the family-owned cows. But all the cows in his care, in his mother's words, were very skinny. His parents arranged for him to marry a woman who was 15 years older than him. His wife had to find crabs in rice paddies to support him and their two children. Another example is Dang Q. T., also in Kim Bang. He was born in 1973 with a severe hernia and cerebral palsy. His hands were crooked and twisted. His parents arranged a marriage with a healthy girl living in the same village. They had two children, but he often beat up his wife whenever he was mentally out of control. The wife left for Taiwan to work and never contacted him since.

These cases show that male AO victims can relatively more easily find a partner through their parents. The parents of male victims are particularly persistent in putting all efforts to follow the norm of communal life that a single male of marriage age is an odd presence. The age gap is easily glossed over by the parents of AO victims. Moreover, another rural convention that holds unmarried women as oddities gives the parents of male victims an opportunity to take advantage of.

The signs of self-imposed biases are relatively easy to spot. Truong V. T., a veteran who fought some of the fiercest battles of the war in AO-contaminated Quang Tri and Khe Son near the demilitarized zone, and his wife, Pham T. H. in Kim Bang, kept repeating the word "shame" as they had one disabled child after another. Shame may be a misnomer since it is a self-inflicted fear that the isolation of the entire family might be deepening, which is also aggravated by the lack of knowledge of other AO families, as pointed out earlier.

The self-imposed stigma may also be the result of an understandable logic in the parents' efforts to keep the fact that they have disabled child(ren) all to themselves, as in the case of N. X. Sang in Kim Bang (May 2006). Sang was born in 1946 and was probably exposed to AO while he was active in and around the Ho Chi Minh Trail during the war. He and his wife, born in 1945, had three daughters and one son. The son was healthy and two of the older daughters grew up to be beautiful women. But the last child, a daughter, was a dwarf and tended to lapse into violent fits. Their parents' fear was that the way in which their neighbours saw the youngest might prevent the older daughters from getting married.

These signs of social stigma, whether they come from outsiders or originate within the families, do cast a shadow over the lives of the disabled children and their families. The mutual isolation of AO families may be reinforced by the stigma they impose upon themselves. This stigma may also highlight the family's awareness that what is acceptable as "normal" to them is by definition inferior to others in the same community.

Hope

Parents in Vietnam and elsewhere, when left alone, are expected-utilitarians of a sort. They invest everything in their children for the possible returns that they will do well at school, become good workers, or even become known as "this Madam, that Mister" (*ong no ba kia*), i.e., become their pride and joy, get married and start a life better than theirs, and become shelter for them in the latter stage of their life. Children are a bridge taking their parents to somewhere other than where they are. In all these hopes, as an economic historian sees it, there is distinguishable value in terms of entertainment, labour, and security.[25]

Hope occupies a unique place in AO families. The minute it is concluded that a child has an incurable ailment, nearly all utilitarian hopes of the parents for the new living creature evaporate. If the cause is determined to be AO contamination, the desperation becomes absolute and stays with them, or so it appears to many.

Yet, after accepting that reality, their desperation may yield to somewhat restrained speculations. "I hope she can walk", "I hope he can support himself", or "I hope we will receive some more help from somewhere for them". Instead of entrusting their better life *to* the children, they become more preoccupied with the hope of moderating the hard life *of* the children. Such hopes border on the intermittent worry: "who will take care of the children when we are gone?" As a result, all the conventional hopes of the parents find their outlet in the normal children as if they are to make up for the disabled children.

That leaves a set of major questions surrounding the role of what the farmers learned from having the AO families in the community unanswered. How potent is it in changing their behaviour or in generating a much broader warning against contact with the chemicals that are in widespread use in rural Vietnam? Before offering answers to these questions, we need to address two problems that accompany the AO issue.

A threat too far: confrontations with Agent Orange

Agent Orange presents two problems: first, AO is often too exclusively linked to the war; and second, because of the damages it is held to cause, scientists and other experts make it their professional responsibility to establish the cause-effect relationship with a smallest possible margin of error. The first underlies the surprisingly limited capacity of the AO experience to generate lessons to be learned. The implications of the second are equally significant. The scientists and experts, who are well informed of the problematic nature of the chemicals and thus capable of issuing warnings, stopped at doing just that, thanks to their obligations to scientific procedures. It suggests a significant void when the actual users of any similar substance have nothing else to rely on but their own educated guesses.

The following pages address these issues: how the rest of Vietnam confronted the AO problem while the contamination victims and their families embraced the immense hardship.

According to Le Cao Dai, Vietnam began investigating the issue of AO and other wartime use of herbicides by the United States as early as 1972 and 1973.[26] Throughout the war, which includes the period of Vietnam's military campaign in Cambodia, however, the research was exclusively conducted by medical and scientific experts. Some of these scientists only later began participating in many international conferences. The product of one such conference in which over 50 Vietnamese experts on health and ecology participated is *Herbicides in War: The Long-Term Ecological and Human Consequences* (1984), edited by Arthur H. Westing.

The Vietnamese government, following these and other scientific efforts, began devising policies and openly addressing the adverse effects of the wartime spraying of AO while remaining alert to the AO issue that was gradually taking shape in legal and political arenas in the United States. The government established the 10-80 Committee in October 1980 under the Ministry of Health. The committee oversaw a wide range of scientific and relief activities for the victims of AO contamination until 1999 when another national body, Committee 33 (Office of the National Steering Committee on Overcoming the Consequences of Toxic Chemicals used by the United States during the war in Vietnam) under the Ministry of Natural Resources and Environment replaced it.

Also, the Vietnam Red Cross Society established the Agent Orange Victims Fund in 1998, which was to be complemented by the establishment of the

Vietnam Association of Victims of Agent Orange in 2004. Both organizations opened their local branches in nearly all provinces, districts, and cities.

A series of decisions and ordinances either paralleled or followed these changes at the upper echelons of the government. In the early 1980s, the Vietnamese government issued directives aimed at providing relief for AO victims and their families.[27] Ministry of Invalid Soldiers and Social Affairs (later the Ministry of Labour, Invalid Soldiers, and Social Affairs) in 1981 directed the Department of Social Affairs across the provinces to support those families who had difficulty in taking care of their disabled children with various birth defects due to the parents' exposure to toxic chemicals in the war.[28] This directive, primarily a call for attention and an appeal for possible help at the local level, was to be followed by a succession of decisions offering upgraded cash allowances for the targeted population.

The government's earlier use of a broad category, the "disadvantaged", to embrace the AO victims also began to change slowly. Decision 167 of 1994 lumped the AO victims with others, such as the homeless, elderly, and orphans as recipients of a monthly allowance.[29] Although the all-inclusive term, the "*crippled* people (*người tàn tật*)", remained intact, Ordinance 26 of 2005 singled out those "with disabilities who are invalid soldiers and their disabled family members, and those (non-civilian) who are recognized as Dioxin victims" for the preferential treatment for their meritorious services, i.e., contributions to the independence and unification of Vietnam.

The Law on Persons with Disabilities came into effect in 2010. It replaced the earlier terminology of the "*crippled* people (*người tàn tật*)" with "people with disabilities (*người khuyết tật*)", and expanded the monetary provisions also to cover those caregivers (including the family members) for those with severe disabilities.[30] Beyond the expanded monetary provisions, the Law addressed the needs of the disabled in a more comprehensive framework for the promotion of their well-being. The areas of government intervention ranged from health care to special education, and from vocational training to support for employment. The Law even aimed at building a barrier-free society for the disabled by 2025.[31]

While these government-led efforts gathered momentum, the most dramatic event that finally caught the attention of the ordinary Vietnamese was a 2004 lawsuit and the developments that followed. A group of Vietnamese AO victims, for the first time, decided to sue the 37 American chemical companies that manufactured defoliants, including AO, for the use of the U.S. government during the period 1961–1971.[32] Suddenly, the issue hit the whole country overnight. The most popular daily newspaper in Vietnam, *Tuoi Tre* (Youth), reported that between September 2003 and January 2008, there were 1,378 pieces of news about AO.[33] The AO issue became a daily topic throughout the country.

Around the same time, several campaigns were calling for the support of people around the world for the Vietnamese AO victims. The most prominent one was probably the effort by Len Aldis, secretary of the Britain-Vietnam Friendship Society, in establishing the society's home page in 2003[34] calling for international support for the lawsuit. This website received 706,000 signatures from all around the world.[35] Moreover, there have been a significant number of documentary films about the consequences of AO through profiles of lives around the country, and numerous campaigns, such as the "White Night Festival", organized by the Vietnamese youth organization in 2004, whose aim was to soothe the pain of AO victims in Ho Chi Minh City. These activities have deepened the understanding of AO as one of the most critical issues, a legacy of the Vietnam War in many corners of the country.

However, these developments may not have been more than a media event for many. The residents in the communities where the AO drama unfolded and is still unfolding exhibited little or no interest in the developments. Addressing AO-related issues in light of these dramatic developments comes with one drawback: the human consequences of AO contamination appear too unusual or rare.

Agent Orange victims are "rare" incidents

There are several points to note here. The first is that a great majority of Vietnamese farmers have not either become aware of, or paid attention to, the link between the AO families in their community and the wartime use of toxic agrochemicals, and if the link emerged in their understanding, the AO families' presence is exclusively tucked away as the legacy of a war from a distant past. Even at an earlier stage of our research, very few residents in the community showed interest in why and how we were conducting research on AO victims and their families. The presence of our research was of interest to no one else but the AO family members.

Second, although not surprisingly, given the monopoly of the research on AO-induced problems by medical and other scientists, a majority of Vietnamese ended up having nothing to do with the problems. The children with the AO-induced defects are seen as too far from their daily life and as outlying cases in the view of the ordinary farmers familiar with childbirth and rearing. They are truly *rare* incidents. There is little doubt that the AO families' efforts to keep the fact away from the public eye, as mentioned above, must have reinforced this perception. More importantly, even some of the parents of AO victims may share this perception, given their very limited knowledge of the link between their disabled children and direct or indirect exposure to toxic herbicides.

Consequently, the presence of AO families, and their hardship, is virtually irrelevant to a majority of the farmers as a warning to be taken seriously in the conduct of their everyday life. The warning that AO may continue to influence human health, that humans and the environment remain carriers of the contaminants, and that some of the agrochemicals in daily use may well be a contemporary, if watered down, version of AO is lost.

Another development reinforces this ironic consequence. It lies in the very behaviour of the AO families. Despite the hardship, many families show no unique pattern of behaviour in the very act that produced the hardship – reproductive behaviour. The usual expectation is that parents will refrain from reproduction once their child is found to be born with a birth defect, and that having more than one child with a birth defect should surely work as an even stronger deterrent. But the expectation is unfounded, as shown in Tables 3.7 and 3.8.[36]

Table 3.7 Effect of Birth Defects (number of children after the *first* disabled child)

	0	*1 Child*	*2 or More*	*NA*	*Total*
Phu Cat	11	14	19	4	48
Thanh Khe	3	7	5	0	15
Kim Bang	4	4	19	1	28
Total	18 families	25	43	5	91

Table 3.8 Effect of Birth Defects (number of children after the *second* disabled child)

	0	*1 Child*	*2 or More*	*NA*	*Total*
Phu Cat	5	4	1	0	10
Thanh Khe	3	1	1	0	5
Kim Bang	2	7	8	0	17
Total	10 families	12	10	0	32

Up to 68 families in the three research sites still decided to have two or more children after the first child with a birth defect (69%, 80%, and 83% of the families in Phu Cat, Thanh Khe, and Kim Bang, respectively). Having had not only one but two such experiences, 22 families still decided to have one or more children.

What do the 18 families who had no child after the first handicapped child (Table 3.7) represent, then? The answer to this question may corroborate, at least partially, the absence of a deterrent effect of having a permanently disabled child. Of the 18 families, 9 already had 4 or more children. A conventional understanding is applicable here: the financial burden of having an additional child *is* a more powerful deterrent.

Many families of the AO victims do admit that they were nervous or scared after it was concluded that the first child had an AO-induced defect. But that fear did not stop them from having more children. The fear stays with them all the way until the day they find out about the condition of the next child. They just pray and wait.

T. V. Nghia is a carpenter in Phu Cat (March 2005, 2007, and 2016). He had three children with T. T. Loan, a farmer who was born in 1970. The first two children were healthy. The last daughter, Thao, born in 1998, had the body of a four- or five-year-old girl with short legs and arms. She slithered on her back most of the time.

When we met the family for the first time in 2005, the parents kept telling us how difficult it was for them to have a disabled child in the house. The parents actually did try hard to keep the floor of their house really clean for Thao to move around on her back. They also said they would never have any more children because they were poor and had enough difficulty. Two years later, in 2007, they had another daughter, born just a few months before our second visit. The house was in a worse condition than the first time we saw it. When asked about the presence of the new daughter, Loan responded with a shy smile: "It was an accident". Nine years later we visited the family again. We detected almost no sign of change in Thao, except that she could at least sit up and had grown to be a talkative girl surrounded by her younger sister and her neighbours' children. The size of her body had remained more or less the same.

The reproductive behaviour of AO victims' families virtually confirms that there is nothing special at work dictating specifically the behaviour of these families. The presence of AO families is *not* prominent in the community in the first place, leaving them to freely act as they please and behave in much the same way as the rest of the farmers. It should not be surprising, then, that the community of farmers as a whole has very little to learn from the consequences of the wartime use of toxic chemicals. After all, the AO-induced disabled children are in the absolute minority.

AO families and their neighbours continue to rely on resources such as food and irrigation water, and others acquired from areas that showed a high level of dioxin as recently as early 2000. People in Da Nang still went to the nearby lake, they told us, for fishing, and people in Phu Cat still fished in the ponds and lakes around Nui Ba Mountains or used that water for irrigation. They were not alarmed by the use of chemicals to remove weeds and insects as this was recommended by the local branch office of the Plant Protection Department, a part of the Ministry of Agriculture and Rural Development, which in some cases offered chemicals with the seeds as the farmers purchase the latter.

Conscious efforts were made to prevent the birth of disabled children. One example was a project by the late Dr Trinh Van Bao around the year 2004: "Building a model of genetic consultation for families exposed to consequences of toxic chemicals in the war". Its actual use reflected the dominant perception by the farmers of AO contamination. The purpose was to help young couples avoid giving birth to disabled children. The advice not to have children was given only when it was nearly 100% medically guaranteed that their children would be born with birth defects or other abnormalities. Out of a dozen cases that were advised not to have children, there were two in which the parents still decided to do so. The resulting children were born with disabilities. There were only a few who responded to the efforts in the first place, and even when the scientific evidence was presented to them, the young couples still decided to ignore the advice.[37]

Agent Orange as a distant legacy

These disabled children are obviously the victims of AO contamination. A closer look at their births also leads us to assert that they may well be the victims of their parents' decision to risk the likelihood of birth abnormalities. And the parents, in turn, may be the victims of something else: the ambiguity surrounding the "probability" of birth abnormalities as determined by the exposure to AO and other wartime use of toxic chemicals. They are the furthest from the position of even guessing the "probable" cause-effect relationship between AO and the various ailments. The lengthy descriptions below show just how far-removed the farmers are from the ongoing developments in determining the toxicity of the wartime chemicals as the cause of death and various disabilities.

The language of "probability" dominates the immensely long and divisive debates. Peter Sills, in his seminal work on the AO litigations in the United States, chronicles the never-ending debate on the cause-effect relationship between the exposure to AO and other herbicides, and numerous types of ailments that hundreds of thousands of veterans of the war, including some U.S. allies, have exhibited.[38] As for the cases of the Vietnamese, the U.S. Ambassador to Vietnam, Michael W. Marine, in response to an enquiry concerning the United States' assistance for Vietnamese AO victims, is quoted to have said as recently as 2007:

> ... [I] cannot say whether or not I have myself seen a victim of Agent Orange. The reason for that is that we still lack good scientific definitions of the causes of disabilities ... that have occurred in Vietnam.... We just don't have the scientific evidence to make that statement with certainty.[39]

The pages below outline what transpired from the divisive evaluations of AO by relying primarily on three major sources: Robert Allen, *Dioxin War: Truth and Lies about a Perfect Poison*;[40] Elmo Zumwalt II, *Report to Secretary of the Department of Veterans Affairs on the Association between Adverse Effects and Exposure to Agent Orange* (May, 1990);[41] and William Buckingham, *Operation Ranch Hand: The Air Force and Herbicides in Southeast Asia, 1961–1971*.[42] In sum, the divisive evaluations are a mixture of scientific discoveries, commercial interests of the manufacturers, and political calculations of the time. The lengthy and divisive evaluations also created a significant void where the use of toxic chemicals was left unchecked.

Long before the Vietnam War, phenoxy herbicides, which produce the toxic dioxin, were first found in research in 1940. Scientists successfully isolated indoleacetic acid, which is supposed to influence plant growth. From there, they developed several plant growth-controlling hormones, including 2,4-dichloro-phenoxy acetic acid (2,4-D) and 2,4,5-trichloro-phenoxyacetic acid (2,4,5-T). The latter contained the most toxic dioxin, 2,3,7,8-T (tetrachlorodibenzo-p-dioxin, TCDD).

Researchers at this early stage of herbicide development discovered that small amounts of these growth-controlling hormones could stimulate the growth of plants, and that if the dose was large, they could also kill the plants. They even realized that some herbicides had different effects on different plants. In 1947, it was discovered that 2,4,5-T and 2,4-D affected broadleaf plants, but they left cereals alone. Phenoxy herbicides were then recognized as tools for removing weeds in the agricultural industry and at the same time as special weapons for the military.

Around the same time as phenoxy herbicides were found, experimentation with new rice varieties (high-yield varieties) was carried out in the United States, the United Kingdom, Mexico, and India to landmark the beginning of the

Green Revolution, which usually comes in a package justifying the removal of weeds and insects.[43]

According to John Perkins, plant disease and weed and insect control were considered "not necessarily a destructive factor every year" in the first place because plant disease, as well as the weed and insect situation, varied with weather and different areas. However, plant disease, and, especially, weed and insect control, gradually "matched the major factors in importance"[44] after herbicides and pesticides started being used. Ironically, the demand for both herbicides and pesticides also increased accordingly. Although the United States was the largest market for these phenoxy herbicides, the manufacturers began selling these chemicals all over the world. Two American companies, Monsanto and Dow Chemicals, nearly monopolized the production and sales of 2,4,5-T.[45] The production of herbicides in the United States kept rising. With the increasing wartime demand for herbicides during the war, the production skyrocketed.

Many warnings followed the spread of these herbicides, concerning their negative impacts on the environment and human health. Monsanto was the first manufacturer of polychloride-biphenyl. They began operations in Anniston, Alabama, by producing dioxin-like substances.

There were several significant incidents along the way, including two factory explosions: one in 1949 in a Monsanto factory and the other in 1953 in a Boehringer factory in Germany. Medical specialists and scientists who examined the severely affected workers in these factories found that the explosions produced TCDD. The problem was that, with or without these scientific claims about the harmful effects of the herbicides, the chemical companies with their massive financial assets were in a position to produce counter-evidence. In defence of a 1949 factory explosion, for example, Monsanto succeeded in producing a conclusion, through a medical doctor whom they hired, that the affected factory workers merely had some skin troubles, called "chloracne". In the case of the Boehringer explosion, a dermatologist, Dr Karl Schultz, examined the affected workers carefully. He concluded that there was definitely toxic dioxin because of the explosion. But his conclusion was published in German. Moreover, the chemical companies, including Monsanto and Dow Chemicals, embraced the conclusion but did not share the findings with the public, and did not take any action to change accordingly. Allen claims:

> Throughout the 1950s, 1960s and 1970s the chemical industry had been able to defend itself against all attacks. If the battles to continue manufacturing their most lucrative products – 2,4,5-T, 2,4-D, penta-chlorophenol – were eventually lost, the war to protect chlorine chemistry was being won. … By pouring billions into medical and scientific research and into the science departments of third-level colleges, the industry held the forward trenches in the battlefield for scientific glory.[46]

Allen's whole book actually deals with these companies' losing attempts to discredit medical and other scientists' efforts to prove and spread the reality of the toxicity of dioxin. But evidence of the toxicity of dioxin and other chemicals was only gradually accumulated over some 30 years.

The usual assumption would be that the actual uses of dioxin or dioxin-like substances should decrease as the warnings against the serious impacts of dioxin on health increased. On the contrary, the reinforced scientific evidence was matched by the increase in the actual use of toxic herbicides. This widening gap between the scientific evidence and the actual use of toxic herbicides is inexplicable since anything scientifically proven, in conventional thinking, would be understood or treated as common knowledge guiding people to act accordingly. Not so.

Table 3.9 summarizes some of the events related to the accumulation of scientific evidence indicating the toxicity of dioxin and the continuous use of chemicals that produce dioxin. In addition to this, the U.S. Department of Veterans Affairs (upgraded Department in 1989) prepared an astonishing list. According to this list, there were 71 events between 1944 and 1977, outside Vietnam, involving AO and other similar dioxin-yielding substances. Some of these events included small-scale experimentations on the effectiveness of toxic chemicals. A few of them were for actual military use, such as those used in the areas near the demilitarized zone in Korea. The U.S. Department of Defense (DOD) was involved in 57 of these events, which took place in seven countries, including Canada, India, and Korea.

These developments leave one nagging question: what was the responsibility of scientists in the interim when the toxicity was not *fully* or even sufficiently established?

One more twist needs to be added, making these developments even more implausible. In 1968, Admiral Elmo R. Zumwalt II (1920–2000) became Commander of U.S. Naval Forces and Chief of the Naval Advisory Group in Vietnam and the Navy's youngest vice-admiral. When he was in Vietnam, he planned to strike "hard and fast" by destroying the foliage along the ponds, lakes, and riverbanks where U.S. Navy men in patrol boats could easily be hit from either side by enemy fire. He had checked with the Army and Air Force about the possible harmful effects on humans of AO, which had been used in other defoliation efforts for the same purpose. He was told there were none. "You trust those things, and I ordered the spraying of Agent Orange". Later, in 1984, the Admiral was given the responsibility of compiling and assessing nearly all AO-related research conducted in the United States up to that point, which led to the publication of the now definitive Zumwalt Report.

In August 1969, his son, Navy Lieutenant Elmo Russell Zumwalt III, arrived in Vietnam as an officer in charge of a Patrol Craft Fast, otherwise known as a "Swift Boat". During his 11-month tour of duty in Vietnam, he "had seen Agent Orange defoliation nearly everywhere [he] had patrolled", "often washed in the waters into which Agent Orange had drained and had eaten local produce which [he] suspected had been doused with the chemical". He developed a skin rash while on the Sea Float (a floating mobile tactical support base on Cau Lon river in the Ca Mau Province in the south). But at that time, he was still "thankful

Table 3.9 An Outline Reinforced Scientific Evidence vs. Actual Uses of Dioxin through the 1970s

	Scientific Evidence	*Actual Uses and Related Events*
1930s	The first discovery that dioxin-like chemicals created dangerous industrial hazards to chemical workers when most of the workers in the Monsanto plant became sick.	Monsanto began manufacturing polychlorobiphenyl in Anniston, Alabama, a process that produced a dioxin-like substance.
1950s	Dr Karl Schultz examined the workers after the explosion at Boehringer trichlorophenol factory (1953), and found dioxin as a contaminant was produced by 2,4,5-T.	Increasing volume of herbicides used in agriculture worldwide. The British used Agent Orange in Malaysia.
1960s	Early 1960. Military scientists were aware of the potential damage to human health due to dioxin contamination by the herbicide. In 1968, scientists, health officials, politicians, and the military began expressing concerns about the potential toxicity of Agent Orange and its contaminant dioxin to humans. In 1969, Bionetics Research Laboratories reported that 2,4,5-T showed a "significant potential to increase birth defects". October 1969, National Institute of Health confirmed that 2,4,5-T could cause malformations and stillbirths in mice. Epidemiologists began noticing the impact on human health.	18 million gallons of herbicide used in Vietnam (1961–1971) with increasing amounts at its peak in the year 1968. Late 1960s: the U.S. sprayed untold volume of herbicides in Laos and Cambodia.
1970s	In April 1970, The U.S. Surgeon General issued a warning the use of 2,4,5-T hazardous to "human health". In 1973, a Swedish medical doctor examined a forest foreman and cancer patient, and began the research that showed a high correlation between exposure to phenoxy herbicide and soft-tissue sarcomas. In the rest of the 1970s, other doctors joined him and established the link. It took them into the 1990s to win the acceptance of their findings by the rest of chemical and medical establishment. In 1977, International Agency for Research on Cancer reported increased mortality rates in animals and humans exposed to 2,4-D or 2,4,5-T.	In May, 1971, 2,000 gallons of "waste oil", contaminated with dioxin, was sprayed as dust suppressant in Times Beach, Missouri. The incident led in ten years to the evacuation of the whole town of Times Beach. In 1976, a factory explosion in Seveso, Italy, released 3,000 kg of chemicals into the air. Among them were 2,4,5-T, used in the manufacture of herbicides, and anywhere from 100 g to 20 kg of dioxin. 37,00 people were believed to have been exposed to the chemicals. 4% of local farm animals died; and 80,000 animals were slaughtered to prevent contamination from filtering up the food chain.

Source: We relied mainly on the following sources for the outline: Robert Allen, *The Dioxin War – Truth and Lies about a Perfect Poison*, London and Ann Arbor, MI, Pluto Press, 2004; U.S. Department of Veterans Affairs, *Report on DoD Herbicides used outside Vietnam*; Zumwalt, *Report*; Le Cao Dai's *Agent Orange in the Viet Nam War*, especially Chapter 3; and Barry Commoner, *Keynote Address at the Second Citizens Conference on Dioxin*, St. Louis, Missouri, July 30, 1994, www.greens.org/s-r/078/07-03.html.

for the defoliation".[47] However, no warning was issued to those in the front-line combat units.

As if to confirm this, one military doctor in charge of preparing the herbicides is quoted to confess:

> Because the material was to be used on the enemy, none of us was overly concerned. We never considered a scenario in which our own personnel

> would become contaminated with the herbicide. And, if we had, we would have expected our own government to give assistance to veterans so contaminated.[48]

The lax attitude, reflecting the ambiguous probability linking the chemicals and their negative effect on human health, resulted in even more irresponsible use of the chemicals. The military use had a much higher dioxin concentration than the version for civilian use, and AO was often sprayed undiluted in Vietnam. Despite the level suggested by the producers, the military sprayed AO in concentrations that were 6–25 times higher.[49]

This attitude, born of the belief that the cause-effect was not firmly established, may also be found in the United States' increasing use of the chemicals as the war accelerated. Table 3.10 clearly shows the increase in the use of the chemicals matching the worsening of the war and its Americanization between 1965 and 1969.

In addition, the use of large quantities of herbicides was not stopped, even when some scientists, who might not have been involved in the dioxin research, began protesting against its use soon after the Americanization of the war started in 1964. The United States began spraying the chemicals in increasing amounts as the war was becoming more difficult for the United States, especially after 1965 (see Table 3.10). The maps of the herbicide spraying in South Vietnam, prepared by Jeanne Stellman in 2003, also confirm the same increasing pattern graphically, reaching its peak later in 1968.[50]

In other words, the period when the scientific evidence was still in the process of building the case supporting the chemicals' accountability for human health problems was the period when the use of the chemicals was almost unfettered.

In early 1967, President Lyndon B. Johnson received a petition from more than 5,000 scientists, including 17 Nobel laureates and 129 members of the National

Table 3.10 United States' Use of Herbicides during the Vietnam War (in $m^3 = 10^3L$)

Year	*Agent Orange*	*Agent White*	*Agent Blue*	*Total*
1961	?	0	?	?
1962	56	0	8	65
1963	281	0	3	283
1964	948	0	118	1066
1965	1767	0	749	2516
1966	6362	2056	1181	9599
1967	11891	4989	2513	19394
1968	8850	8483	1931	19264
1969	12376	3572	1309	17257
1970	1806	697	370	2873
1971	0	38	?	38
Total	44338	19835	8182	72354

Source: From Arthur H. Westing, "Herbicides in War: Past and Present", in Westing, ed., *Herbicides in War – The long-term Ecological and Human Consequences*, London and Philadelphia, Taylor & Francis, 1984, p. 7.

Academy of Sciences, urging him to stop using anti-personnel and anti-crop chemicals in Vietnam. Again, in early 1968, American scientists, health officials, politicians, and the military itself began to express concerns about the potential harm of AO and other herbicides to human health. These rising voices of concern were met with increasing use of such herbicides.[51] Only in October 1969 did the National Institute of Health finally confirm that 2,4,5-T could cause malformation and stillbirth in mice. This finding eventually forced the DOD to recognize and issue a public warning about the toxicity of dioxin, six months later, in April 1970. Although the warning was initially limited to the use of herbicides in the United States, on the same day, the DOD also announced the termination of AO spraying in Vietnam.

Incidentally, a few of our informants, including Dr Truong Quang Dat, then head of the Phu Cat Health Centre, testified that he and others still witnessed the spraying, even in the years between 1972 and 1973. By April 15, 1970, the increasing awareness among scientists and some government officials of the harmful herbicides and the mounting scientific evidence pushed the Surgeon General of the United States to issue a warning that the use of 2,4,5-T might be hazardous to "our health".[52]

The slow and haphazard way in which these toxic chemicals found their way into people's awareness is a further illustration of how "distant" the threat of dioxin was in everyday life. Around the same time when the United States decided to terminate the use of AO in Vietnam and warned against the use of dioxin at home, the seeds for the eventual destruction of an entire town in the United States, Times Beach in Missouri, were planted. "[O]ne of the greatest tragedies in America's secret toxic history"[53] took over ten years to unfold.[54]

Russell Martin Bliss owned a company, the Bliss Waste Oil Company, which used oil waste and other industrial wastes. The company collected discarded motor and lubrication oils from gasoline stations, factories, garages, trucking companies, airports, and similar establishments. The company also disposed of chemical wastes and used waste oil, especially mixed with others, to control dust by spraying it over dusty roads or yards. One company handling chemicals asked another to dispose of hexachlorophene residue from its storage tanks, and the latter asked Bliss's company to take care of the "waste oil". Sometime between February and October 1971, one year after the Surgeon General's stern warning, Bliss's company disposed of at least 18,500 gallons of waste that was heavily contaminated with dioxin. He mixed these with more waste oil to make the dust suppressant, and sprayed it on truck terminals, trailer parks, and unpaved roads in eastern Missouri and on the small town of Times Beach. He did this at least twice a year from 1971 to 1982, spraying around 40,000 gallons each time. From early on, some of the animals and people in this area began showing all sorts of health problems. Later, even Bliss himself checked a sample of what he sprayed. All he did was use his eyes to observe what was happening and he found something suspicious. But his suspicions disappeared after he was told that what he had sprayed was regular waste. In 1971 alone, almost 20,000 gallons of what was supposed to be waste oil were sprayed on the soil in a nearby horse arena in Missouri.

Strikingly, the mayor and others from the town were not informed that the town was contaminated with dioxin until 1982. The Environmental Protection Agency notified the mayor of the finding and said that it would take another nine to ten months for the Agency to finally determine the level of contamination.[55] Eventually, the whole town was evacuated in 1983. The place had become synonymous with dioxin contamination; it was guarded initially by state troopers and visited only by curious sightseers who were warned to stay outside the fences that enclosed its deserted roads, homes, and offices.

The laxness was challenged only ten years after the toxicity of the wartime dioxin was formally recognized. In the early 1980s, a group of U.S. veterans of the Vietnam War decided to pursue a lawsuit again dioxin manufacturers, including Monsanto and Dow Chemicals. But the challenge was only half met. The suit resulted in an out-of-court settlement from the manufacturers of AO, with the latter agreeing to set up a fund of $180 million to help the victims of AO among the former for ten years. That settlement was only the beginning for those on whose shoulders fell the responsibility of proving that they had been exposed to AO, "leaving tens of thousands of veterans who were not yet sick with dioxin poisoning without access to settlement" and "the largest cash payout to any of the individual plaintiffs was a lame $4,000".[56]

There may be one more factor that makes AO and other toxic chemicals appear to be a distant threat. Traces of toxic herbicides are dispersed in a massive complex consisting of different types of chemicals, their manufacturers, the purposes of their use, and numerous user and producer countries, among others. Their massive worldwide sale, easily in billions of dollars, resulted in a constant and big jump from a few billion dollars in 1960 to close to 35 billion dollars in 1999.[57] The jump partially paralleled scientists' efforts to prove the toxicity of some of the chemicals. It implies that any effort to establish the level of toxicity of certain chemicals, among many, that are harmful to human health would require years and an untold cost. The effort is also tantamount to challenging the beneficiaries of a huge growing market. The United States' expenditure on herbicides alone accounts for half of the world's expenditure. From 1982 to 2001, the United States almost doubled its spending on herbicides from $3.8 billion to $6.4 billion.[58] The increase matches the global increase.

Allen suggests that there *is* more than what the aggregate data show, i.e., the political interferences taking advantage of the absence of a definite cause-effect linkage between the chemicals and harm to human health. The absence makes any watchdog on the environmental issues susceptible to various pressures unrelated to the scientific findings. He gives one example of the EPA's susceptibility to various pressures. Since the early 1970s, long before AO caught the attention of war veterans, the EPA had known that dioxin was a contaminant of pentachlorophenol (an organochlorine compound used as a pesticide and a disinfectant). One EPA report in 1975 revealed that workers who had handled pentachlorophenol contracted chloracne. An EPA researcher, Cate Jenkins, uncovered the fact that chemical companies like Dow Chemicals tried to hide this revelation. At that time, chemical companies such as Dow, Reichlold, and others were producing 79 million pounds of pentachlorophenol annually. In 1978, the EPA ordered the manufacturers to prove that the benefits of pentachlorophenol outweighed its risks to human health. A similar order led to a ban on the use of the highly lucrative 2,4,5-T in 1979.

Then, Ronald Reagan came to power in the United States in 1981 and things changed. His administration wanted to promote a free-market principle even in the production of chemicals like pentachlorophenol. They appointed pro-industry people to the top EPA posts. Cate Jenkins was moved to an irrelevant position. By the summer of 1982, the EPA was prepared to terminate the banning order on the use of pentachlorophenol.

There was a significant amount of time between the actual scientific findings and the time when these findings were made public. During that time, all kinds of political manipulations were carried out by the EPA. Gerson Smoger, a lawyer actively supporting the U.S. veterans' legal actions since the 1984 out-of-court settlement, is quoted to have argued that "the dioxin reassessment still hasn't come out. The draft has been approved and they still have not released it. That is one of the things going on in the EPA – stopping everything that is going out". This susceptibility, if not an outright corruption of the EPA, shows that even for the scientists, scientific evidence alone is not the decisive factor in establishing the high "probability" that the chemicals threaten human health.

The point of this lengthy discussion on how AO and other toxic chemicals have survived waves of efforts at their elimination is simple enough. Efforts are mostly made within the scientific community, which is fragmented in the first place because of its susceptibility to various non-scientific pressures. Ordinary farmers are obviously deprived of access to this reality. So was Admiral Zumwalt until after he completed his *Report*. Neither are they in a position to draw "lessons" from the most obvious incident of chemical warfare threatening human well-being. For them, AO is a thing of the past; the parents of AO victims, the most likely candidates for changing their behaviour accordingly, exhibit virtually unchanged behaviour, and after all, the victims are too few and too rare in their eyes. AO alone is a distant threat, and agrochemicals as potential threats may be even farther away in the eyes of the majority of Vietnamese farmers.

It has been thirty years since the end of the war of unification as of the beginning of our research and 45 years as of the writing of this book. The war itself receded into the distant past. And with it went AO. The research on AO and other toxic chemicals still goes on within the secluded scientific community. The great majority of farmers have no way of benefiting from the findings or even from the ongoing research. All that the AO victims represent is as far removed from their life as the war itself.

Disturbing findings are now available. Arnold Schecter and his associates, who have been actively involved in AO contamination research, recently found that AO as a source of dioxin contamination is beginning to become indistinguishable from other sources, such as industrial production and wastes, even in the former hot spots of established AO-induced contamination, such as Bien Hoa, north-east of Ho Chi Minh City.[59] There is a high possibility that efforts to multiply wealth by way of economic development may occur with collateral damage to the health of the beneficiaries of the increased wealth. And yet they are still perceived as distant and unaffected by the threat.

Notes

1 H. W. Lewis, *Technological Risk*, New York, W.W. Norton and Co., 1990, p. 123.
2 Le Khe Son, in Scott-Clark and Levy, *Guardian* interview on March 29, 2003, www.guardian.co.uk/world/2003/mar/29/usa.adranlevy. We also had a few opportunities between 2004 and 2010 to talk to him in Hanoi, which confirmed the *Guardian*'s story. There were also Agent Purple and others with different degrees of toxicity.
3 Cao Dai, *Memoirs of War: The Central Highlands, A North Vietnamese Journal of Life on the Ho Chi Minh Trail 1965–1973*, Hanoi, The Gioi Publishers, 2004.
4 It is not the purpose of this study to examine the war at the ground level. However, Colonel (retired) Harry G. Summers' appraisal of crucial battles in the war offers a succinct ground-level view of this unique characteristic of the Vietnam War, *Historical Atlas of the Vietnam War*, New York, Houghton Mifflin, 1995. Novels such as Philip Caputo's *A Rumor of War* and John Del Vecchio's *13th Valley* also help capture the utter uneasiness among the U.S. soldiers accompanying this unusual characteristic of the war.
5 For the official account of the operation behind the use of chemicals such as Agent Orange and other herbicides, see William A. Buckingham, *Operation Ranch Hand: The Air Force and Herbicides in Southeast Asia, 1961–1971*, Washington D.C., Office of Air Force History, US Air Force, 1982. Also, Edwin A. Martini gives a critical account of the AO problem, though mostly from the U.S. perspective, in *Agent Orange: History, Science, and the Politics of Uncertainty*, Amherst and Boston, MA, University of Massachusetts Press, 2012.
6 Arthur H. Westing, *Ecological Consequences of the Second Indochina War*, Stockholm, Almqvist & Wiksell International, 1976.
7 For a brief but succinct account leading to the 1984 out-of-court settlement, see Gerson H. Smoger (undated), "Agent Orange Lawsuit: Knocking Down Windmills", www.agentorangelaw.net/agent_orangelawsuit.html. A comprehensive account of Agent Orange litigation, including the renewed round in 2003, is offered by Peter Sills, *Toxic War: the Story of Agent Orange*, Nashville, TN, Vanderbilt University Press, 2014, which has not seen its end yet. Also see Martini, *op. cit.*, and Michael F. Martin, "Vietnamese Victims of Agent Orange and the US-Vietnam Relations", *CRS Report for Congress*, 2009, pp. 1–32.
8 Dr Phan briefly describes Hanoi Medical University-based research activities, which leaves a strong impression that Vietnam's systematic and large-scale research efforts started in the early 1980s. Tran Duc Phan, "The Consequence of Agent Orange in Humans, Some Methods supporting Agent Orange Victims", no date, *mimeo*.
9 Admiral Elmo R. Zumwalt II, *Report to Secretary of the Department of Veterans Affairs on the Association*, 1990, p. 4 (hereafter, *Zumwalt Report*).
10 Cao Dai, *Agent Orange in the Viet Nam War: History and Consequences*, Hanoi, Vietnam Red Cross Society, Hanoi, 2000, p. 53.
11 Buckingham, *op. cit.*
12 Stellman et al., "The Extent and Patterns of Usage of Agent Orange and Other Herbicides in Vietnam", *Nature*, Vol. 422, 2003, pp. 681–7; see also Michio Umegaki, Vu Le Thao Chi, and Tran Duc Phan, "Embracing Human Insecurity: Agent Orange-Dioxin and the Legacies of the War in Viet Nam", in Umegaki et al., eds., *Human Insecurity in East Asia*, Tokyo and New York, 2009, especially, pp. 22–8.
13 *Zumwalt Report*, p. 52. Cao Dai, *op. cit.*, 2000, pp. 109–125.

14 The Canada-based Hatfield Consultants found that the level of dioxin contamination of the lake is alarmingly high. See Thomas Boivin et al., "Agent Orange Dioxin Contamination in the Environment and Human Population in the Vicinity of Da Nang Airbase, Viet Nam", unpublished paper presented at *Dioxin 2007: International Symposium*, Tokyo, September 2–7, 2007.

15 Madame Nguyen Thi Binh, former Vice-President of Vietnam, quoted in Scott-Clark and Levy, the *Guardian*, *op. cit.*

16 The decision on population and family planning, announced on October 18, 1988, was to become effective three months after the chairman of the Council of Ministers signed it. The policy appears to have become official even before the three months had elapsed, as the Council's December 1988 report to the Eighth National Assembly indicated that the policy had already been formally promulgated by that time. The reversal of the policy comes later in 2017 in Resolution 21 NQ/TW (by the Sixth Plenum Party Central Committee VII) issued on October 25, 2017.

17 See en. 16 of this chapter.

18 The international poverty line, estimated by the World Bank, is equal to $1.08 a day, roughly equal to 17,270 VND a day and 518,400 VND ($25) a month (Asian Development Bank Institute, www.adbi.org/discussionpaper/2005/01/14/869.malnutrition.poverty.indonesia/poverty.line/). The new poverty line of Vietnam, applied in 2006, is 230,000 VND/($12) month for urban residents (Thanh Khe) and 200,000 VND/($11) a month for rural residents (Phu Cat and Kim Bang). Vietnam News, http://vietnamnews.vnanet.vn/showarticle.php?num= 08SOC210305.

19 For a reference, the Vietnam Red Cross's Binh Dinh provided us with a list of recipients, which shows an increased amount varying from 405,000 VND to 945,000 VND, depending upon the certified degree of seriousness of the disabilities.

20 Finn Tarp, ed., *Growth, Structural Transformation, and Rural Change in Vietnam: A Rising Dragon on the Move*, Oxford, Oxford University Press, 2017; in particular, Chapter 7 by Gaia Nariciso on internal labour migration provides a picture of the background.

21 According to the World Health Organization, *World Health Statistics* 2007, pp. 56–63, there are 0.53 medical doctors per 1,000 people in Vietnam (2001) whereas there are 0.37 in Thailand (2000) and 1.98 in Japan (2002).

22 Truong Quang Dat, "Health Service Utilization of the Phu Cat District Residents", unpublished paper presented at the Fourth International Workshop on Human Security in East Asia, Keio University at Shonan-Fujisawa Campus, February 25–27, 2007.

23 Note, here, that regardless of the total number of medical establishments, the closest medical services to the villagers are those Commune Clinics.

24 Tran T. H. had never seen Binh again until we volunteered to take her daughter to visit her for the first time after almost 15 years in August 2006. The mother was speechless and just looked at her first daughter. At that moment, a thin man was walking through the village, only 30 m away from where we were sitting. The mother said: "Binh's father". He walked past us and headed straight to the rice paddy ahead. Binh was unable to grasp what was going on and kept smiling at Mai, her younger sister whom she had met for the first time in her life.

25 For a succinct summary of these utilities that having a child offers, see Harvey Leibenstein, "An Interpretation of the Economic Theory of Fertility: Promising Path or Blind Alley?", *Journal of Economic Literature*, Vol. 12, No. 2, 1974, pp. 457–79.

26 Cao Dai, *op. cit.*, 2000, Chapter 6. Also, the correspondence with Dr Tran Duc Phan, then Director of the Agent Orange Victims Fund in the Vietnam Red Cross Society, December 13, 2007.

27 Quoted in the Ministry of Natural Resources and Environment, Committee 33, "Conference on Consequences of Toxic Chemicals used by the US in the Vietnam War", 2007, from the government document, "Implementation of Supporting Policies towards Victims of Toxic Chemicals – Dioxin and Activities to Improve the Awareness

of Consequences of Toxic Chemicals among the Communities", pp. 23–44. See also Le Ke Son and Charles R. Bailey, *op. cit.*, pp. 91–4, for a brief outline of the developments described here.

28 Document No. 399/CTXH.

29 Decision 167/1994 on Amendment on Allowances for Social Welfare Recipients, issued by the (Vietnam) Prime Minister April 8, 1994.

30 The Law defined "persons with severe disabilities" as "those whose impairments lead to partial loss or deficiency of their functions, self-control or make them unable to move, to dress, to keep personal hygiene and to complete other everyday tasks without other people to watch, to help and to take care of". In article 3 clauses 1 and 2 of Decrees detailing and guiding several articles of the Law on the Disabled (No. 28/2012/ND-CP, 2010).

31 Articles 22, 27, 32, 33, and 40, respectively.

32 The best summary of this lawsuit until now is "Agent Orange Lawsuit filed by Vietnamese Victims: Update of the Lawsuit", www.ffrd.org/Lawsuit/Lawsuit.htm. Judge Jack Weinstein of the New York Federal Court, on March 10, 2005, however, ruled that the use of the chemicals during the Vietnam War did not constitute a "chemical warfare" and therefore did not violate international law. For more recent developments concerning Vietnam's demand for compensation on the chemical companies, see Ralph Jennings, "Vietnam's Latest Demand for Agent Orange Compensation Described as Last Resort", August 2018, www.voanews.com/east-asia-pacific/vietnams-latest-demand-agent-orange-compensation-described-last-resort, accessed August 2019. See also Edwin A. Martini, *Agent Orange: History, Science, and the Politics of Uncertainty*, Amherst and Boston: University of Massachusetts Press, 2012, pp. 23–30.

33 www.tuoitre.com.vn/

34 www.petitiononline.com/AOVN/petition.html

35 www.nhandan.com.vn/english/life/170707/life_b.htm

36 Both from Umegaki et al., 2009, *op. cit.*, p. 37.

37 Correspondence and conversations in 2005 and 2006 with Dr Tran Duc Phan, a disciple of the late Dr Bao, who worked for Vietnam Red Cross Society's Agent Orange Victims Fund, and then moved back to Hanoi Medical University. See also Phan, *mimeo*, op. cit.

38 Sills, *op. cit.*, especially Chapter 17.

39 Quoted in Martini, *op. cit.*, p. 207.

40 Robert Allen, *The Dioxin War – Truth and Lies about a Perfect Poison*, London and Ann Arbor, MI: Pluto Press, 2004.

41 Available at www.gulfwarvets.com/ao.html, 1990.

42 *Ibid.*

43 John H. Perkins, *Geopolitics and the Green Revolution – Wheat, Genes and the Cold War*, New York, Oxford University Press, 1997, p. 256.

44 *Ibid.*, p. 211.

45 Allen, *op. cit.*, pp. xv–xvi, pp. 26–7, and p. 149.

46 Allen, *op. cit.*, p. 29. Admiral Elmo Zumwalt also claims in his *Report* that similar attempts were made to manipulate scientific evidence by the chemical companies, including pressure on government agencies such as the U.S. Environmental Protection Agency and the Centers for Disease Control.

47 The quotes are from Admiral Zumwalt and his son, Elmo Zumwalt III, "Agent Orange and the Anguish of an American Family", *New York Times Sunday Magazine*, August 24, 1986.

48 Zumwalt, *op. cit.*, p. 6.

49 Jeanne Stellman et al., "The Extent and Patterns of Usage of Agent Orange and Other Herbicides in Vietnam", *Nature*, Vol. 422, 2003, pp. 681–7.

50 www.columbia.edu/~jms13/video.html

51 Buckingham, *op. cit.*, and Zumwalt, *Report*, op. cit.
52 Zumwalt, *op. cit.*, pp. 7–8.
53 Allen, *op. cit.*, p. 46.
54 Allen, *op. cit.*, Chapter 3.
55 See the account by the last mayor of the town, Marilyn Leistner, "The Times Beach Story", *Synthesis/Regeneration 7–8*, Summer 1995, www.greens. org/s-r/078/07-09. html
56 "Agent Orange – The Time-Release Poison", *Veteran: Vietnam Veterans against the War*, Vol. 38, No. 1, Spring 2008, p. 8. For a broader and detailed description of the litigation, see Sills, *op. cit.*
57 See for example, George N. Agrios, *Plant Pathology* (5th edn), Burlington, MA, Academic Press, 2005, accessed through https://ourworldindata.org/fertilizer-and-pesticides.
58 www.epa.gov/oppbead1/pestsales/01pestsales/historical_data2001.htm.table5_1
59 Schecter et al., *op. cit.*, 2001, "Recent Dioxin Contamination from Agent Orange in Residents of a Southern Vietnam City", *Journal of Occupational and Environmental Medicine*, Vol. 43, No. 5, 2001, pp. 435–43.

4 Farmers in Post-*Doi Moi* Vietnam

We move closer to the life of the farmers in Post-*Doi Moi* Vietnam and capture it in their local context. Changes in their living environment are opportunities for them to exploit to their advantage. At the same time, these opportunities come with elements of uncertainties, or risks, which make the farmers more apprehensive, or at least cautious, about taking any path deviating from the past, familiar course of action.

The site of our closer observation is Phu Cat District, with a population of 210,000, one of the original three research sites. The District, a nondescript, mostly rural community, had its share of turmoil during the war. Late in 1965, a fierce battle took place between the U.S. ground forces, on the one hand, and a large number of units of North Vietnamese Regular Army and of Liberation Front, on the other hand, in Ia Drang Valley, 100 km southwest of Phu Cat, in Gia Lai Province. Another battle of an even larger scale soon followed in Bong Son, the northern end of Binh Dinh Province, much closer to Phu Cat, involving division-size forces from both sides.

These two battles, marking the beginning of the Americanization of the war, dragged Phu Cat residents into its unpredictable unfolding. The battles were the unmistakable signs of deep penetration by the North Vietnamese Regular Army units into the South, with the National Liberation Front (NLF) either leading the way or tagging along with them. The District was a stage as many other rural communities in the South where the forces supporting the South and the North crossed their paths at an alarming frequency. The residents had no choice in siding with either but went along with the dominant side at any given time. They, with no apparent partisan loyalty, sometimes helped the forces for the South, and, other times, those for the North and the NLF.

Consequently, the farmers sustained their daily activities as farmers with great difficulty. They needed to stay alert to any signs of disruptions and often suspended their work in rice paddies whenever spotting troop movements near and around their backyard. The farmers in the North suspended their familiar, family-centred, life under the collective farming method; the Phu Cat farmers intermittently put a moratorium on their family-led daily activities as they faced unpredictable turn of events in their backyard.

The two battles also drew Phu Cat into the middle of the war in another way. Recognizing the need to secure the basis for troop's air mobility, the United States installed an airbase in the middle of the District. The airbase and its surrounding areas quickly became one of the three "hot spots" of the toxic herbicides spray, along with Bien Hoa near Ho Chi Minh City and Da Nang to the north. The end of the war did not help the farmers restore their familiar life. It merely extended the moratorium on the family-centred rural life as the collectivization of agricultural production replaced the war.

Against this background, the District, in many ways, represents the changes that *Doi Moi* reforms triggered, and some of the characteristics of farmers' lives that remain untouched by them. Phu Cat also embraces both the families of Agent Orange (AO) victims and those who were spared the misfortune. As such, Phu Cat and its farmers offer an opportune focus for our examination of how the farmers behave.

The focal point of the observation is the farmers' attitudes towards the choices that may change their standing with wealth and health. The standings on these two fronts are not as self-evident as they seem for two reasons: that wealth cannot be so readily captured as increased profits alone, and health even less so, as we discuss it later. More importantly, neither concern, wealth or health, consumes the farmers' cares, worries, hopes, wishes, speculations, or attention on its own. Both are only among many areas that the farmers find worth investing their time and resources in.

Phu Cat, Binh Dinh Province, Vietnam

We came to Phu Cat for the first time in 2004, ten years after the Land Reform of 1993, to develop research on AO. There was not much hustle and bustle in the narrow streets in the business section, Ngo May, 15 km north of the Airport, or on either side of the main North-South thoroughfare, Route 1, along which the District stretches. Seemingly prolonged blasts of horns from heavy trucks and long-distance buses passing by did not seem to disturb anyone. The residents, in pyjamas or casual rolled-up khaki trousers and dirty T-shirts, were walking around or riding bicycles or motorbikes. They seemed to be just wandering at a leisurely pace to the extent that we began to doubt if they had a destination in mind. Away from Route I, the whole area was a green mosaic of rice paddies, peanut farms, and tall and drooping bamboo bushes, all with the Nui Ba Mountains rising in the background. It was a picture-perfect rural landscape of Vietnam.

The Nui Ba Mountain range, we soon learned, was known as the "Man Eater" because it had been a target of AO spraying since around the battle in Bong Son in early 1966, and numerous ponds and lakes on it were badly contaminated. The discoloured "No Trespassing" signs were everywhere near these bodies of water. The name, of course, was given only recently and usually shared only by a few who came into contact with some of the medical and social research teams like ours.

A few farmers returning from their farms with hoes and forks or spades on their shoulders looked at us with curiosity but did not forget to throw a friendly smile with a slight nod. A group of kids quickly gathered right behind us, calling out "hello, hello" as they caught us riding into the villages in a District Health Centre ambulance, which served as a makeshift limo.

Not much has changed since then. Several new cafes and eateries have opened up at both ends of the Ngo May section, and two 30-room hotels, including Anh Phu, the first of its kind, now stand at its northern end. As if to justify these new additions, an industrial park is being built on the former rice paddies. One wide paved-road runs through the park, although the park remains mostly unoccupied. There is a world of difference between this and the vast Nhon Hoi Economic Zone further to the south around Qui Nhon, the largest development project of the province, which began in 2005.[1]

Phu Cat Airport has gone through rounds of renovations. What was once a small attachment to the air force base now has the look of a major regional airport, with its entirely new, stylish terminal, complete with decent restaurants. Most of the eye-catching changes are along the road to, and the areas around, the beach, which is poised to become a major tourist attraction. An enormous statue of Buddha overlooking the South China Sea (East Sea, as the locals call it) completes the list of changes over the past 15 years or so. These changes are mostly to the east and south of the airport. Everything else has remained more or less the same, the farmers included.

Phu Cat: a farming country

Phu Cat is a district in Binh Dinh Province, which is one of 90 provinces, and located in central coastal Vietnam. Binh Dinh is an emerging economy. In the first several years of our research, the province was enjoying a high annual growth rate of about 10%, with per capita income of around $900 in 2010 (doubling that of 2005). The reliance on agriculture and forestry was still heavy (35%), although their contribution to the province's economy had been on the decline, from 42.2% in 2000. The rise of development parks in Nhon Hoi continues to push this relative decline.

In the long run, the development projects in the Nhon Hoi Economic Zone may lift the province's economy. As of now, however, the new economic zone and its neighbouring Quy Nhon, a port city and tourist spot, is no more than a place for occasional weekend visits for the majority of Phu Cat farmers. In addition, part of Binh Dinh's major contributions to the national income comes from servicing the export of coffee, rice, cashew nuts, textiles, minerals, wood, and seafood (Figure 4.1 and Table 4.1).

Nonetheless, the earlier phases of our close observations offered plenty of opportunities to see a few signs of change, though fragmented, in this rural community. The farmers in this district represented, as they do now, any combination of the rural poor and transitional farming.

The majority of the farmers never questioned the meaning of seasonal rituals such as the Tet (Lunar New Year), regardless of the costs they might incur, and

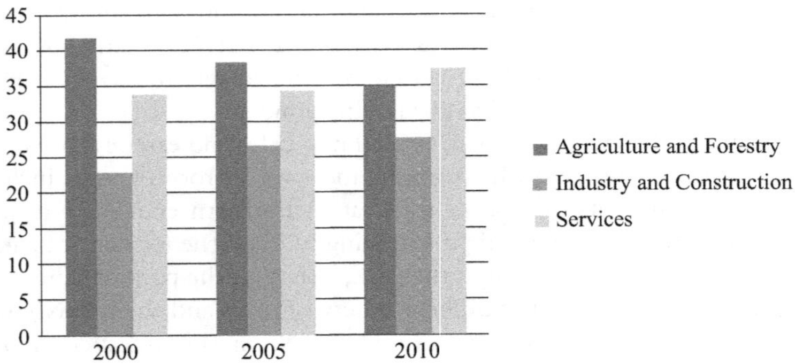

Figure 4.1 Economic Structure (%) of Binh Dinh 2000–2010.
Source: http://binhdinh.vietccr.vn/xem-tong-quan/thong-tin-kinh-te-xa-hoi-binh-dinh-default.html

Table 4.1 Binh Dinh: Facts and Figures

	Binh Dinh
Land area	6051 km^2
Forest land area	3065 km^2
Agricultural land area	1315 km^2
Population	1.5 million
Agricultural population	30% (2009)
GDP	$159.7 million (2010)
Value of agricultural production	1% total production value
GDP per capita	$900
Export	$304.6 million (2011)

Source: Collected from different sources including General Statistics House, ASEM Connect (http://asemconnectvietnam.gov.vn/infodetail.aspx?infoid=11184), Binh Dinh Industrial Zone http://kktbinhdinh.vn/default.asp?id =0&ID_ tin =1963); Science and Technology Department of Binh Dinh, www.dostbinhdinh.org.vn/Magazine NewsPage. asp?TinTS_ID=495&TS_ID=48

they routinely and fastidiously observed the reciprocity of mutual help at harvest and other busy time of the year. Beyond these practices, however, they differed from each other in just about everything they did. Some supplemented their income by producing and selling Che and other snacks at their neighbourhood market; likewise, others sold the fruits from their yard. Still, others might keep what they claim were the "convenient stores" in small spaces facing a street. A few of them even sold cigarettes individually. Some parents wished their future to be with that of their children away from farming, and others were perfectly happy to see some of their children already capable of taking over the farming chores. These farmers, in short, spoke for the diversity behind their uniform self-identification as farmers. Not much has changed since.

The first inkling of a common thread was that the farmers were not as concerned about how much wealth their farms brought in. As we mentioned earlier in Chapter 3, all signs were that any question concerning income had little traction on their mind. One farmer, H. Ngoc, even gave precisely the same income figure in 2005 and 2009: "between 2,000,000 and 3,000,000 VND" (March 2005 and September 2009).

There was no doubt that they were concerned about whether their farms could support their families' daily consumption, including sufficient food, or if their subsistence was secured. What mattered to them was that they were above the "subsistence" level, although what they considered "subsistence" varied from one family to another. Beyond that, the "income" seemed to be a concern of secondary significance among the full range of other factors inundating their daily lives.

The absence of efforts to reinforce the basis of household income illustrates this point. Nearly all farmers purchased and kept cows and pigs for future extra cash income. However, purchasing them was as far as their purposeful actions went. One farmer, Dang N., testified, "It would be nice if this cow gives birth to two or three calves". He had acquired the cow by using a two-year loan from a local bank of 3,000,000 VND, approximately $150. Then he added: "That would be a big surprise". "What?" was our unspoken response to that. So why did he bother with borrowing money? "Uh, everyone else does. Besides, I have plenty of livestock feed from the field" (March 2005). Conscious efforts to strengthen the basis of the household income in order to launch rounds of investment for more gains were conspicuously missing.

"Farming" was a typical response, and remains so, when asked about their vocation. And that response, too, can be somewhat misleading. It speaks first and foremost of what the farmers *own*: the land or, more precisely, the right to use it. Maximization of that right for profit, again, is not their top priority. Many produce cashew nuts, peanuts, and other products for sale, in addition to rice. Nevertheless, they exhibit little or no sign that they are engaged in efforts to produce surplus beyond what is needed to support the household. If anything, the additional income offers a safe distance for their life from the threshold of subsistence. It makes the difference between an easier and difficult life.

Looking at the peanut farm, which was nearly as large as a parcel of his rice paddies, one farmer, Mac C.T., who still considered himself poor, confessed that he and his family did not wish for anything more. His wish did not change between several visits in 2005, 2009, and now. A secure life, and not prosperity, occupied his mind. His wife, who was seated next to him, concurred (March 2005 and March 2009).

Farming occupies much of what these farmers do. Farming, however, is often a part of the social relations within a community that owning the land, or the right to use it, has necessitated. Some parts of Phu Cat farmland are better irrigated, allowing them to carry out the biannual harvesting of rice, thereby doubling the opportunities for, or *burden* of, farm work. Regardless of the sizes of farms they own, it is customary for the farmers to offer each other a helping hand in ploughing, growing and planting seedlings, weeding, and harvesting. It is a custom that goes hand in hand with a tightly knit community with untraceable origins, or a practice reinforced by the collective farming era, especially of the decade following the unification in 1975. It is a common-sense understanding of the farmers that a free ride is not a choice for the majority of landowners, as the consequence of that would inevitably be that they would have to face their farm work alone.

In other words, whether to fulfil the collective obligation (reminiscent of the days of collective farming or of traditional communal duty) or to respect mutual help practices, farming is that much removed from the inspiration for producing "surplus" for profit. Farming is deeply embedded in communal life, so much so that it is "not just an economic activity", to borrow economist Michael Todaro's observation; "it is a way of life".[2]

Their efforts to produce more than they need, of course, come from their being farmers. In Phu Cat, a substantial proportion, if not the majority, of the farmers produce for self-consumption ***and*** for the market. From a development economics perspective, they may be at the second stage of a three-stage progression of agricultural transformation, with subsistence farming at first and commercial agriculture at the end.[3] Except, the farmers' behaviours, or their narratives, show no signs that they are eager to move to the final stage.

Nui Ba Mountains

Given the overall picture of Phu Cat as a farming country, the presence of the Nui Ba Mountains in the middle of the District offers a sharper focus on our examination of the farmers' behaviour. Opportunities for commercial gains had never seemed to cross the farmers' minds, even when the Mountains opened up its vast forestland to the farmers from the collective management in post-unification Vietnam.

As mentioned earlier, the Mountains are often identified with the AO contamination. But this is so mostly for outsiders like us and medical professionals in the District. The majority of the farmers, especially the middle-aged and older farmers, associate the Mountains with the recent yet bygone "collective farming" days: how the authority installed the cooperative's mode of production after the war, changed over the years after *Doi Moi*, and eventually discarded it entirely. The changes in the agricultural activities in and around the Mountains illustrate more closely how the farmers have lived with the changes on the perimeter of their lives.

In 1978, the government established a state-owned farm, *nong truong Nui Ba*. Farmers were recruited from the lowland Phu Cat to work in the Farm. Once employed, they moved to live around the farmland in the Mountains, and received a piece of "livelihood" land, or a "household plot" to build houses, to grow vegetables, and to raise pigs to supplement their livelihood. The Nui Ba State Farm, a large-sized cooperative, coexisted with regular collectives in the lowland of the District. The main activity of the Farm initially was the production of pineapples, sugarcane, tea, and coconuts. Later, the Farm added eucalyptus and cashew nuts in its production line. Like elsewhere, in 1985, the Farm started product-based contracts among its workers by allocating the forestland to the workers' households and assigning product quota to each.

Towards the end of the 1980s, some of the families on the Nui Ba Farm began to leave the Mountains when its operation began dwindling. An ironical and additional push for the farmers' departure was the Land Reform itself, initiated in 1988 and formalized in 1993. The Reform restored the farm household as the principal agent of agricultural production and assured the farmers of their right over agricultural land. It completed the departure from the collective mode of agricultural production in the eyes of the farmers and helped them resume their familiar agricultural activities more openly in what now appeared to be their *own* lands.

Under Instruction 64-CP (September 27, 1993), each family member in Phu Cat (born before 1993) received rights over one "*sao*" of agricultural land (the allocated farmland), equal to 500 m^2 for 20 years. They were among the 10 million households who received certificates for the agricultural land, representing about 87% of farming households and 78% of the agricultural land in Vietnam.[4]

Against this background, the forestland in the Nui Ba Mountains offered ***additional*** opportunities for farming. Earlier in 1968, North Vietnam had begun allocating forestland to the cooperatives as the North had firmly established the collectivization. As specified in Resolution 272/CP in 1972, the purpose for allocating the forestland was threefold: agricultural production, forest protection, and forest resources development. When the government began the forestland allocation elsewhere in 1983, the allocation was pushed through the existing cooperatives. The establishment of the State Farm in Nui Ba, in place of the use of an existing cooperative, appeared to be an exception in this push. However, the Farm's function was the same as that of any other agricultural cooperatives. Nationwide, a total of 4.4 million ha of forest was allocated to 2,638 communes, 7,442 cooperatives, and 432,500 households in the early 1990s.[5]

By the late 1980s, as in the regular allocated farmland, the farming households had almost replaced state enterprises in managing forests. In order to formalize and promote this trend, the government pushed further programmes targeting the forestland in quick succession. In 1992, the government announced Decision 327 concerning the distribution and use of land, including bare hills and mountains, forests, and alluvial ground by the sea, which again confirmed the "households" as the principal unit for the production activities of the forestland.[6]

Forestland allocation to each family was based on the family's capacity (for growing perennial or annual trees). Families moving to these new zones or new land had the choice to transfer the right to use their farmland and housing land if they wished to secure funding for their new ventures. This provision was indicative of the difficulty of moving a large number of farmers to mountainous areas. The government, nonetheless, expanded this provision in 1998 through the programme known as the Five Million Hectare Reforestation Project (5MHRP) or Decision 661. The new version had a numerical goal to achieve: reforest 5 million ha of land, of which 2 million ha was earmarked for special-use forest and protection forest and 3 million for production forest.[7] Furthermore, in 1998, the joint Vietnam-UN reforestation and food programme, known as "PAM", pushed even more the allocation of the forestland among the farmers with immensely generous conditions, such as support for an initial investment fund and taxation favourable to the farmers.[8]

Finally in 2005, the government launched a World Bank-backed afforestation programme known as WB3, specifically for the four provinces south of the former DMZ including Binh Dinh. The programme offered technical training in rearing trees and saplings, among others, and investment support of 10 million VND/ha (about $500) distributed over three years.[9] One catch was that those who had not participated in the earlier forestland allocation programmes were not qualified to be part of this final one, the WB3 programme.

In the meantime, many of the farmers who had initially worked on the Nui Ba State Farm left the Mountains as the right of land use was secured in lowland Phu Cat through the land reforms. Some had decided to stay on. Also, new farmers, though still at a modest rate in the early years, volunteered to go to the Mountains, receiving the assigned land from these afforestation programmes and began their new life in this mountainous area. The number of local farmers moving to Nui Ba increased somewhat in the 1990s, although no local officials could offer even a vague figure as regards the total.

Despite all these efforts in the Mountains, the government finally and permanently closed the State Farm in Nui Ba in 2006. Part of it was transferred to the People's Committee of Cat Trinh Commune at the foot of the Mountains, while the mountainous area became Phu Cat Forest Farm (*lâm trường Phù Cát*). Cat Trinh People's Committee began to sell this lower part through TV ads, and "red books" (land title) were to be provided to the buyers. This motivated some farmers to acquire land and/or move closer to this area while keeping the allocated farmland mainly to support the household. However, the fact that the Committee has repeated the efforts to lure farmers to the forestland in the Mountains suggests that the response has been disappointing to the planners.

The termination of the State Farm marked the end of de-collectivization in Phu Cat. It also meant that the vast forestland in the Mountains could have been exploited by the farmers to their gain, if they had wished. The gains that the farmers sought, however, were not commercial.

Land and the farmers: farming as a way of life

Land is one of the primary production factors in economics parlance.

However, the farmers seek more from the land than efficient production. They see the land as the basis for family life and its continuity and for practising communal obligations. More importantly, the farmers see the land where their actions secure the expected returns in many dimensions of the family and community life.

In the post-Land Reform Vietnam, as mentioned in Chapter 2, there are three types of land that the farmers possess or have access to: the allocated farmland, the auctioned farmland, and the allocated forestland. The first of the three is a constant, or a given, as everyone born after 1993 has at least one in his or her possession. In the eyes of the farmers, the other two present extra opportunities to calculate the gains and losses to the minimum basis of life, which is already secured by having the first. As such, how the farmers deal with these two additional lands tells us more about how they see where they are going: preservation of, or improvement of, the status quo. They maybe even taking steps to commercial farming.

Additional resources: the "Auction" land

Following the Land Reform and its associated changes in the early 1990s, the majority of the Phu Cat residents acquired at least a parcel of the "allocated" farmland to cultivate rice and have maintained their residence close to their farmland. Some of them may have become office workers since and moved their residence closer to the Ngo May section of the District but have still kept the land and hire somebody, if necessary, to cultivate it for them. Mr Phung, the assistant physician and our active liaison, is an example. He worked at Cat Trinh Commune Clinic until his recent retirement and his wife helped him run an Internet shop for online games from home. Between them, they still keep a 1,000 m^2 rice paddy.

The eight informants – those active in farming in the Mountains and lowland (plus one "middleman", as shown in Table 2.7 in Chapter 2 and below) – all have at least 1,000 m^2 of the allocated farmland for rice cultivation. Without exception, they all are the beneficiaries of the 1993 Land Reform.

Legally, the farmland is the state property, and the farmers have the right to use it for 20 years. During the tenure, the farmers can exercise the right to inherit and transfer it. After the 20 years, they can extend the land tenure so that their production activities will not be disrupted, as stated in the amendment to the 1993 Reform Law in 2003. Moreover, they did not need to pay agricultural tax. This exemption was again extended for another ten years in 2012. In reality, therefore, the farmers nearly automatically assume the allocated farmland to be part of their assets and committed themselves to the production activities seamlessly. The eight farmers are no exception. The table below presents a list of the landholdings of the eight (plus one "middleman", No. 1), as of 2010.

Table 4.2 Sample of the Size of Landholding among Selected Farmers in the Mountains

	Total	*Allocated Farmland*	*Auction Farmland*	*Allocated Forestland*	*Others*
No. 1	na	na			
No. 2 No. 6	2.1 ha	1500 m^2	0	2 ha	na
No. 3	3.2 ha	2000 m^2	1 ha	2 ha	na
No. 4	8.5 ha	5000 m^2	0	8 ha	na
No. 5	1.6 ha	1000 m^2	3000 m^2	1.2 ha	na
No. 7	2.85 ha	2000 m^2	1000 m^2	2.4 ha	1500 m^2 for house
No. 8	2.25 ha	2500 m^2	0	2 ha	na
No. 9	1 ha	2000 m^2	3000 m^2	0.5 ha	na

Binh Dinh Province, in general, and Phu Cat, in particular, are not known for large-sized operations of commercial agricultural production. The farmland is mainly used for growing rice and seasonal produce, mostly for household and local consumption. Surplus products, including rice, are usually sold in small domestic markets.

If they do not produce enough rice for self-consumption, they can rent more land, called *ruộng đấu giá*, "Auction land", from the local People's Committee. It is similar to the traditional type of communal land for shared use. Local People's Committee manages and rents out the "auction land" in Phu Cat to those households that may not produce enough rice even for self-consumption from their allocated farmland. To highlight the purpose, the land has another name, "*ruộng công ích*" (land for public use). As can be seen from Table 4.3, the farmers with smaller landholdings (ranging from 1,000 to 2,000 m^2) go for the "auction land" (four out of eight farmers). The rent per year for "auction land" is about 30 kg of rice grain per *sao*.

However, this "auction land" is usually of poor quality, ranked between the fourth and the seventh (out of seven ranks). According to the national standard, ranks one, two, and three are considered from "good" to "fairly good".[10] It is usually also located far away from residential areas, and sometimes way back into the Nui Ba Mountains and, therefore, good only for one-crop-a-year cultivation of rice and growing vegetables. The farmers grow rice on the "Auction land" in the Mountains only in the rainy season (winter-spring crop) and often leave it unattended for the rest of the year because they cannot afford irrigation costs for all seasons. Some farmers take a risk by growing rice in October. In one of our visits, they reported the flooded rice paddies and could not do much about it. Mr Phung insisted, "[I]t is a stupid idea to grow rice in that land in this season".

Auction land is designed for those families in need, who do not produce enough for their household consumption. In reality, anyone can join the bidding for it. Since the quality of land is not that great, well-to-do farmers usually do not participate in the bidding.

Table 4.3 Rice Production by Selected Farmers

Farmers	*Allocated Farmland*			*Auction Farmland*		*Total (year)*
	Crop 1	Crop 2	Crop 3	Crop 1	Crop 2	
No. 1						
No. 2	1 ton	1 ton	200 kg	0	0	2.2 tons
No. 6						
No. 3	2 tons		0	6 tons	Vegetables	8 tons
No. 4	3 tons		0	0	0	3 tons
No. 5	400 kg		0	1.2 tons	Vegetables	1.6 tons
No. 7	250~270 kg	180~200 kg	0	150 kg	Vegetables	~620 kg
No. 8	1.1 tons	0	Not much	0	0	1.1 ton
No. 9	6–700 kg	200 kg		150 kg	Vegetables	~1 ton

Crop 1: Winter-Spring, Crop 2: Summer-Autumn, Crop 3: Occasional.

A closer look at the accounts given by these farmers reveals that they do not to go for the "Auction land" bidding in order to secure subsistence. A farmer no. 3 in Table 4.2, H. H. Gian, born in 1967, is one example (November 2010). He was not desperate to secure enough to feed his family of five. Nevertheless, he contracted 20 "sao" (one hectare) of the "Auction land" to grow rice during the winter-spring crop and cassava and peanuts for the rest of the year. The reason was simple: convenience. That piece of land happened to be near his home since 1993 when his family moved to the mountainside while retaining his 4 "sao" of the allocated farmland in the lowland part of the District. Besides, no one else wanted it since it was in the mountainous area.

Another case is that of no. 9, Vo N. K. (November 24 2010), who had had two children and tried to keep the land in the Mountains ever since 1984, in addition to the regular allocated farmland for rice production. In 1984, he received 1 "*sao*" to build a house to live and 1 "*mau*" (equivalent to 10,000 m^2) from the local cooperative to grow coconuts as the "Three Interests coconut farm" campaign (in the interests of farmers, cooperatives, and the state) was launched locally. The coconut farm did not last long because the productivity was not high, and after seven or eight years, the land used for coconut farming had to be returned to the local cooperative and became the "auction land". Since then, he had continued to rent part of the land, except he grew cassava instead of coconut trees. He neither gained nor lost much.

On paper, farmers have to return the auction farmland after four years and the land is auctioned again. In practice, farmers usually get the same piece of land so that their cultivation is not disrupted, and nor is their previous investment wasted. Mr Vo. N. K. had always participated in bidding for the same piece of land and managed to keep the land right through until now to grow cassava. Our guess is that no one wished to compete for the land with him.

What emerges from these and other similar accounts is the consistency and continuity in the farmers' efforts to acquire and/or keep their land and production going. An unwritten law underlying their action is mutual respect for each other's efforts to sustain consistency and continuity in their life; no serious competition is seen among the farmers during the bidding for the auction land. One obvious reason for non-interference may be that the auction farmland is usually not of good quality, and therefore not many farmers go after it. But a more important reason is reciprocity, as Mr H. H. Gian once put it: "*tình nghĩa*" (appreciation) among the farmers to respect the continuous thread running through each of their lives. There was not even the slightest hint that the farmers looked at these additional lands from an investment angle.

Additional resources: the forestland

A confluence of a few factors makes the allocated forestland in the mountains of Phu Cat a particularly intriguing probe for the farmers' behaviours. For one, as mentioned earlier, the forestland in the Mountains is mostly barren and is located well into the Mountains away from the residential lowland of the District.

And, the land is fit for growing produce whose value fluctuates with its market price. It is not that the land had been entirely neglected as it had seen various afforestation and reforestation programmes. However, to lure the farmers, an extra incentive was needed: free and/or with government financial aid.

Even now, a visit to the forestland in the Mountains usually takes almost an hour from the Ngo May section of the District on a small bike to the former Nui Ba state-owned Farm area. A car ride would make no significant difference. The ride would be far from smooth, bouncing constantly on a dirt road with many bumps of different sizes and puddles of muddy water if it rained the day before. Without rain, the road is like a collection of tyre tracks of small pickup trucks and bikes twisting and crossing each other imprinted on the hardened surface. In other words, the road must have been well used, but is not part of the improving infrastructure, which is more visible in the lowland of Phu Cat.

Under these unfavourable conditions, cashew nuts, one of the key products of the land, went through some changes. They started as one of the main ones along with eucalyptus. The latter was, and is, considered highly promising commercially as it is the raw material for oil and paper and other synthetic goods. There was a period when the farmers in Phu Cat, including some in the lowland, went back and forth between these two products. By the early 2000s, the farmers had begun to opt for cashew nut production over that of eucalyptus. After all, cashew nuts were starting to make the most significant contribution to Vietnam's foreign currency reserves.

According to a cashew nut collector (no. 1 in Table 4.2) – a middleman between the growers and the buyers, residing in Cat Trinh Commune – about 10% of the Commune's farmers (3,400 households) were involved in growing cashew nuts, as of our first visit (November 2010). The collector from Phu Nhon village in the same Commune testified that 80 households out of the total 320 had joined the cashew nut production, while in An Duc village, 100 out of 800 had done so. These are not negligible numbers considering the additional burden that the cashew production generates tacked on to the rice production, and the burden is multiplied since the farm is in the forestland. In other words, these farmers might be signalling that the commercially oriented farming had begun taking hold of some of the Phu Cat farmers' guarded views of themselves as farmers.

Our initial interpretation was too hasty.

H. H. Gian, who had moved to the Mountains in 1993, recalled that "there was still no electricity and no paved road" in the Mountains back then. The conditions have not changed much since. Our guess initially was that he, and many others, had a clear "gain" in mind as compensation for the difficult conditions when extending their activities to cover the forestland. They were willing to risk even the fluctuating market price of cashew nuts. Their actions were indicative of the new consciousness. Or were they?

The important point to note is that the negative impact of the fluctuating cashew nut price was limited to the forestland, their asset in the Mountains, which is auxiliary to the allocated farmland.

A puzzle still remains: why then did some farmers bother to move to or add the forestland when the living conditions were inhibitive in the Mountains then as now, and when in particular the idea of commercial agriculture or forestry was still in its early days. What could have been the "gains"?

Guard against the uncertainties or fear of losses

With the landholding in the Mountains gradually turning into a somewhat promising asset, at least for some, the farmers' behaviour remains as consistent as that of the farmers without such extra assets. The farmers exhibit little or no deviation from the past, a familiar course of action, where surviving the constant changes, and thus uncertainties, has become the norm. Changes in the legal framework for land-farmer relationships and the purpose behind the changes give little or no incentive for the farmers to change their lifestyle. They merely prompt small adjustments. The farmers' narratives reflect this cautious, if conservative, outlook. Their efforts at adjustments are aimed at making the noticeable changes in their living environment "unproblematic", to borrow from Berger and Luckmann,[11] to the lifestyle they have fastidiously observed and protected.

The story of N. V. Thom, born in 1959 (interviewed in November 2010, August 2015, and March 2017), illustrates this remarkable consistency. Like those of many of the farmers with additional assets, his life in the Mountains began as a worker at Nui Ba State Farm in 1981 and survived the Farm's termination in 2006. As mentioned earlier, Nui Ba State Farm gradually shifted its production strategy to concentrate on cashew nut growing. Along the way, in 1985, Nui Ba Farm introduced product-based contracts among its workers by allocating them land. The amount of land allocated depended on its quality. If the land was ranked first out of the seven land quality ranks, it was 4 ha per person. If it ranked second or third, the families could receive more, say, 6–7 ha per member. These families were allowed to keep surplus products and sell them locally, or they could ask the State Farm to sell the surplus for them.

N. V. Thom lived through these earlier years and the eventual dismantling of the State Farm's collective production system. He found himself in the end with the rights of over 8 ha of land and has done just about everything himself, including the construction and improvement of a road to a nearby reservoir. Now over 60, he produces rice and grows cashew nuts. In the past, he had grown eucalyptus around the cashew farm. Most recently, he began producing peppers. He comfortably supports his family of five and even some relatives well up in the Mountains. Over the past 30 years, he moved from stage one to stage two and was poised to reach the final stage of Todaro's three-stage agricultural transformation. Or so it appears.

Mr N. V. Thom is among the most senior of the farmers, with his experience of working at Nui Ba State Farm since the early 1980s. Initially he was a worker in a State Farm production unit tasked to produce pineapples, sugarcane, and cashew nuts. He met his wife there. They married and have since built their life in this forestland. The Farm shifted production to concentrate on cashew nuts, which, at times, was susceptible to market fluctuations. Regardless, his family's livelihood was "secured" by a small landholding in the Mountains, reserved for producing rice and other things for self-consumption. Soon after *Doi Moi* in 1986, his family took on the responsibility of the whole production process within the assigned land, which was about 1.5 ha. Thus, Decision 10 of 1988 did not come as a surprise to him and his family, nor did it cause any disruption in their life. It merely reinforced what he and his family, with occasional help from his relatives, had been practising – the family as the principal unit of production and of life generally.

The 1993 Land Reform and its amendments in 1995 and 2003 formally institutionalized his land use and other rights over the 1.5-ha area. He was only slightly older than 30. He along the way acquired the right to use an additional 7.5 ha in exchange for 20% of any profit from the acquired land to the state under Decision 327, the forest land allocation programme, aimed at both land reclamation and reforestation. In 2006, Phu Cat People's Committee took over the management responsibility of the State Farm's land. The Committee presented Mr Thom with the choice of leaving the area or purchasing the land he had cultivated since 1993 for a token sum of cash; he chose the latter. He does not remember how much he had to pay.

He always seized the opportunity to acquire the use of more land. However, this was more an act of adjustment than of investment. He is now unofficially called the "land millionaire" by the local farmers. He owns a vast land in the Mountains but exhibits virtually no signs of him and his family being endowed with rich assets. His house in the Mountains is not any better or larger than any average farmer's house, with only limited improvements in plumbing and lighting.

Likewise, N. X. Tien (no. 8 in Table 4.3), born in 1957 in Phu Nhon village in Cat Trinh Commune, happened to be in the right place at the right time where the acquisition of the forestland was concerned. He retained the allocated farmland at the foot of the Mountains. But when the State Farm ceased to function and its forestland became available, Mr Tien acquired part of it *free* on the condition that he did not build a house on it. On paper, the size of land he received was 1.4 ha, but in fact, he received 2 ha, on which he grew 300 cashew nut trees. He did not need to pay any tax. By having this land, he was qualified to be part of the WB3 programme and even enjoyed support from it.

The fact that he lacked a sense of management or interest in expanding his forest operation, however, was evident when we asked him about the "lease" on the land and the contribution (quota) of the products to the Commune: "I am not sure", he said. He only recently began harvesting cashew nuts somewhat more systematically. Before, he was not "growing the nuts much", even when acquiring the seeds from a nearby farm free.

A brief sketch above shows that concern other than investment for profit underlies Thom's and others' moves in acquiring the forestland, and their relocation and settlement in the Mountains. The decisions may be a little more involved, at least for Mr N. V. Thom and his wife, than merely going along with the changes in the land system as handed down from the highest authority. After all, they began their life together in 1980, a year before moving to the Mountains and developed a special attachment to the forestland.

Even then, there was little or no sign of business speculation on their part. What mattered to them at the vital decision-making junctures was that the choices they made to acquire more land did not come with a sense of uncertainty, threatening to disrupt their lives.

In much the same way as Mr Vo N. K., the consistency with which N. V. Thom's family has remained the principal actor of production and life, in general, has survived the test of an unpredictable turn of events in the mode of agricultural production since the 1980s. That consistency has become an irreplaceable goal throughout *his* changing status from a collective farm worker to a head of an independent production unit, his family. The size of the productive land at his disposal would have placed him closer to the final stage in Todaro's three-stage agricultural transformation, mentioned earlier. However, he would be the last to admit that he is conscious of the approaching final stage.

Starting "way of life"

Unlike Mr N. V. Thom or Mr Vo N. K., Mr H. H. Gian was too young to go through the whole range of changes in agriculture generated by the collectivization campaign to the south of DMZ. In 1993, he moved to the Mountain area, part of Nui Ba State Farm, long after the heyday of the cooperatives was over. The physical conditions were inhibitive then. He quickly added, as if to insist that there were more than economic opportunities: "I was young". Mr H. H. Gian was only in his mid-20s then.

He had married in 1990 and had the allocated farmland through the cooperative in Phu Nhon village in Cat Trinh Commune. When he acquired 2 ha of forestland through the cooperative in 1993 in exchange for 5% of whatever he made, he and his wife moved to the Mountains and began producing "bricks" for housing construction. Their efforts to raise eucalyptus did not pan out and they sold the trees even as firewood for cooking. They then began growing cashew nuts as the State Farm in the Mountains shifted its emphasis from raising eucalyptus to growing cashew nuts. They asked the Farm for cashew seeds and later began selling the products through a middleman in the Mountains. They now usually made around 40 million VND – about $2,000 – per year off the cashew nuts and other operations, which was more than a decent income.

What appears to be a success story, nonetheless, did not fit well with Mr H. H. Gian's far more modest and low-key narratives of their life in the Mountains. For one, the forestland was an alternative that presented itself at the right time in 1993 for him and his wife of only two years. They wanted to take on the task, however adventurous it appeared, of building the basis of their house away from their parents'. Having tried to produce bricks for years, growing eucalyptus trees and then cashew nuts were part of a navigation for a new and young household to establish itself, and the navigators, the husband and wife, were especially alert to the opportunities and threats influencing the course of navigation, such as shifting operations of the State Farm and its eventual closure. The navigating eyes were always animated by the commitment to protecting their new household, something they did not wish to endanger at any cost.

N. N. Tien (no. 5), who was 40 years old at our first meeting in 2010, three years younger than Mr Gian and with forestland a 20-minute bike ride from Gian's residence (November 2010), may have been a little more "business" conscious than the others. He had allocated farmland in the lowland Cat Trinh Commune but added forestland from the Commune's People's Committee, which took over the management responsibility of part of former Nui Ba State Farm in 1997. N. N. Tien and his wife, who married two years earlier, moved to the Mountains then. Two years later, they acquired 1.2 ha of PAM land from N. N. Tien's sick uncle, who found it difficult to manage the land. The case of another opportunity presented itself. The price, or what he called the "family price", was 2.5 million VND ($110), or six "*chi vang*", the equivalent of 0.72 ounces of gold, according to Mr Tien.

His uncle used to grow eucalyptus on this land as it was in high demand in the first half of the 1990s. The eucalyptus business began dwindling soon afterwards to the point that the farmers had to cut down nearly all eucalyptus just to make firewood. Cashew nuts became a promising alternative then. Despite limited experience in the production of cashew nuts, Tien monitored this trend, as well as the price of cashew nuts, and decided to grow them soon after he moved into the area. After ten years of living in the Mountains, Mr N. N. Tien and his wife are quite content and financially secure.

With the size of the land being over 1,000 m^2 for his housing alone, it may have given any visitor an impression that their household is a cut above that of the average farmer in the District. Nothing else, however, corroborates that impression, with pigs, a few hens, and children in raggedy clothes making up the rest of the scene.

In Tien's case, a few factors were at work leading to where N. N. Tien and his family are, some of which were fortuitous: the fact that they had been married only for a short period of time before moving to the Mountains, that the former state-owned forestland became available through his Commune's intervention, and that he had a sick uncle who had acquired a large forestland free as part of the PAM programme. What enabled him to exploit these factors was his wish, much like Mr H. H. Gian's, to start and solidify his new household, i.e., there was less to lose by the move in the first place. Beyond this commitment, he exhibited no apparent interest in exploiting these and other factors to expand his family's operations.

Mr N. N. Tien observed that this year's (2010) cashew nut yield might be low because, as he casually commented, his "investment [in fertilizers] is low". He spread pigs' dung as manure, instead, over the cashew nuts' roots. The underlying concern was the launching of a new life with his family and protecting it. A commercially motivated move, which may still come into his perspective later, may have been considered more as a risk to their young venture.

Exceptions to the rule or new breeds

Some farmers' behaviour is indicative of concerns beyond protecting their life against disruptions or establishing and promoting the family. N. T. Tung (no. 6, b. 1957) and L. D. Cuong (no. 7, b. 1963) may be a case in point as their narratives hint more at concerns with production than concerns with protecting their families.

Mr Tung was 58 years old and vice-chairman of Cat Trinh's People's Committee at the time of our first visit and had been in a unique position to add a cashew nut-growing operation through greater access to the forestland development programmes and "in-house" information. Alternatively speaking, he was in a position where he could not refuse to go along with the nationwide programmes. That position over time has landed him a large forestland and the position of Head of the Management Board for the WB3 programme in the local Commune. The result is the emergence of, at least in appearance, a commerce-oriented farmer.

Mr Tung had been a People's Committee in Cat Trinh Commune long before becoming its vice-chairman in 2004. He was also Head of the Management Board for the WB3 programme in Phu Cat. He benefited from his official position, although he did not openly admit it. The joint Vietnam-UN reforestation and food programme (PAM) provided him 2 ha of forestland in 1998, with a generous provision that 80% of the profit went to the farmers and the rest to the state.

He said he "is overwhelmed by the administrative works on the People's Committee and running the WB3 programme and has no time to take care of the cashew nut farm [of 2 ha]". He thus left all the farming work to his wife, Cao T. H. (b. 1957, no. 2 in Table 4.2). Cao, in turn, hired other farmers to take care of the nut farm because the rice farm alone was too much work for her at the age of 53. Their farms, for both the rice and the cashew nut production, did produce a surplus, but the surplus was primarily the means to keep the production going, as they saw it. In other words, despite the appearance of commercial farming with the hired farm "workers", Mr N. T. Tung and his wife were not too different from the other farmers we interviewed. Their work is more focussed on maintaining their current quality of life, on the two fronts of cashew nut production and rice production, rather than raising it.

For a truly outlying case, we would have to bring in the other of the two, Mr L. D. Cuong. He had a daughter studying at a college in Quy Nhon and a son working at a bike shop in the Ngo May section. With the future of the youngest son, 17 years old, still uncertain, his family appeared more in line with "transitional" farmers moving up in Todaro's three-stage transformation: farming activity was the means to change his family's future status to something other than that of a "farmer" (November, 2010).

Like many other farmers in the Commune, Cuong's family had its share of allocated farmland, with at least one crop of rice a year or two if and when irrigation from a nearby reservoir presented no problem. However, he began growing cashew nuts in 2004, learning through perhaps the first-hand experience of a former worker on the State Farm, his uncle, Mr N. V. Thom, the "land millionaire". Then, in 2006, by spending more than 100 million VND ($5,000), of which he borrowed 20 million VND, he acquired (the right to use for 50 years) 2.4 ha of the forestland from the People's Committee in the Commune, which was then taking over part of the defunct State Farm in the Mountains.

We heard and learned about Mr L. D. Cuong as his name was often mentioned in many of the conversations with the cashew nut growers. Mr Cuong was a "professional chemical sprayer" for their cashew farms. He was so busy with his spraying schedule for his friends and neighbours because it was just a month or so before the pollination period (usually in January) at the time of our visit. We could not meet him in the Mountains or on the rice farm, but we eventually met him after his day's work at a café next to the hotel in Ngo May where we usually stayed.

He was acutely aware when the harvest was not good and alert to what causes the decline in production, and adopted ways to resolve the problem: the trees have been harvested for too many seasons during the State Farm era and after, and needed a lot more fertilizer to be more productive. He was not reluctant to make use of bank loans to sustain a reasonable level of productivity, the most recent loan being 30 million VND (about $1,300) from the local Rural and Agricultural Bank. It is also noteworthy that he developed the family-based operation of chemical spraying into something of a small-business venture.

Perhaps a few words are in order concerning the cashew nut production that goes hand in hand with Cuong's small "business". The former is one of the many activities of commercial farming that picked up about ten years ago, around the Land Reform. In Vietnam in general, the cashew nut industry started in the 1980s. In 1990, the Vietnam Cashew Association was founded under the auspices of the Ministry of Agriculture and Food Technology (now the Ministry of Agriculture and Agricultural Development). Soon after that, Vietnam began exporting cashews to China and to the United States in 1994, even before the relationship was normalized. In 1996, Vietnam stopped exporting raw cashew nuts to India and instead began importing raw cashew nuts from Africa because cashew nuts produced domestically did not meet the growing demand for processed cashew nuts for export. In 2006, Vietnam became the world's first cashew nut exporter, surpassing India. After that, Vietnam held that position for another four consecutive years. The largest markets are the United States (over 36%), China (18%), and the EU (20%), as of our visit. In 2010, the export turnover reached $1 billion for the first time, even though the world financial crises spanning the EU and the US reduced the demand, and the price.[12]

Local reactions to these developments may be found in the latter years of Nui Ba State Farm. It first engaged in the production of eucalyptus and cashew nut, and then concentrated on the latter. Some of the farmers we interviewed closely had seized the opportunities presented by the changes in the operation, and the eventual closure, of the State Farm. WB3 and other local afforestation programmes helped multiply the opportunities. Table 4.4 shows the results of these

Table 4.4 Cashew Nut Production in Nui Ba Mountains

Farmers	*Land Size for Cashew Nuts/Total Landholding*	*Investment (VND)*	*Yield per Land*	*Profit (VND)*
1 Middleman–collector				
2 6	2 ha/2.15 ha	9 mil	2 tons	36 mil $1600
3	2 ha/3.2 ha	NA	7~800 kg	15 mil $750
4	7 ha/8.5 ha	NA	10 tons	160~180 mil $8000~$9000
5	1 ha/1.6 ha	1.5~2 mil	1 ton	16~18 mil $800~$900
7	2.4 ha /2.85 ha	12 mil	1.6 tons	26~29 mil $1300~$1450
8	2 ha/2.25 ha	~ 3 mil	1 ton	7 mil ~18 mil $350~$900
9	0.5 ha/1 ha	Not much	150 kg	3 mil $150

(Collecting price for the middleman, #1 informant, for cashew nuts at the given time in 2010 was 16,000 VND ~ 18,000 VND/kg. $1 = 20,000 VND).
Investment = agrochemical input and hired labourers to spray chemicals;
Profit is estimated by interviewees, not on any fixed price for 1 kg of cashew, therefore different outcomes of profit.

changes, i.e., allocation of the land for cashew nut production, investment in the input (labour, fertilizers, herbicides, and pesticides), yield, and cash income generated from the production.

There are several points to note. First, the allocated forestland tends to be large in size, and thus tends to occupy the largest portion of these farmers' landholdings. This may give the impression that these farmers allocate proportionately more time for cashew nut production. The farmers' accounts, as shown above, however, do not support this impression.

Second, there are discrepancies among their yields per ha, while cash earnings per yield show only a narrow margin of differences. We wondered why those with the low-yielding farms would not do anything to improve their productivity. We soon realized that they were not aware of the higher yield in other farms. This point suggests that the farmers did not see cashew nut production as a commercial venture and hence did not let it consume them. Of course, they thought of ways of keeping the production going when the production declined. However, the decline was damaging to their possession and not to their "business". The view that holds cashew nut production in a lesser light is a corollary to having secured the family's livelihood through the use of the allocated farmland.

Third, there is a variation in the figures in the "Investment" column. Some could not even quote the figures, while others allocated a large or small amount of resources for investment purposes. The variations in investment indicate that there are no coordinated efforts among these farmers to raise or sustain the productivity, even though they are dealing with the common product for commercial gains. It is clear that each farmer relies on his or her own counsel, which, in turn, explains the discrepancies in the yields per hectare.

The last point may explain how Mr L. D. Cuong started his chemical spraying operation exclusively as part of his family business. When he acquired part of the former Nui Ba State Farm in 2006, he quickly realized that the land had been of "impoverished quality" because of the prior "overexploitation", and decided, on his own accord, to purchase a large spraying tank for fertilizers together with supporting equipment such as long tubes and a generator to support his production on the new land. He had no idea that he was taking the steps towards a small business venture.

The expansion of the spraying operation was almost fortuitous as it hinged upon convenience and coincidence. The physical proximity to the neighbours was among such conveniences. The neighbours found it expedient to ask him to extend the spraying operation. L. D. Cuong then formed a spraying team with his brother and a friend. He now did the job for eight or more neighbours a year out of 41 cashew nut growers in the former Nui Ba State Farm and an additional two or three of his neighbours at the foot of the Mountains. The venture now earned him about 60,000 VND ($3) per ha, multiplied by four or five rounds for each.

Although the neighbours called him a "professional" chemical sprayer of cashew nuts, he had not bothered to acquire a work permit or qualifications for what he did. His operations may have reached the scale of a small business, but in the minds of the farmers, including *his* own, he was not engaged in a commercial venture.

The varying performances in cashew nut production more generally tell us something intriguing: farming *is* predominantly and exclusively a family affair having survived the recent 30-year experience with collective farming. There seems to be very little or no concerted effort among the farmers to secure key inputs such as seeds or fertilizers, or to raise productivity, or to ensure better prices for the products.

Many who missed out on the opportunity to acquire the forestland, especially through the more recent WB3 programme in 2004, may now look at some of the cashew nut growers, or for that matter even eucalyptus growers, with a degree of envy. Nguyen V. T., the father of Liem – an AO victim – planted a few eucalyptus trees in the backyard where the land was apparently too barren to grow anything else. Yet, he and his wife did not think of gaining any profit out of it. They planted it just because some farmers were growing it, and his wife summarized their decision, saying, "just in case some overnight luck knocked on our door".

A similar indifference may be found in another farmer's approach to cashew nut production: that of Mr Vo N. K., the smallest forestland holder (0.5 ha) among the eight. While concentrating almost exclusively on rice production in both allocated (0.3 ha) and auction (0.2 ha) farmland, enough to support the family, he said he did not have sufficient time and, of course, capital to invest in cashew nut production. What was left for him to do was to purchase some seedlings from middlemen for the land he had acquired from his parents and leave them to grow on their own without much care. Our conversations with him left us convinced that he either grew cashew nuts just because he did not want to leave the land unused, or because it was what others did. It is hard not to assume that he had no incentive to raise productivity on the cashew nuts farm.

Phu Cat: home of AO victims and agrochemicals

The behaviour of the farmers needs to be analysed in the context of Phu Cat's being a farming state that is also home to AO victims. The farmers in the Mountains generally lack business acumen, even while using the forestland, which they consider an asset in addition to their allocated farmland. Their use of agrochemicals, some of which are toxic, also lacks caution as they rely more on their routine than on careful handling of the chemicals.

Do the farmers in the Mountains represent Phu Cat farmers generally? What does the presence of the large number of AO victims tell the famers about the use of agrochemicals and their impact on health?

War legacy

The farmers' contact with AO and other toxic chemicals may be best summarized by Mr H. H. Gian's anecdote. When he was in sixth grade (the early 1980s), he went to Nui Ba and saw a barrel filled with a white substance. Vaguely remembering hearing of the spraying of chemicals over his country by the United States during the war, he gathered that the white substance was some pesticide and decided to bring back a bag of about 2 kg. Later he went fishing and threw the white powder into the river. It did not take long before dead fish started floating to the surface, covering the length of nearly 1 km. He was stunned at how powerful the substance was. That was the last time he touched it. Vo N.K. also blamed AO for the problematic soil in the forestland that he had inherited from his parents. The tea trees that his parents had planted had failed to grow, and soon everything was dead. They'd had no idea that the substance, or whatever prevented the tea trees from growing, was the toxic herbicide known as AO. They learned the word only after Phu Cat Airport and its surrounding areas were designated as one of the "hot spots" i.e., the areas suspected of having been heavily sprayed with toxic chemicals such as AO.

The hazardous spots identified through the actual encounters with what may have been residue of AO were duly highlighted in a 1.5 m × 2 m map of the Mountains in the Phu Cat District Health Centre. The small and large dots on the map indicated the reservoirs in the Mountains where, as of our initial phase of research, people had been warned not to enter because of the contaminated water. The farmers also paid attention and acted accordingly "not to enter" the areas marked with "No Trespassing" signs. We quickly speculated about the signal that these signs might be sending: as long as one stayed away from the closed-off areas, one would be safe from the toxicity of the chemicals.

Agent Orange, well-understood as "chemicals to kill weeds" (*thuốc diệt cỏ*), has no place in the daily life of the farmers. More telling is the fact that Mr H. H. Gian, or for that matter everybody else among the nine people we interviewed closely, did not even think much about AO-dioxin contamination in human bodies until we brought it to their attention. Pressed further on if they knew of any AO victims' families, they said "yes". What they meant by "yes", however, was that they had seen these "families" now that we had identified them by name.

The acknowledgement did not mean a higher level of consciousness about the problematic agrochemicals. The AO victims and their families, rather, symbolized what had gone on in the distant past, which was now sealed within the areas with "No Trespassing" signs. Their significance, too, stops there in the minds of the farmers who are spared its devastating impact on the human bodies among their family members and relatives.

The increasingly frequent and more substantial use of agrochemicals did reach the farmers in Phu Cat, especially after the early 1990s, when Vietnamese agriculture was opened up to more commercial ventures. Their use, however, exhibits no trace of what AO may have signified in the present-day context.

Chemicals and health: muted guard

The statistics around our initial phase of research showed how Vietnam, including Phu Cat, has been exposed to a disturbing worldwide trend. About 3 billion kg of pesticides was used globally at a purchasing price of nearly $40 billion in the beginning of the twenty-first century.[13] This resulted in 26 million cases of non-fatal pesticide poisonings, of which 3 million cases involved hospitalization. There were approximately 220,000 fatalities, and about 750,000 chemical-induced chronic ailments every year.[14] As mentioned earlier, the costs of chemical-induced ill health and other damages in Vietnam were equivalent to 2% of the total GDP in 2006.

In Phu Cat, though the corresponding figures are not available, the use of chemicals was spreading widely both in rice paddies and in the fields for cashew nuts and other products. A narrow path we walked between the fields was often littered with empty chemical bags of unknown origin. The walk was indeed an unnerving experience, especially for us, with our special interest in the negative impact of chemical abuse on health.

A lack of close attention to AO and its implications, however, does not mean that the Phu Cat's farmers are entirely ignorant of, or indifferent to, the potential health risks of the daily use of agrochemicals. When asked if they were concerned about health, the farmers, including the members of AO families and cashew nut growers, responded almost instantaneously: "Of course I care about health". They also reported wearing cloth gloves, cloth masks, and motorbike helmets. Table 4.4 indicates that some of the farmers can even quote how much they invest in pesticides and other chemicals, *and* the cost of hiring personnel for spraying them. These signs suggest a certain degree of alertness to chemical-induced health risks. Mr L. D. Cuong claimed that at least those who could afford to hire someone for chemical spraying did so because they "[were] afraid of getting sick", and he quickly added that he took "every caution as much as [he] can".

From the observations of the farmers, we were left with the impression that for the majority of them, health risks may be a collateral but tolerable damage from the chemicals, which they consider to be their "salvation" in their efforts to secure a constant yield or prevent crop failure. To that extent, the farmers' guard against chemicals is somewhat muted.

In the early 1990s in particular, partially because the country was still recovering from the prolonged turmoil of war, the farmers may have looked for inexpensive chemicals or whatever was available. Mr H. H. Gian recalled purchasing a 100-ml bottle of a red "chemical" for his rice paddies. He did not remember what it was or in what proportion he diluted it with water because "everything was written in Chinese". The chemical was "amazing, the first time when it worked", he said, adding, "it may have been just a matter of luck" as it stopped working the second time, and he stopped using it (November 2010).

More recently, if a warning or a rumour reached them, saying that the use of questionable chemicals might trigger food poisoning, they would rush to defend their action by saying, "Oh, we always wash our food carefully". Alternatively, some of them found solace in the fact that they saved part of their land to produce vegetables and other produce for the family's consumption. Not far from this sort of muted caution against the chemicals was hiring somebody else, such as Mr L. D. Cuong and his small team, to spray the chemicals. Mr N. V. Thom, the "land millionaire", insisted that he monitored the mixing process before the chemicals were ready for spraying. As long as they did not touch the chemicals *directly*, it seemed that they presented no threat to health.

As examined in Chapter 2, nationwide efforts to curtail agrochemical-induced health problems began around 1992 and 1993 through a series of actions initiated by the Ministry of Agriculture and Rural Development (MARD), including the installation of Plant Protection Centres in various regions. A 2006 World Bank Report shows that the effects of these measures still remained far from satisfactory. The presence of a Plant Protection Centre in Phu Cat serves more to direct the traffic of chemicals than to raise the farmers' awareness of the chemicals' risk to health.

The farmers, both in the Mountains and in the lowlands, invariably responded with "Plant Protection Centre" to the question of where they procured the chemicals. They preferred the Centre to the local cooperatives now offering some agricultural inputs, such as fertilizers and pesticides. The latter offered products of local origin, similar to those of the Centre's, but they were of a "lesser quality and higher price", they claimed.

The presence of the Centre is significant. Here is a situation where its presence is ubiquitous beyond its local location. The farmers ask for the same varieties of chemicals as the Centre's, especially when they go to regular retail shops because of a shortage of cash. Regular retail shops are sometimes willing to wait for payment until harvest time.

Nonetheless, a nagging feeling has never left us concerning how seriously these farmers took chemical-induced health risks. We often came across instances of casual use of chemicals. An episode such as the following popped up in our interviews with an alarming frequency.

The farmers often, if reluctantly, admitted to having a "secret formula". We suspected that its use was, and is even now, fairly widespread. Mr N. N. Tien was embarrassed to bring up this topic, but after being pushed by Mr Phung, who was accompanying us, he revealed the use of a certain liquid: a liquid in which to soak mosquito nets (*thuốc nhúng mùng*). Farm workers frequently used the nets for the prevention of malaria in highland areas such as Gia Lai.[15] Mr Phung declared that this chemical worked like a "miracle". Mr N. N. Tien did not know how toxic the substance could be. He bought it from long-distance truck drivers at a price of 600,000 VND/litre ($30), which was relatively expensive compared to other pesticides. Therefore, he used it only once or twice a year. He said that the label on the bottle had been removed so he could not tell what it was. He just diluted 8 litres of water to 10cc of the substance before spraying it.

Mr L. D. Cuong, a "professional sprayer" and no stranger to agrochemicals, claimed that it was "berberine" (which he claimed had antibiotic, anti-inflammatory, and anti-diarrheic effects for malaria and dengue fever patients). He added that he bought it at a much lower price (450,000 VND/litre ($23)) from the city, presumably Quy Nohn. N. X. Tien, another Tien, reported having used the same substance, and he acquired it from the Malaria Centre in Quy Nhon at a price of 50,000 VND ($2) for a small bottle. It didn't have any smell, but it was very toxic, he had heard. He mixed it with water by himself (20 cc with a tank of 16 litres of water) and used it only for a small patch of cashew nut plants because he didn't have enough money to spray the whole farm. They all believed that since these chemicals were used in hospitals, they must be safe to use to kill pests.

The fact that the farmers paid varying prices for the "miraculous" chemical confirms one of the earlier points in the chapter that their production activities are maintained more or less independently of each other. There were no concerted effort to coordinate the acquisition and use of land or pesticides and fertilizers. The use of chemicals, therefore, is tailored to the needs of the individual households, and so are the measures of caution against the chemicals. Little or no thought is invested in the health complications induced by AO contamination (Table 4.4). For example, the low cashew nut yield (600~700 kg) on H. H. Gian's forest land (2 ha) did not bother him. He could not quote how much he had spent on fertilizer and pesticides, but he felt he had invested "well enough" as he contentedly showed us the labels, bags of chemicals, and a spraying tank (of the professional kind) he had bought from the Plant Protection Centre. His allocated and auctioned farmlands offered plenty of resources to fall back on, and he was content maintaining the cashew nut farm the way he always had. It was, and is, difficult to see how any use of the chemicals stood out in his mind and served as a reminder to him of the more devastating consequences of the wartime use of the toxic chemicals.

Evidence of risks

To the extent that the herbicides and other chemicals, and their use do not figure prominently as a crucial production factor, the chemicals are not even a remote threat to health. Despite the presence of AO families – the clearest evidence of the abuse of herbicides in their community – the farmers in Phu Cat are little inclined to protect themselves against health risks presented by the abuse or misuse of agrochemicals and *far less* predisposed to draw any hint from the exposure to wartime toxic chemicals.

Additional factors lie behind the lackadaisical reactions to the possible warnings represented by AO families and the casual use of agrochemicals. For one, evidence of the wartime chemicals' devastating effect is isolated and present only with very few families as they, although significant in number, are scattered in a large rural district. Consequently, and ironically, the farmers, and indeed almost everyone else, might hope that the evidence supports the *un*likelihood of the misfortune happening to them. Therefore, farmers who were spared the misfortune view victims' families as having been struck by bad luck, *so phan* (fate), another factor that helps them to be less concerned by the toxic chemicals. Conversely, this convenient narrative of *so phan* is monopolized not only by the farmers with healthy family members but also by AO families with multiple victims, who may think that they might be struck, next time, by good luck, and therefore do not think that there is a likelihood of having another disabled child *after* the first and/or the second. Evidence that could have led the farmers toward a more cautious use of agrochemicals is too few or too remote.

There is something more to this convenient way in which the farmers avoid the confrontation with health risks that the use of agrochemicals presented, so symbolically represented by AO. Farmers made *exceptional* use of the chemicals. One Plant Protection Centre official casually remarked, with a snigger, that the farmers used the agrochemicals to "kill themselves", and such incidents often took place around the Tet time, when family reunions (with those who had moved to the cities for jobs) failed to materialize (March 2009). The fact that some farmers resort to such an extreme measure must have been fairly well known in Phu Cat. Such incidents probably have a similar effect upon their perception of health risks induced by chemical such as AO: too extreme to raise ordinary farmers' awareness.

In the absence of *meaningful* evidence alerting the farmers to health risks that underlie what appears to be their overly casual attitude towards agrochemicals, the observations and remarks of some medical specialists on our team, such as "we need to educate them", point to a difficulty that both parties have to face.

Rumours of food poisoning motivate some farmers to set aside a small patch of land for producing food exclusively for the family's consumption. The usual evidence that may faintly arouse suspicion comprises "skin rashes, headache, dizziness", as Mr L. D. Cuong, among others, testified. These symptoms could well be those that "chemical poisonings can mimic" often at the earlier stages.[16] There is no means available, at least for the farmers, to see if these earlier signs are signals of something more serious than food poisoning.

Furthermore, the establishment of the cause-effect relationship between the chemicals and farmers' health in and of itself is part of an enormous and complex process within chemical-medical establishments. As examined in Chapter 3, it took a few decades, not even years, to determine the toxicity of dioxin and ban its production and use. That leaves a major question: what should the users of these toxic chemicals do when scientific evidence does not yet suggest deadly consequences beyond reasonable doubt?

Phu Cat's farmers are very much like everybody else on this matter. They are caught in a curious void created by the availability of chemicals and the "findings" that their use may damage their health. In the void, the farmers were left only with their own limited resources. In the end, the ultimate responsibility for the use of chemicals rests with the farmers, though they have little scientific knowledge. Mr N. V. Thom, who monitored closely how the sprayers mix the chemicals with water, and L. D. Cuong, who gives it "a few days" to see if "rash, headache, and dizziness" last long or become serious, are examples of Ulrich Beck's "individualization" of responsibility in a modernized world – of farmers leading a life within and despite their limited resources.

Farmers in Phu Cat: a summary

Our account of the life of a Phu Cat farmer does not entirely discredit economists' argument that efficient production, with an appropriate return, is a driving force in *changing* behaviour. We did see indications of this force at work in the life of the "sprayer" or the "land millionaire". Nonetheless, their behaviour does not nearly conform to that of the farmers transitioning towards Todaro's final stage. Their acquisition of land, in addition to the allocated farmland, was hardly an act of pursuing more profit. That the land remains state property may have kept any idea of profit-making from crossing their minds. Fortuities, such as having an ailing relative with a vast amount of land, had a great deal more to do with their acquisition of additional lands.

Farmers had even less say in selecting what to produce in the acquired land. If the State Farm concentrated on eucalyptus production, they went along with it. Likewise, when the Farm added cashew nuts to the production line, the farmers went along with that too. The only exception, in which the farmer took the initiative in changing or adding a new product, was the case of the "land millionaire", who recently added the production of pepper trees to his land. But his case is the exception that proves the rule.

There was no sign of the farmers' treating agrochemicals as "capital goods". Some almost unconsciously used herbicides and other agrochemicals just because others did, without really examining the contents. A few acquired a spraying machine, but they were more the exception. If there is anything common in their use of chemicals, it is their attempt to prevent a given level of production from falling. We rarely heard of chemicals' being used for the improvement of land quality.

Farmers' disinterest in profit, or surplus gains beyond their needs, was puzzling. Some farmers earned more than others. It did not occur to the latter that a better use of chemicals or machines might improve yield because the disparity in yield and earnings did not bother them, as in the case of Gian or N. X. Tien.

The reward for efficient farming and improved earnings in the manner of Theodore Shultz did not even seem to cross the farmers' minds. Relief from "work[ing] so hard and long", and freedom for their relatives and friends "[to] move to town to earn their living" were no part of the expectations the farmers had of themselves.[17] They were acutely aware that some of them undermined the very rewards they were seeking: secured earnings and a cohesive family.

"No, she [who had gone to Ho Chi Minh City] does not send us money regularly. She must be busy taking care of herself" (March and December 2012), a lowland farmer, the oldest son in the family, testified. Some had not heard from their loved ones who had moved to the distant cities "for such a long time" that they "don't know how they are doing there". Shultz may have agreed if he had had his field of research in a developing area that release from hard labour in agriculture only resulted in enlarging the "informal sector" in the cities where the *surplus* labour from rural communities barely survives as a day labourer.[18] A casual remark by a Plant Protection Centre official that suicides were common around the Tet (the lunar new year) belies the gravity of "losing" family members to big cities.

Inquiries into the farmers' reactions to the use of chemicals elicited only casual responses. Agrochemicals and their aftereffects did not figure prominently in their minds. Their use was mostly part of a routine, and the farmers rarely re-examined its impact. After several interviews in Phu Cat, which houses a large number of victims of the wartime use of herbicides, the farmers' wide-spread indifference to the disastrous health consequences ceased to surprise us.

Their indifference alerted us to their health, which usually escapes the careful consideration of even alert users of the chemicals. Phu Cat's farmers are not the only ones guilty of being disinterested in heeding the warning signals from AO victims and, in turn, neglecting their health. Their indifference has a lot to do with this particular area of anyone's concern. Health, like wealth, is a state of conditions that profoundly influences one's well-being. Health, unlike wealth, is a state of physical and mental conditions that particular behaviour and habits, in addition to innate biological characteristics, have cumulatively built over time through their complex interactions in a changing living environment. A given state of these conditions thus has an almost untraceable path, leading it to where it is.

In other words, it usually takes a health crisis for someone to realize what being healthy entails. Consequently, while some may react to every incident by protecting their health, fearing its loss, others may pay no attention to it until it is irretrievably damaged. Inevitably, everyone in Phu Cat was at a point somewhere between the two extreme reactions: overreacting and being indifferent.

Phu Cat's farmers represent a society whose well-being is at stake. We explore the farmers' behaviour from a health-care perspective. This is a necessary step before we can press further the argument that the farmers' behaviour is "reasonable", given their living environment, past and present.

Notes

1 http://binhdinh.vietccr.vn/xem-tong-quan/thong-tin-kinh-te-xa-hoi-binh-dinh-default.html
2 Michael Todaro, *Economic Development in the Third World*, New York, Longman, 1989, p. 313.
3 *Ibid.*, p. 313.
4 Michael Kirk, Nguyen Do Anh Tuan, "Land Tenure Policy Reforms – Decollectivization and the Doi Moi System in Vietnam", *IFPRI Discussion Paper*, 00927, International Food Policy Research Institute, 2009, www.ifpri.org/sites/default/files/publications/ifpridp 00927.pdf.
5 Tran Duc Vien, *Forestland Management Policies in Vietnam: An Overview*, no date, Center for Agricultural Research and Ecological Studies (CARES), Hanoi University of Agriculture, www.cares.org.vn/webplus/Article/Forestland%20management%20Policies%20in%20VietNam%20An%20Overview.pdf.
6 See "On a number of guidelines and policies to use vacant land, hills, forests, alluvial and coastal water", www.moj.gov.vn/vbpq/Lists/Vn% 20bn%20php%20lut/ View_Detail.aspx?ItemID=11124. See also Wil de Jong, Do Dinh Sam, and Tieu Van Hung, *Forest Rehabilitation in Vietnam: Histories, Realities and Future*, Jakarta, Center for International Forestry Research, 2006 and Nguyen Tan Phat and Nguyen Tien Dung, "Vietnam's Land Policy in the Transition Period", *Tokyo Jouhou Daigaku Kennkyuu Ronsou*, Vol. 15, No. 1, 2011, pp. 9–25.
7 See Thi Que, *op. cit.*, 2005, p. 184.
8 www.na.gov.vn/sach_qh/chinhsachpl/phan2/p2_b_iv_48.html
9 Interview with Nguyen Thanh Tung, local manager of WB3 programme in Cat Trinh Commune (November 2010).
10 The government provides instructions on how to rank the land depending on its location and quality using a ten-point ladder scale. However, it is also up to local authorities as well as local customs to have their own standard for ranking and calling. For the research, we mainly rely on the local sources (the interviewees, including farmers, medical workers, and local officers) through interviews and casual discussions.
11 Berger and Luckmann, *op. cit.*, p. 37.
12 Vietnam Cashew Association, www.vinacas.com.vn/content/ detail/id/38
13 PAN-UK, Current Pesticide Spectrum, Global Use and Major concerns, 2003, www.pan-uk.org/briefing/SIDA_Fil/CHap1.htm
14 See, for example, David Pimentel, "Environmental and Economic Costs of the Application of Pesticides Primarily in the United States", *Environment, Development and Sustainability*, Vol. 7, 2005, pp. 229–52.
15 The Central Highland Provinces remain malaria hot spots, accounting for 50% of malaria cases and 80% of malaria deaths in the entire country. www.monre.gov.vn/v35/default.aspx?tabid=675&CateID= 54&ID= 116473&Code=ZFL4116473
16 Sasumita Dasgupta et al., "Pesticide Poisoning of Farm Workers: Implications of Blood Test Results from Vietnam", *Policy Research Working Paper*, no. 3624, 2005, p. 6.
17 Schultz, *op. cit.*, p. 1.
18 The issue of the informal sector, and how to identify and measure its presence, has been one of the critical development issues since the late 1960s. See, for example, S. V. Sethurman, "The Urban Informal Sector: Concept, Measurement and Policy", *International Labour Review*, Vol. 114, No. 1, July–August 1976, pp. 69–81.

Part II

Farmers' choices and behaviour

5 Health and elusive risks

Most of the farmers in Phu Cat do not behave as residents of a rural community that practises commercialized agriculture. Deviation from expectation was even more apparent in their use of agrochemicals in a community with unmistakable evidence of the wartime use of toxic chemicals, displayed by a large number of Agent Orange (AO) victims, even in second and third post-war generations. The farmers are not, however, entirely indifferent to these opportunities to exploit for their gains or for caution against hazard.

One reason for the deviation is the distance that separates the experts in the agricultural, medical, and agrochemical professions on one side from the farmers on the other. The former may not be solely responsible for this divide, which shows no signs of disappearance: they are fully engaged in honing their expertise. In the meantime, the latter is absorbed in rural life, which encompasses more than agricultural production in that it is their "way of life", to repeat Todaro's and others' observations. The farmers are engaged in multidimensional activities stretching from the observation of communal obligations to the protection of their families' well-being. Agricultural production is only part and parcel of their lives.

The division, in other words, is characterized by the different responsibilities of the professionals and the farmers. Those of the former end when they prepare the necessary recommendations, fortified by scientific findings at any given time. Those of the latter begin where the former's end and start with interpreting and examining the utility of the recommendations through an exercise in evaluating this utility in the specific contexts of their lives. These contexts are much broader than those in which the professionals prepare their recommendations. The exercise is an integral part of the latter's responsibility as it leads to their decision to go along with, customize, or ignore the recommendations *and* live with the consequences of that decision. It is a disproportionately heavy responsibility for those who may be the least informed of scientific findings.

In this division of responsibilities, the farmers have no choice but to go through a wide range of interpretations of the professionals' recommendations, which, in turn, makes them seem to behave independently, or irresponsibly, in the eyes of the professionals.

In the area of health, the division of responsibilities leaves the farmers with an even wider margin for interpreting the professionals' recommendations and, thus, prone to "independent" behaviours. As mentioned in the previous chapter, health is a set of mental and physical conditions. It is only when one feels sick or less than ordinary that he or she becomes aware of something interfering with that set of conditions. He or she appreciates health only in its absence. Besides, farmers are not consumed by the concern of their own health; concern only arises in full force when it begins to interfere with the other demands and needs of their well-being. It is an entirely foreign exercise for them to examine if and when they feel, or are, healthy, especially when they think they are healthy.

While medical professionals may readily offer a long list of warning signs, the farmers usually lack a coherent framework with which to interpret their health conditions. They are not cognizant of the need for staying alert to any changes in that set of mental and physical conditions alone. The only exception to this underlying attitude towards health may be a sporadic concern that something might happen to their health in the indefinite future: a concern of a "future loss" in a given set of mental and physical conditions.

Health and risks

A casual exchange with the farmers illustrates how easily the demands of health elude their attention. "Of course, I care about my health" was the usual response to our query. This carried no more weight than daily greetings. We pressed further on whether they had prepared for any health contingencies. The farmers pointed to a Clinic staff accompanying our research and said, "these people" (May 2005).

Elusive health

Among health professionals, debates on understanding health never cease. A general understanding of health as "the key resource for everyday life"[1] to facilitate human activities is widely shared and beyond debate. The World Health Organization (WHO), as early as 1948, had an added dimension to this understanding: health is a state of complete physical, mental, and social well-being and not merely the absence of disease or infirmity.[2] The definition is clear enough. Health is "the absence of diseases or abnormalities".[3] Conversely, health thus defined can, after all, be perceived and appreciated in its absence. Besides, a degree of ambiguity follows expressions such as "complete", leaving health to a wide-open debate.[4]

There have been efforts to turn this understanding into a more operational concept. Among the efforts to capture health in an operational concept, Johannes Bircher, Bern University health specialist, proposes:

> Health is a dynamic state of well-being characterized by a physical, mental, and social potential, which satisfies the demands of a life commensurate with age, culture, and personal responsibility.[5]

Health, in this conceptualization, is the making of the balance between the "biologically given potential" and "personally acquired potential"[6] on the one hand, and the demands of life on the other. When the latter surpasses the former, Bircher calls it "disease", whereas when the first two surpass the third, it becomes "health".[7] The "potentials" and the "demands" can vary with age, social status, and familial environment, among others, which makes this particular definition a little more useable.

However, all these definitions have left a principal question unanswered: who determines if "health" is present or absent, i.e., when the demands are lower or higher than the potentials? Is it up to how the individual feels or up to what the doctors or specialists with particular expertise determine? Until now, the common assumption has been that the determining role for health belongs exclusively to medical professionals. This practice does not help define health in more explicit terms. Instead, stricter definitions of health by medical professionals make health an almost impossible condition for anyone to achieve and sustain.

One medical commentator sees this irony in the following way. The microscopic search for negative factors such as illnesses, diseases, and abnormalities has been the means for medical doctors to discuss health. Consequently, "finding more abnormalities" and "narrowing the definition of normal" has become a "great strategy for [their] industry [medical–pharmaceutical complex]". For example, even "failing to do the laundry or to stock the kitchen with food because of procrastination and dawdling" can be the "routine traits of a mental disorder". The monopoly of the means by medical experts to decide what abnormalities are creates a world in which "we all harbour abnormalities". This monopoly is untouchable as it has been accompanied by an increase in "diagnostic technologies that are able to find smaller and smaller abnormalities".[8]

That leaves us with another, discomforting question: is there a threshold that separates "healthy" from "not healthy"? Our contact with AO victims through the weekend classes – *Lop hoc Uoc Mo*, Dream Class – offers plenty of opportunities to observe "disabled" children. They are concluded to be so by the medical establishment and hence by their parents. Some of these children are perfectly capable of behaving with almost no trace of medically defined defects. The difference between these and other healthy children seems to be one of degree.

If Phu Cat's farmers, or anyone for that matter, live in a world where medical professionals rule and where they could spot health problems in everything they see, everyone would have to be only either sicker or less sick. Without a means of measurement, everyone is either obsessed with or otherwise indifferent to any health-related phenomenon. It is too complex to grasp in his or her own terms how he or she is. Regular farmers are not medical specialists. Health is a given, which they take as something to start with and not something to question. Therefore, to them, the pursuit of that which is a given would have to be an extra, and odd, endeavour. Another specialist comments on this irony. For a healthy individual or those who may think they are healthy, the pursuit of health is, thus, a "symptom of unhealth"[sic]. The same specialist goes on to say:

> Health, like love, beauty or happiness, is a metaphysical concept, which eludes all attempts at objectivisation[sic]. Healthy people do not think of health, unless they are hypochondriacs, which, strictly speaking, is not a sign of health. Similarly, when our organs perform their functions perfectly, we are not aware of them. It is the absence of health that gives rise to dreaming about health, just as the real meaning of freedom is only experienced in prison.[9]

In practice, therefore, a risk to health is usually non-existent, since when one sees it, *it* has already damaged health. Thus, health that can be captured through its absence is a conceptual nightmare, especially for healthy individuals or those who rarely question whether or not they are healthy like Phu Cat's farmers.

The only practical argument that one can make for protecting health is to learn either from the past or from somebody else – to search for empirical evidence of the failure to acknowledge the deteriorating health, i.e., the presence of risks to health. That argument is still open to a circular argument – how convincing could the empirical evidence be for those who have never doubted their health? Therefore, the elusive health makes health risks, too, elusive.

This problem of health may be highlighted in another way: by contrasting it with wealth. Adam Smith sees wealth as the "annual produce of the land and labour of the society to satisfy human needs and wants of utility",[10] which is similar to health's being defined as the "key resource for everyday life". Gains in wealth can be measured in terms of increments such as cash income and fixed assets. There may not be a limit to the increment as in "[n]o matter how rich one can get, there is always someone richer".

By contrast, gains in health mean no change for healthy individuals. If anything, no change is proof of the increment. That may be all the more reason why some medical professionals make it their calling to find something, anything, wrong with ordinary people, as the commentator above points out.

Therefore, the difficulty of capturing health, as opposed to wealth, is graphically presented in Figure 5.1.

Elusive risks

Health is elusive, and what threatens it – risk – is also elusive. Human poisonings and serious illnesses can be the highest price that the use of agrochemicals such as pesticides or herbicides may exact from the users and from the consumers of the goods benefiting from the use. But the chemicals alone are not the

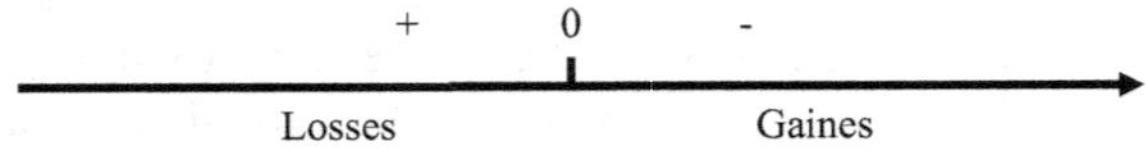

Figure 5.1 Gains and Losses in Health and Wealth.

risk. Somebody must use them carelessly before they threaten health. The usual users, on the other hand, have no ground to grasp what risks the chemicals involve. The only push for cautious use comes from the instructions on the labels of the containers, which in some cases are ineligible, as shown in the previous chapter.

There are a few more factors that push health risks to elude the attention of even alert farmers. The use of chemicals usually takes a long roundabout route before it actually begins to show damages to health, variously called “collateral damage”, “unintended consequences”, or “side effects”.[11] The time that elapses between the use and the actual negative results may take a few hours, days, weeks, or even months: the longer the lapse, the less obvious the causes of the negative results. The sense of health risks, accompanying the use of particular chemicals, has no traction on the minds of the users or even the consumers of the products for which the chemicals are used.

Worse still, the negative consequences may not be so obvious nor alarming to the users or the consumers of the contaminated products. Farmers use the agrochemicals to kill pests and weeds, *and* to protect or increase production. In turn, the practice may leave a negative impact on human health and the environment. However, a chain of effects follows, setting off the “risk trade-offs”: Successful efforts to combat a “target risk” (removal of pests and weeds) result in an increase in “countervailing risks” (side effects on human health and the environment)”.[12] Some users may make light of the latter while emphasizing the benefit only of the former.

In reality, such a self-serving act is unnecessary when the beneficiaries of the use of chemicals and the victims (damaged health) are not the same. All farmers need to do is to procure food away from the usual distribution system. As seen before, some farmers inadvertently admitted that there might be other farmers suspected of abusing, or of careless use of, the chemicals when they casually remarked: “We grow the vegetables we eat in our yard”. That is an uncanny way of protecting themselves against the “unintended consequences” of others’ chemicals as well as a way of diverting their attention away from potential health risks outside their yard.

Health risks from toxic chemicals evade the farmers’ attention in the following manner. At present, farmers may have experienced some effects, such as rashes or headaches, but after “three to four days”, they may still be doing “okay”. The farmers recognize these symptoms, but they are not sufficiently prepared for speculating on whether the symptoms are threatening enough to warrant preventive or corrective behaviours. They even tolerate these side effects and disregard them as long as they gain in wealth (more yield, or at least prevented losses), attributing this gain to the use of pesticides.

The law of diminishing returns in the use of agrochemicals does not cross the farmers’ minds since the use of chemicals is not meant to maximize their gains. Phu Cat’s farmers use chemicals more as a routine. Regardless of the incremental changes in wealth (increase in yield or even the absence of a decline in yield), the farmers keep using the chemicals. Health risks remain elusive.

The symptoms suggesting damaged health may become alarming after a while. Still, the farmers, either as the producers or as the consumers, do not see anything beyond their eyes can catch. If they are the producers, they may be away from the site of the actual health damages that their products may cause, and if they are the consumers, they are facing the intractable path of chemical contamination only eventually leading to damaged health. The evidence of "risks" lies in the eventual damages. The eventual damages are, ironically, the proof that there are risks.

Consequently, before the damages materialize, the farmers settle with the relief that the front cover of Deborah Lupton's *Risk*[13] best represents: "IT'll NEVER HAPPEN TO ME". Phu Cat's farmers find ample evidence reinforcing this relief in the presence of AO victims.

Risks in division of labour

To uncover where health risks are hidden, we need to broaden our perspective and reconstruct the lives of Phu Cat's farmers from that perspective.

Time and physical distance separating the cause and effects of the use of agrochemicals are integral to a larger whole of production, distribution, and consumption, of which the farmers and others are part. It is a whole where the individuals are expected to act according to the "roles" that only collectively contribute to its continuation. That is a whole, also, where and what one does is often detached from its consequences and from what the others do. Elusive health risks, or more precisely the difficulty in recognizing health risks, are rooted in this whole where parts are detached from each other. In this massive whole, and given the nature of health, only the damaged health conditions or "losses" in a set of mental and physical conditions prompt us to speculate on the presence of *preceding* health risks somewhere.

Even in Phu Cat, which is still far from becoming fully engaged in commercializing agriculture, the presence of that whole is relatively easy to recognize. Farmers produce and consume, the Plant Protection Centre offers good seedlings, chemicals, and other agricultural inputs, and the middlemen distribute the products to markets near and far. Each has a specific role to perform: production, procurement of agricultural inputs, distribution of the produce, and consumption. For a brief period, even within the process of production, the individual farmers of Phu Cat performed distinct roles, which collectively contributed to the performance of the whole, that is, the production brigade of the collective farming era.

One may also see the ubiquitous Commune Clinic staff as integral to this whole. Their role may be at best auxiliary: they offer a cursory diagnosis on the signs of minor ailments, which the farmers bring to their attention. Given the relatively low-level medical expertise, the staff's role in most cases appears to signal that nothing is *serious* in that whole or else to offer a conclusion that the whole needs extra-role players or medical professionals with *more* highly specialized training.

Lost risks

Ulrich Beck and others offer the contours of the ground in which the "whole" described above has emerged and persisted.[14] It is the whole in which the division of responsibilities, described above, also has its roots.

The world's population grows, but the resources offered by the earth can increase only so much, threatening a demand-supply equilibrium. The scarcity of resources has multiplied the pressure for technological innovations for more production *and* more efficient distribution of them. Individuals based on their skills, or the abilities to perform specific roles, are integrated into the whole process of making the scarce resources last longer or of enriching them to meet the demands of the growing population. Division of labour is a human answer to what little nature can provide. It is also a process that has antiquated the term "subsistence activities" – activities to produce enough for self-consumption where the producers and the consumers are one and the same, and the place of production and consumption are one and the same.

Differentiation of the producers and consumers inevitably necessitates another role that somebody needs to perform – the role of linking the production and consumption, the producers and consumers, i.e., the intermediary or mediators. Mediators of all kinds would have to be capable of striking a balance between what is consumed and what is produced, *and* of taking into consideration all the costs of striking that balance. Ironically, the need to cover the costs justifies the mediator's efforts to lure producers into producing more and consumers into consuming more. Supply no longer means meeting demand; it often dictates demand leading to overproduction and overconsumption. The classic supply-demand equilibrium disappears, and so does the awareness of who is doing what for whom. A division of labour complicates the cause-effect chains, thereby giving birth to the basic backdrop of "side effects", "risk trade-offs", and "unintended consequences".

We produce and use cars, among others, to make the distribution of goods more efficient; cars emit carbon dioxide; carbon dioxide contaminates the air. Those who are in the car assembly line are rarely aware that their productive activities contribute in no small part to cancers attributable to environmental factors. We began producing pesticides and herbicides long before the Second World War and since have kept, outside their production lines, "millions of people ignorant of the danger to their health".[15]

The differentiation between the producers and the consumers (users of the products) blinds us to another division: that of responsibilities. Producers of toxic substances may not feel secure about the fact that "there is no evidence of a threshold – a dose below which the chemical is harmless".[16] They would feel slightly relieved by the possibility that "the statistics of small effects make it unlikely that we would ever find [the threshold], even if it existed".[17] But their sense of relief becomes stronger when they realize that the responsibility of sufficient warning against the potential danger could be easily replaced by another responsibility, that of proper use (consumption) of the product which belongs to the users. The producer's responsibility does not cover the use of the product. As shown in Chapter 3, the chemicals were often used in a more concentrated combination than recommended. Or else, a U.S. military doctor's confession unwittingly poured out a sense of relief, though it was laced with a degree of regret, that he and others "would have expected [their] own government" to do something about the use if the U.S. soldiers were to be exposed to AO.

In short, risks to health lie somewhere in a seemingly seamless flow of producing, distributing, and consuming a problematic substance. The question, then, remains if there are ways as to how we capture them in a manner that induces everyone involved to change his or her behaviour.

Risks as presented

Smoking leading to lung cancers may be an exceptional example of health risks' being explicitly presented, leaving the entire responsibility of absorbing the devastating impact of nicotine addiction to smokers. However, millions of smokers signify one more kind of distance between the cause and the effect: not all smokers contract the deadly disease. The restrained language of the health risk warning, the use of "may" or "likely", for example, on the label on a cigarette packet, does not represent the cigarette maker's false modesty. It represents the fact that scientific evidence can support only the *likelihood* of contracting the disease, and that the scientific evidence cannot put an end to the indeterminacy of that likelihood.[18]

In other words, risk signals possibility, and the question of when a risk becomes a reality – actual "losses" in health – is a matter of probability. The role of scientists and experts has been to identify and examine conditions under which the chances of a risk turning into reality can be estimated. Any other risks beyond "probability estimates" are called "uncertainty".[19] Modernization is an effort to diminish this uncertainty by enriching probability estimates. Thus, there is an almost zero-sum relationship between risk and uncertainty, or as Anthony Giddens sees it, the world of uncertainty has been like a "territory to be conquered or colonized" by extending probability estimates.[20] All risks are usually thus presented as *Risk = Danger × Probability.*

However, this is where risks, as presented to influence people to act in a certain way, pose real difficulty in practice. For one thing, the habitual responses are almost exclusively to the first half of the equation to the neglect of the second. A statement such as "the chances of a destructive earthquake hitting Tokyo are xx% within x years" usually elicits no responsive action. While "a destructive earthquake" may grab the attention of ordinary citizens, millions continue to reside in the city. Tens of thousands of people continue to reside in areas adjacent to active volcanoes such as Mount Merapi, one of our research sites in Indonesia, in a very similar way to the millions who continue to smoke.

It is difficult to decide whether they ignore the danger presented as a possibility *despite* the warning or *because* of the warning. In the latter case, people do count on the part of the probability – i.e., the remaining possibility of risks not turning into a reality. Or, at least, the probability leaves a margin for indifference in the minds of ordinary people, leaving them to conduct life as if a final push turning a risk into a reality is something over which they have little control. In other words, the final and perhaps the most critical piece in the puzzle, when and to whom the risk turns into a reality, is lost in an infinite range of probability.

Another reason for the equation – Risk = Danger × Probability – to have only limited traction on people's mind is an unconscious assumption of the experts' warning that theirs alone matters or matters the most. No message is in their warning that the use of resources to prepare for the damages may cut into the resources which others in other professions may consider indispensable to address their "risks", showing a high probability of them turning into reality. Caught in the crossfires of risk warnings, ordinary people have very little to rely on for their selection of which warnings they should be alert to, and hence let them sit on the back burner, so to speak, of their consciousness. The experts, in the meantime, engage themselves in refining their techniques and technologies in order to reduce the margin of errors in probability calculations in the "trenches", to borrow from Ulrich Beck,[21] of their narrowly defined concerns to the neglect of others.

Among the experts within their "trenches" of expertise, specifics of when and to whom a risk might turn into a reality belong to the realm of uncertainty, and thus efforts to diminish it continue. They do extend their efforts to cover even the contextual specifics of when (time of day, climate conditions, geological features, and others) and to whom (physical make-up, age, sex, income, education, and others). Nevertheless, these efforts are part of strengthening the probability estimates. Thus, when and if a risk turns into a reality, the experts may not blame particular individuals for having failed to heed their warnings. Instead, they merely add more "cases" that justify their efforts to refine the probability estimates, thereby diminishing uncertainty that much more. While each expert may increase the confidence in estimating the period between risk detection and occurrence, ordinary people face the crossfire of various scientifically supported warnings in the interim.

Ordinary people face the impossible task of confronting many risk equations simultaneously while each expert may treat them as his loyal followers. They are left with only their own counsel, while there is no expert on risk who may offer appropriate counsel on which risk equation may be more urgent or essential, and on how to strike a balance among many equations.[22] They face an overwhelming flood of warnings, in which risks are presented as no more or less than possibilities. The decisions that they make carry all the weight of choosing the right *course(s)* of action. Moreover, in all likelihood, there may be contradictions among at least some of the suggested courses of action. Consequently, some, if not all, of the risks may turn into realities, but that is not part of the experts' responsibilities, nor a consequence of miscalculated probability by scientists or experts.

There is an irony to this division of responsibilities where the experts refine the probability estimates, and the ordinary people make final decisions – supposing that people heed the warnings and may take preventive actions within the resources at their disposal. The likes of consuming fewer alcoholic beverages, exercising, and not smoking may top the list of preventive measures for health.

Storing emergency food and medicine, reinforcing the structure of a house or a building, securing an evacuation route among others may not be so taxing to people's daily life as preventive measures against a natural disaster such as earthquakes. These preventive actions are the insurance, a means by which to moderate, but not to prevent, the projected damages to health or their assets. The insurance may be more or less costly, depending upon the resources at people's disposal. However, regardless of the cost, the insurance does not *stop* a risk turning into a reality, which remains a matter of probability. When and to whom a risk turns into a reality would have to be the making of something over which ordinary people as the final decision-makers have very little control. They may call it "fate" in the absence of a scientific term for it. Here, the scientists and experts, who refuse to offer definitive conclusions as to when and to whom a risk turns into reality, are allowing this highly unscientific notion of fate to play the decisive role in much the same way as the ordinary people.[23]

Risks in life: Phu Cat's farmers

These observations on "health" as an almost ethereal framework for action may help capture the twin puzzles about the Phu Cat farmers in a different light. Why don't AO families change their behaviour, despite the most unequivocal evidence of health damages being presented amongst their own? Why does the presence of the AO families not have any significant impact on the rest of the farmers in the District? On the other side of the same twin puzzles, there is another set: (1) what is more potent in dictating the farmers' moves than reinforced caution against the agrochemicals, a means of higher productivity, and (2) what risks do the farmers (AO families included) see *in* obviously more cautious reactions to toxic chemicals?

We have already touched upon one self-defence "mechanism" against the fear of health risks. These risks are, in the eyes of residents, an integral part of the war that ended in 1975. The majority of Phu Cat's farmers lived through wartime confusions and difficulties partly because of their location: south of the Di-Militarized Zone, not far from the branches of the Ho Chi Minh Trail, the main artery for transporting war material, food, and soldiers from the north. The war was fought in a manner, i.e., dictated by the search-and-destroy strategy, that effectively erased the mark separating the front and the rear. AO and all that it has brought about are part of this past, which is unlikely to repeat itself; they are the "legacies" of the war.

Within this overall framework in which AO is conveniently swept into oblivion, however, other factors deprive the farmers of the "lessons", retrievable from AO complications.

Agent Orange impacts as isolated incidents

Whenever we interviewed AO victims' families, we were rarely alone. There were always either a "platoon" of neighbourhood kids or adults standing by out of curiosity; the adults occasionally joined in our discussions, sometimes actively. Their presence sometimes helped us to make conversations with the families lighter by not focussing exclusively on the AO victims. But more importantly, it helped us recognize how their neighbours interacted with the victim's families: with understandable sympathy and sense of safety that they were spared of the misfortune, or, as we read from their fragmented comments, that the AO families were too exceptionally unfortunate.

These neighbours know about the families, not just about their children, but also other aspects involving their production activities, the healthy kids' whereabouts, and their social relationships in the neighbourhood. To the neighbours, the AO families are merely unfortunate. They are willing to help them when needed, such as by fixing their houses or babysitting their disabled children. There was an odd kind of reciprocity between the AO families and the rest of the farmers that helped make the evidence of the consequences of AO less capable of generating lessons to be extracted.

Physical distance from AO families only reinforces the effect of this reciprocity. After all, Phu Cat has a land area of nearly 700 km^2 with a population of 210,000. Moreover, small villages would look like isolated dots in a map, and the rest are Nui Ba Mountains and mostly rice paddies. The population density of 290 per 1 km^2 is nowhere close to hinting at how sparsely Phu Cat is populated.

The "distance" exists not only between the AO families and the rest but also among AO families. As mentioned earlier, none of the parents of AO victims recognized that others had experienced the same misfortune, at least at the beginning of our research. Only after our prodding as to their knowledge of other AO families did they remember *hearing* something about some other families. This lack of communication among the AO families is indicative of the strength of their will to keep their affairs all to themselves. The effect of this reciprocity has an additional impact: a reinforced belief that an AO-induced ailment is an isolated incident.

Apart from the presence of AO victims, the farmers are always willing to speak about *their* encounters with what they now believe is AO or something similar to it. Some claim to have had direct encounters before and after 1975. However, each story never develops beyond their *personal* story.

N. S. Thuc is among the very few who were very straightforward. "I must have been exposed to Agent Orange in the Nui Ba Mountains" while he was active in the militia in 1966. Later he even saw three barrels of white substance in the Mountains and saw some villagers bring them back to kill rats. He blamed the health condition of his sixth son (with a stiffened body, difficult to turn over) on AO. He did not call it "fate", as often heard from other AO families. He believed that having one of his children affected by AO was his personal matter. "I have to do something about it", he uttered in one of our interviews. What he meant was that he had to do something about his family having a severely disabled child, not about the child's disability. Neither did he think much of the other AO families. He did not know any of them. Agent Orange, Nui Ba Mountains, and a disabled child are all *personal* matters to him (July 2005).

Another villager, Dao V. T. of Cat Thanh Commune, located in the northern foothills of the Nui Ba Mountains, related a story about cow herders from the commune. The incident had happened in the mid-90s. The herders had led their cows to the Mountains and let them graze there. Soon after they returned to the commune, nearly all the cows had died, one after another. The villagers had been stunned and terrified since the cows were important assets for the farmers. Since then, the villagers have stopped using any part of the northern slope of the Mountains for feeding their cows. They now attribute the mysterious deaths to AO or similar chemicals (July 2005). This story has a metaphorical quality to it: the deaths of their cows, much like dead fish floating in H. H. Gian's personal story in Chapter 4, are evidence of how seriously the "No Trespass" sign was meant to be taken.

These and other stories about encounters with AO never extended beyond *personal* memories and, instead, have the effect of indicating to the villagers that they are *isolated* incidents.

Agent Orange as an irrelevant lesson

Then there are the families of children with AO-induced ailments. As seen before, many of the parents of AO victims went ahead and had a child or more after being confronted by clear evidence – one or even two children with severe congenital disabilities. The parents face more opportunities to re-examine the warning represented by a disabled child and reconsider having another. The additional opportunities include seasonal use of fertilizers, herbicides, and other chemicals for their rice paddies, cashew nuts, or peanut farms. However, they have exhibited no precaution.

A closer look at their reproductive behaviour is in order.

Of the 98 AO families we examined in Phu Cat, Thank Khe, and Kim Bang, the number of disabled children per family was 1.27, which is much higher than the estimated 0.22% national average as of 1979.[24] The figures for each district are 1.16 for Phu Cat, 1.26 for Thanh Khe, and 1.8 for Kim Bang.

The extremely high rate of incidence of birth abnormalities alone is alarming, especially to the medical experts. The risk of having a child with congenital disabilities should have alarmed also any couple contemplating having a child. But many did not hear the alarm.

The parents of AO victims are no exception, as shown before. Many of them had one child or more, even after a child adversely affected by AO contamination was born. Beyond the physical distance separating the AO families, the fact that they keep AO-induced health issues to themselves also accounts for the lack of responsiveness to the alarmingly high probability. They rarely have the opportunity to compare what happened to them with what may be happening to other AO families, i.e., those in the same "risk" group. The experience of having a child with birth abnormalities is either irrelevant or not potent enough for them to reconsider having another.

How much time did these parents allow themselves to think of the risk of giving birth? How much time did they give the precedent (within their personal world) to sink in? Table 5.1 presents average figures for the intervals between births.

Table 5.1 Birth Spacing after the First Child, Year (healthy and disabled)

	Birth Spacing after the First Healthy *Child*	*Birth Spacing after the First* Disabled *Child*
Phu Cat	*3.64*	*3.75*
Thanh Khe	3.20	5.28
Kim Bang	2.60	2.25
Total	3.88	3.92

Note: The target group is 74 families, 18 less than the original 92 AO families. Eighteen were removed from the list for various reasons, such as the parents' ambiguous memory.

The first child means a great deal to the parents because it is the very first experience for them. The child embodies great expectations, hope, and excitement as well as anxiety. Would that excitement dissipate after the second or the third? Or, more to the point, would having a disabled child entirely alter their view towards reproductive activities? Almost none of the parents of this category gave up on having more child(ren) after the first disabled child, with 2.18 more children on average to follow. Not only that: the first disabled child seemed to rush these parents to have more children, especially in the cases in Kim Bang, in the north. Birth spacing after the first disabled child (2.25 years) is noticeably shorter than birth spacing after a first physically fit child (2.6). This tendency may be partly attributable to their being relatively older parents – the former North Vietnamese regular army soldiers fitting Madame Nguyễn Thị Bình's portrait of the survivors of the War of Unification, cited earlier.

Among the three areas, Thanh Khe families responded distinctly to the birth of a first handicapped child. These families were more cautious when having their next child, as shown by the longer interval of 5.28 years, compared to 3.1 years after a non-handicapped first child. This may attest to the fact that Da Nang is an urban dynamic emergent economy. The more developed the market, the more available and the better the services, including health services, though this also means that access to these services is costlier. In Thanh Khe, people have choices beyond the 11 Commune Clinics; they are also able to access private health services or larger health facilities. Most of the 15 families we interviewed reported that they took their children for regular check-ups or therapy sessions. The reliance on cash income, for that reason, becomes more critical. Even without a disabled child, the parents cannot afford to have many children. This financial concern is particularly true for younger couples (in their 40s). The parents, given the presence of one or two disabled children, cannot simply go ahead and continue pursuing a healthy child. They need to decide based on full consideration of all their choices after overcoming their initial reaction to intuitive feelings – the desire to have a healthy child. If they take a risk, it is a calculated risk after taking into consideration costs from all aspects, including medical costs, daycare costs, and education costs.

Among the five young couples in Thanh Khe, two had two disabled children. After their first disabled child was born, these couples had given it one more try, but they'd stopped after this since they had also failed at the second attempt.

Only one family whose first two children were disabled had decided to have one more.

In Phu Cat, there is only a marginal time lag between births after having the first healthy child (3.64) and after having the first disabled child (3.75). This is the group representing the responses to one unanswerable question: "why us?" But the questioning itself did not deter them from trying to have more children. Our conjecture may not be ungrounded: the idea may have crossed the parents' minds that if the decisive factor of turning risks into realities (children with birth defects) is fate, it could well be also fate that the risks remain just risks.

Taking these findings and adding them to another on the limited deterrence effects of AO-induced disabled children on reproduction (in Chapter 3), one point becomes clearer: the incidents of birth abnormalities are seen by their parents as an irrelevant lesson from which little is to be learned (with a few possible exceptions among AO families in Thanh Khe). No matter how recent the birth of a disabled child may be, it is still in the past and irrelevant to the present.

Agent Orange as irrelevant evidence

A rare event is, by definition, an infrequent and unpredictable occurrence. How could such an event be a signal for anyone to change his or her behaviour? Health, as discussed earlier, is a difficult value whose gains often mean no change, especially as far as people who consider themselves to be healthy are concerned. How could AO and all that surrounds it signal a risk that needs to be heeded?

Furthermore, the usual probability estimates are arrived at by removing cases too far outside of a probable standard deviation. Inclusion of the rare cases seriously distorts the probability estimates. Not only ordinary people but also scientists and experts within their "trenches" reconstruct a world in which a risk is likely to turn into a reality by eliminating the cases deviating from reasonable standards and expectations. Rare events, like "outliers" in statistical observations, are considered irrelevant.

Epistemologist Nassim Nicholas Taleb developed an argument in his *Black Swan – The Impact of the Highly Improbable* (2007) that our cognitive capacity often fails to consider "outliers". Rare events, in his argument, usually lie outside "the realm of regular expectations, because nothing in the past can convincingly point to its probability". Rare events do have an extreme, or shocking, impact. However, whether or not they actually interfere with life is not important to most of us as they remain outliers. Finally, even though rare events may lie outside our conventional expectations, they nonetheless trigger our predisposition to look for explanations for their occurrences, to make them "explainable" after they occur. To illustrate a "rare event", Taleb uses the analogy of "sighting a black swan in Australia", which has changed the unassailable belief that swans are all white to highlight the "extreme impact" of the event. Despite this "impact", according to Taleb, people tend to turn a blind eye to the event due to "the highly improbable" nature or uncertainty of it. To Taleb, "[a black swan] illustrates a severe limitation to our learning from observations or experience and the fragility of our knowledge".[25]

Given our cognitive tendency, as summed up by Taleb, the consequences of AO exposure trigger different reactions among people. Medical and other scientific experts are not entirely immune to the cognitive trap of the "black swan", but they have become accustomed to the unusually high rate of birth abnormality incidences. So, to them, a flock of "white swans" in Phu Cat still includes the thousands of disabled children. These children are not the "black" swans but the "white" ones as they represent the "expected" results of the reproductive behaviours of the parents in the risk-laden living environment. Healthy children among the AO families are the "black" swans. Accordingly, their expectation for the others living in the same living environment is that of restraint from reproductive activities.

Their scientific minds do not stop operating just because they have established a high correlation between the high rate of birth abnormalities and the parents' living environment, i.e., Phu Cat in the middle of the risk area, as the contaminant – dioxin – remains active not only in the Mountains, the soil, and water sources but also in human bodies. In their minds, the "contingencies"[26] that may interfere with their risk probability are the reproductive behaviour of the farmers, which is, to the medical professionals, unexplainable.

On the other hand, to the majority of Phu Cat's farmers, the incidences of congenital defects are isolated and thus "rare" events: 1.16 disabled children per family, spread thin over a 700 km^2 area, seems like virtually no instances. Families struck by AO-induced health complications do not seem to signal anything. They, or more likely one or two AO families within the immediate living environment, are cases of exceptional misfortunes. AO victims and their families are "black" swans for the majority of Phu Cat's farmers.

Neighbours who gathered around during our visits to the AO families often expressed their sympathy for the unfortunate families as well as their admiration for the families – "Oh, this family…they are doing fine, though". This and similar statements sent us the neighbours' sub-textual message, which we could put together from the fragmented statements thrown into the interviews: that the neighbours felt they were out of harm's way.

For the AO families, the disabled child(ren) is (are), first and foremost, a black swan. Once the families are convinced that the birth of a disabled child is "improbable", they see their child not as a case from which to learn something. In turn, however, families with disabled children *are* black swans for the rest of the farmers. The families are *sui generis.*

The victims' families usually learned about the relationship between AO exposure and the current conditions of their children. The medical experts gave the parents an explanation for the misfortune. We often raised a rhetorical question: "Do you know why your children were born with birth defects?" This received various but firm answers: "the doctor said it was because of Agent Orange", which was followed by "my husband used to be a soldier in (the sprayed areas like branches stemming out from the Ho Chi Minh Trail)", or "my husband used to go to the Nui Ba Mountains to raise cows".

Having a handicapped child or two is hard enough for these AO families. Therefore, these efforts to explain away the births of disabled children still leave them with an understandable puzzle, demanding an answer. "Why us and why not others" who have been leading nearly an identical life in a nearly identical living environment? The desire to seek an explanation is clearly evident, albeit intermittently. The desire for an answer betrays their view of the disabled child(ren) as the "black" swan(s).

Here the AO families' responses reveal an intriguing narrative about themselves, which underlies the oft-uttered statement: "we have to live with it [the fact of having a disabled child]". On the one hand, the statement speaks for the families' resignation to the birth of a disabled child(ren) as something beyond their control. The statement is a companion to the frequent resort to fate, *so phan*, an all-too-common Vietnamese response to a situation over which they have no control.[27] The parents repeat the statement as they cannot do anything about the disabilities, and as they, and nobody else, had the children with the birth abnormalities.

The statement, on the other hand, also speaks to the families' resolve. It signals their acceptance of the *disabilities*, which make their child(ren) a "black swan" and an unchangeable or undoable given in their life. This acceptance of their disabled child(ren) enables the families to go on with and sustain their life *as usual*, albeit with the additional burdens of care. The disabled children are as integral to the families' normal life as a black swan is in a flock of white swans.

Of course, just because the AO families manage to embrace their misfortune as a "black swan", the presence of the highly improbable, it does not mean that their life becomes easier. An interesting and poignant case is the behaviour of a couple, Kim and Hien, in Kim Bang in the north: in order to deal with *their* being a black swan in the community, they hid their first two disabled children inside the house. They initially just felt "ashamed". But after two more children (and a couple of miscarriages and a stillbirth in between), the wife developed a fear that no one would want to marry their younger and *healthy* children because of the label of an AO victims' family (May, 2005). Our initial thought was that their efforts to hide the disabled children were carefully designed to conceal the traces of abnormality from outsiders' watchful eyes. The black swan metaphor helped us to see that there was more than an attempt at concealment. Theirs were the efforts to isolate, reduce, and confine the working of that fate within the first two children.

To call this and other similar actions the parents' thoughtlessness may belittle something more fundamental to the process by which the parents come into contact with and digest the implications of the "rare" event – AO and its human consequences. Their reactions are merely parts of keeping their everyday life free of changes, or protecting it from a demand of an "extreme transition", as Berger and Luckmann would call it.[28]

Having a disabled child(ren) does not consume their life, which consists of other equally important needs and concerns such as the household economy and caring for their healthy children, among others. Here lies one more consideration that needs to be added to Taleb's black swan metaphor.

In real life, there are many *flocks* of white swans that impose upon ordinary people a set of regular expectations. Complete acceptance, even of just one "black" swan in a flock, may consume a great deal of time and other resources. An instinctive act, such as the neglect of the "black swan" or its root cause, is an act of balancing the cost of doing something about it and of doing nothing within this multiple set of regular expectations.

The overloaded cognitive capacity of AO families usually has no place in medical and other professionals' concerns. As we saw earlier, it is not surprising that the young couples with one disabled child, or those living in an area suspected of AO contamination, often ignore medical experts' insistence on refraining from conceiving another child. The couples are inundated with other equally important demands such as meeting the expectation that a farmer has as many children as their household economy demands and allows. The disregard may be irrational, given the fact that the couples are from an area that has a record of a high incidence of birth abnormalities. It is irrational, however, only from the perspective of one set of regular expectations, that of the reproduction experts. It is less so when the disregard is thrown into a broader range of concerns that consume the young couples' resources.

Agent Orange contamination is undoubtedly a significant health issue. With nearly 2,000 victims of the contamination and the Mountains that are suspected to be still contaminated, Phu Cat should be the best candidate for efforts to launch a warning campaign against the abuse of agrochemicals. Moreover, Phu Cat is not like the other contamination "hot spots", such as Bien Hoa near Ho Chi Minh City, where the effect of the dioxin-yielding AO is becoming increasingly indistinguishable from other sources of dioxin due to the encroachment of industrial and other complexes.[29]

However, we developed a nagging feeling about possibly one ironical consequence of the medical specialists' efforts to establish a more accurate "probability" of chemicals causing health damages. Their research focussed upon the reproduction-related health records of a sample of Phu Cat's farmers, and identified a pattern – higher incidences of birth anomalies. The research efforts with the prominent, yet isolated, presence of the medical researchers may make the AO-induced abnormalities even *blacker*.

After two years of research in the early 2000s as part of national efforts to address AO-induced health problems, Dr Trinh Van Bao and others reported results where the samples from Phu Cat exhibited much higher scores in all categories, including miscarriages and stillbirths. Dr Truong Quang Dat and others' research ten years later corroborated Dr Bao's team's findings on Phu Cat.[30] Dr Bao's team had a little over 13,000 respondents, and Dr Dat's had 1,644 (for congenital deficiencies). The findings suggest the relatively higher incidences of birth abnormalities among the samples from Phu Cat. They also show that the actual total of AO victims in Phu Cat might have been larger than 1,857 *certified* victims at the time of their research.

Behind the findings, however, these numbers conceal one important implication. The total number of the samples for either research is perfectly acceptable.

Sometimes, the researchers invite dozens of informants to a large conference room at the Phu Cat Health Centre. They explain the intent of the research to the informants and circulate pages of questionnaires to be filled in carefully by the informants. A team of research assistants stand by to answer questions, as raised. Occasionally, the researchers visit some of the informants at their homes.

All these efforts are the basis of the researchers' findings that the health anomalies are *common*, i.e., *unusually* high among the samples. The differences between 1% and 2%, or 0.1% and 0.4% catch the attention of medical experts – a slight difference is *enormous* for those who are looking for it.

However, the respondents are spread thin over the vast Phu Cat District. The findings have not been widely circulated beyond the circle of researchers. The anomalies shown in the findings remain unknown to the informants. Regardless of a specific method of identifying correlations between the living environment and health anomalies, the research efforts, too, remain an isolated event that has very little to do with the informants' everyday lives. Therefore, there is only a limited effectiveness in the medical professionals' claim that the samples (informants) *represent* the rest of the farmers in the District.

While the efforts of medical professionals might be considered steps to prevent the occurrence of another "black swan", the research operations themselves appeared as a "rare" event to the majority of farmers. Issues pertaining to chemical contamination seemed unconnected to their everyday lives. The researchers had not foreseen such an effect; however, it is likely that the medical research that was conducted has left the black swan even *blacker*, its relevance limited to a small group of farmers and their families.

Notes

1 World Health Organization (WHO), Ottawa Charter for Health Promotion 1986, http://www.who.int/healthpromotion/conferences/previous/ottawa/en/
2 *Ibid.*
3 Susan J. Simmons, "Health: A Concept Analysis", *International Journal of Nursing Studies*, Vol. 26, No. 2, 1989, pp. 155–61.
4 Johannes Bircher, "Towards a Dynamic Definition of Health and Disease", *Medicine, Health Care and Philosophy*, No. 8, Spring 2005, p. 338.
5 *Ibid.*, p. 336.
6 *Ibid.*, p. 336.
7 *Ibid.*, pp. 336–8.
8 Christopher Lane, "What is Health? Increasingly, the Absence of Abnormality", *Psychology Today*, http://www.psychologytoday.com/blog/side-effects/201012/what-is-health-increasingly-it-s-defined-the-absence-abnormality
9 Petr Skrabanek, *The Death of Humane Medicine and the Rise of Coercive Healthism*, Social Affairs Unit, 1994, p. 15.
10 Adam Smith, *The Wealth of Nations* (1776), Oxford, Oxford University Press, 1976, p. 12.
11 John D. Graham and Jonathan Baert Wiener, eds., *Risk vs. Risk: Tradeoffs in Protecting Health and the Environment*, Cambridge, MA, Harvard University Press, 1995, p. 2, and Beck, *op. cit.*, p. 23.
12 *Ibid.*, pp. 1–2.

13 Deborah Lupton, *Risk*, London; New York, Routledge, 1999.
14 Beck, *op. cit.*, and Anthony Giddens, "Living in a Post-Traditional Society", in Ulrich Beck, Anthony Giddens, and Scott Lash, eds., *Reflexive Modernization: Politics, Tradition and Aesthetics in the Modern Social Order*, Cambridge, Polity Press, 1994, pp. 56–109.
15 Allen, *op. cit.*, pp. 136–8.
16 H. W. Lewis, *op. cit.*, p. 123.
17 *Ibid.*, p. 123.
18 H. W. Lewis, *op. cit.*, p. 32.
19 Lupton, *op. cit.*, p. 7.
20 Anthony Giddens, "Risk", BBC Reith Lectures 1999, http://news.bbc.co.uk/hi/english/static/events/reith_99/week2/week2.htm
21 Beck, *op. cit.*, p. 29.
22 *Ibid.*
23 Giddens, "Risk", *op. cit.*
24 Cited in Tran Duc Phan, *mimeo*, undated, p. 6. The figure is based on a study done by Nguyen Thi Ngoc Phuong in 1983 at Ho Chi Minh Obstetrics and Gynecology Hospital.
25 Nassim Nicholas Taleb, *The Black Swan – The impact of the Highly Improbable*, New York, Random House 2007, p. xx.
26 Lupton, *op. cit.*, p. 78.
27 There are not many works on the relationship between Vietnamese "traditions" or culture in general and the AO families' and victims' ways of dealing with their inner pain caused by the Agent Orange-dioxin contamination. One example we have come across is Jacques Maitre and Bernard Doray, "The Experiences of the Families of AO Victims", a paper presented at the International Scientific Conference: "Victims of Agent Orange/Dioxin in Vietnam – the Expectations", Hanoi, March 16–17, 2006.
28 Berger and Luckmann, *op. cit.*, p. 23.
29 Arnold Schecter et al., "Food as a Source of Dioxin Exposure in the Residents of Bien Hoa City, Vietnam", *Journal of Occupational and Environmental Medicine*, Vol. 45, No. 4, 2003, pp. 781–8.
30 The research placed Phu Cat in a comparative framework which included Da Nang and Thai Binh. Trinh Van Bao, Tran Duc Phan, and Nguyen Ngoc Hung, "National Project on Establishing a Genetic Consulting Model for the Families Affected by Warfare Chemicals", 2003, cited in Tran Duc Phan, *mimeo*, pp. 10–11. For Dr Dat's team's findings, see Truong Quang Dat et al., "Reproduction-related Abnormalities in Phu Cat", uploaded on the official website of the Department of Science and Technology of Binh Dinh Province, July 19, 2013, http://skhcnbinhdinh.gov.vn/?p=4452

6 Health and the farmers

Whose responsibility counts?

Risk is merely a probability, as shown in *Risk = Danger (damage or losses) × Probability*. Phu Cat's farmers may readily agree on a given danger but often debate on its probability. The debate remains a debate among the experts, and occasionally among ordinary farmers. However, no matter how sound scientific evidence may be, the point of debate is the probability, not the risk.

From the previous two chapters, it is evident that the behaviours of the Phu Cat farmers vary, even when they are expected to behave more or less in a similar manner, faced, for example, with opportunities to increase earnings or prepare for threats to health. Even when health is, or appears to be, at risk, they still do not react solely to health risk warnings. They often do not take preventive action even when the risk, if materialized, might mean severe damage to their health.

The farmers usually acquiesce to the blame as the final trigger for a risk turning into a reality. The medical professionals of the Phu Cat Health Centre, who often accompanied us on our research trips, or the doctors on the preceding research teams, often repeated, "We need to educate the farmers". As far as these experts are concerned, the farmers do not see the obvious, i.e., as entomologist David Pimentel puts it, "human pesticide poisonings and illnesses are clearly the highest prices paid for all pesticide use".[1] The blame goes back to the beneficiaries of the warning. The only difference among the beneficiaries, then, lies between those who do and those who do not heed the warnings. As Ulrich Beck puts it, they carry the ultimate "responsibility for performing the task *and* for the consequences of their performance" (italics added).[2]

Health experts' efforts to motivate the farmers to act in a certain way are a reminder of those efforts by the old development planners or economists, such as Theodore Schultz, as examined earlier: why do the farmers not see the benefits of efficient production? Likewise, in the eyes of the medical professionals, why do these farmers not see health risks as the health experts see them, and act accordingly?

One of the reasons, as discussed in Chapter 5, is the ambiguity in communicating a risk turning into a reality. Another reason, to be discussed in this chapter, is that the farmers are in a position to take ultimate responsibility for the action – including non-action. Medical experts may be better at treatment when a risk becomes a reality, that is, when they have complete authority over their patients. When it comes to preventing a risk from turning into reality, however, medical experts often face unresponsive people. In many cases people – the *potential* patients in their eyes – do not even think they are the potential patients. People do not take the prescriptions for preventive behaviours seriously, thereby depriving the medical experts of the very basis of their authority.

One earlier point becomes more critical in this ironical twist in the question of who is responsible for the farmers' health. The point is that one single concern does not consume the farmers' time, energy, intelligence, and mental and physical resources that make and keep them as farmers. The multiple concerns in the farmers' life mean that, given the limited resources at their disposal, they can rarely satisfy all sorts of pleas or recommendations coming from discreet "trenches" of expertise where various experts address various issues in life separately. To satisfy all would require what Sven Ove Hansson calls a "unified calculation", cutting across all risks, which is an impossibility in practice.[3] The "individualized" responsibility, in the manner of Beck, for the consequences of many decisions underlies the farmers' behaviour.

Individualization of the ultimate health responsibility does not mean that the medical experts abandon their responsibility, nor that the farmers insist on being the authority. There is a broader framework to consider for health management and its transformation that ultimately places the most critical decisions on health squarely upon individual farmers.

Health *for* the people

Medical and health experts may be most successful when dealing with the kind of risks endangering a large population and clear evidence of the failure to heed the warning is ubiquitous. Pandemics such as HIV or bird flu are cases in point. These examples may be associated with the advent of modern clinical medicine and pharmaceutical research. However, the success in preventing some, if not all, of the pandemics in recent times has a long history. Here, we rely on a few secondary sources to place the problem of individualization of health responsibility into perspective.

Hippocrates, as early as 400 BC, noted that "human well-being was influenced by the totality of environment factors: living habits, climate, and the quality of air, water, and food." Here, there is already a notion of a confluence of many factors leading to damaged health.[4] When faced with almost infinite combinations of the factors leading to the outbreak of a communicable, i.e., devastating disease such as yellow fever, smallpox, or measles, the adopted method was one that lumped together and shut out all suspicious factors including human bodies from coming into contact with healthy bodies. In 1348, Venice, a contact point through commerce and other activities with the Orient, adopted the method we generically called "quarantine".[5] Variations of this initial catch-all approach may be found in colonial America throughout its eastern seaboard.

The distinct boundary of the habitat of suspicious elements (such as incoming ships) would soon disappear, and in its place, the living environment in general was found potentially guilty of embracing communicative and other diseases. An all-embracing approach, that is, a sort of expanded version of "quarantine", emerged by the mid-nineteenth century. In 1842, the idea of "sanitary" was introduced in the *General Report on the Sanitary Conditions of the Labouring Population of Great Britain*,[6] alarmed by the poor working conditions of the Industrial Revolution leading to infectious diseases such as typhus, typhoid, and cholera, among others. When the wealthier people were found to be less affected, policies informed of the notion of sanitary were promoted to improve the infrastructure for a clean drinking water supply and sewers for waste disposal *for* the poor.

The fight against infectious and debilitating diseases found a new turn with the "germ theory", usually associated with discoveries by Louis Pasteur and Robert Koch. They represent a series of discoveries in the late nineteenth century linking germs (bacteria) and infectious diseases. These discoveries added another step in controlling the spread of diseases, that is, monitoring and controlling disease carriers – agents. The earlier efforts to improve the living and working environment were now pushed together with the efforts to keep healthy human bodies from becoming the carriers and/or to protect them from contact with the carriers. The development of immunization that followed these discoveries marked another peak in the organized efforts to protect health and prevent health from harm, i.e., public health.[7]

The emphasis up to this point has been on what the health professionals could do for people, a position that makes the professionals the protectors and providers of health. Ordinary people are passive beneficiaries of the services rendered by the health professionals, in addition to at least potentially being the hosts of disease-causing agents. The responsibility of the health professionals is to reduce the *likelihood* of the disease-causing agents striking healthy human beings by improving the living and working environment, by preparing effective immunization, and by reducing the number of people who remain untouched by their efforts.[8]

Health *by* the people

The role of the beneficiaries of health policies is still ambiguous in the development of health management above. Medical and health professionals could push to improve the living environment. They could multiply vaccinations. However, these efforts have not addressed one type of health problem – the diseases that result from personal habits such as drinking, smoking, eating, or a lack of exercise, i.e., those whose roots are in the daily routine of an average individual and its cumulative effects. The excesses in these habits, lumped together as "lifestyle diseases", may catch the professionals' attention. The attention, however, falls short of offering a fine line beyond which the habits become excessive.

Public health historians usually draw attention to the publication of one U.S. document, *Healthy People: The Surgeon General's Report on Health Promotion and Disease Prevention* (1979), as the first of its kind to address this absence.

The Report conceded that individuals may not have complete control over, or take responsibility for, their health in part because of socio-economic and other factors. *The Report* was still emphatic that healthy behaviour was the individual's responsibility with significant consequences.[9]

Furthermore, the *Report*, or for that matter any similar documents', has a paternalistic undertone in its view towards the individual's responsibility. The responsibility that it emphasizes is that of heeding the appeal; it falls short of referring to the equally important responsibility for medical and health specialists that the individuals *are* assured of positive consequences of being responsible, of heeding the appeal. The assurance, however, lies outside the "trenches" of medical and health professionals.

Responsibility as an individual sees it

It should be remembered that health is a physical and mental state best captured in its absence, or in the loss of certain conditions; to many, pursuing health while healthy is an unnecessary practice. While some may still go ahead and invest, say, time for physical exercise, flossing, or weight watching, they do not receive immediate "returns": the results of what they do are not marked by recognizable changes. For healthy individuals, the return on investment is *no* change.

If the investment means cutting into precious time and other resources, the returns would have to be recognizable changes, especially for Phu Cat's farmers, to whom time and money are scarce resources. Consequently, the farmers, at least, appear to be irresponsive to the appeal for certain actions. Their irresponsiveness is not a sign of ignorance, but it is a result of their trying to maximize the use of mental and other resources to satisfy their multiple needs. Health is one of those needs and one without obvious return.

There is another factor that we need to consider: a strange sort of distance between medical and health professionals and the farmers. The distance abets, at least partially, the latter's irresponsiveness. Medical staff from either the Phu Cat District Health Centre or local Commune Clinics often accompanied our earlier visits to the farmers. The Health Centre even provided one of their two ambulances as means of transportation. Although the medical staff never donned the usual white uniforms, their presence should have been motivating enough for the residents. Over nearly 15 years, first as part of the Keio University-Hanoi Medical University cooperation and then as an independent research team, we have visited some of the farmers more than once or twice. Our presence was an addition to the other visits by medical authorities, such as teams from Hanoi Medical University dating back to the early 2000s. The frequent presence of these personnel should be alarming enough. Yet the farmers exhibited no such sign or curiosity. They all remember the earlier visitors not for *why* they were there, but for how they acted – "Oh, Dr Bao always stayed in a tiny inn in town" (March 2009).

Clearly, the risk warnings did not stick, or if they did, they did not stay long in the minds of the farmers. The research teams' repeated visits, including ours, should have aroused at least some nervousness among the farmers leading to some corresponding changes in the farmers' responses. Something must have been missing. The credibility of the message sender, Hanoi Medical University teams, was unquestionable. So was the quality of the information that their *presence* was sending. All the ingredients for making a "persuasive message" heard were present, or so it appears. Except one thing was missing: the predisposition or inclination on the part of the recipients, of the "audience",[10] to heed the warnings.

As discussed in the previous chapter, Agent Orange (AO) and its consequences merely represent a "black swan" to the audience. The nervousness or fear alone, as triggered by the outlying case, is not nearly sufficient to invite a protective behaviour.

Perhaps there is something in our presence, especially that of Hanoi Medical University teams and by extension the medical experts from the District Health Centre, that contributed to barring the audience from seeing the risk warning entirely. As we mentioned earlier, often the research, especially by the Medical University teams, was conducted in a large hall in the District Health Centre away from the informants' homes and villages. The setting was definitely an elaborate stage for the experts to exhibit their authority. But it is an isolated stage, away from the farmers' daily life. This is all the more reason why one of the team leaders, the late Dr Bao, was remembered by the farmers as being unusual for his unauthoritative presence exhibited, e.g., in his choice of a humble inn in town.

This distance is virtually insurmountable. On one side are the farmers without the benefit of heeding the warnings, that is, the utility of the action recommended by the professionals. They are without the test of efficacy of the recommended action. On the other side are the professionals who, like the sales personnel, assume that the right products need no sales pitch to the customers.

There are health specialists who captured the significance of this part of health warnings in their "health belief model". Of the four points below, especially point three matters where the "customers" of health warnings are concerned.[11] They are: (1) perceived susceptibility, i.e., the subjective perception of risk or vulnerability to a health threat; (2) perceived severity, i.e., one's perception of the seriousness of the health threat; (3) perceived benefits, i.e., the efficacy of an action designed to prevent or reduce the health threat; and (4) perceived barriers, i.e., the negative consequences that might be associated with preventive or ameliorative behaviour. A variation of this health belief model draws closer attention to the influence of additional (or new) information upon the recipients in a manner that changes their expectations towards preventive or ameliorative actions they might take.[12]

These observations suggest that medical and health experts are unaware that scientifically sound warnings alone cannot induce their "clients" to *buy* them and that there is the stretch of responsibility beyond the view from their "trenches". The ultimate responsibility for health management by an individual starts where that of medical and health specialists ends.

This brings the examination of the farmers' behaviour into a sharper focus: where a health risk stands in their everyday life, and how much it matters to them.

Farmers' responsibility

The conventional approach to public health is to concentrate on delivering the incentives for people to change their behaviour. The role of experts is to prepare and enrich the evidence of the positive consequences and reinforce that evidence. Here, there is an untested assumption behind this role of experts. To use an analogy, the better the products are, the more willing the consumers are to purchase them. Given this basic assumption, there are roles for the government to play too: (1) to establish infrastructure such as clean water, clean air, safe food, decent housing, safe working conditions, safe roads, among others, i.e., the fundamentals for a healthy life; (2) to enforce a legal framework for actions that may impinge upon the individual's freedoms, such as enforcement of seat belts or banning smoking in public spaces; and (3) to regulate various commercial activities that may directly or indirectly compromise health (such as product standards, labelling, pricing, advertising, and marketing). When properly performed, these roles definitely help construct an environment where the individuals are protected from health hazards. These roles are still those of a "steward",[13] a guardian of those who are receptive to health warnings and willing to act accordingly. In other words, they help protect the benefits that accrue from health-conscious action.

All these efforts leave a large margin of responsibility for health that remains untouched by the government and health and medical experts: the responsibility of how to convince oneself of the need for health-conscious action. The clearer the responsibilities become for the government and for the experts, the less margin for the farmers is left for interpreting what is promoted and pushed on their behalf, and the weightier their responsibility becomes. The individualization of the responsibility is there for the farmers to live with. That responsibility is not something from which they can opt out.

One fact remains, however, that health experts, who are preoccupied mostly with "their risks", ignore that health and health risks are just one concern among many that occupy the farmers' minds, or anyone's for that matter. This neglect may be a vocational predisposition and may be even more hardened when presenting the risk to a high-risk group. Nevertheless, how individuals respond to health risk depends on how they see it among many other risks in their individual contexts, thereby exhibiting various behaviours in response to the risk.

This tendency towards a dispersed risk perception is especially prevalent when the probability of the risk turning into a reality is not in a clear-cut cause-effect sequence as in the cases involving the use of agrochemicals where the threshold of toxicity is at best ambiguous.[14]

The perception of risk does matter, and so do the factors that help shape that perception. Health education from early on may help people view health-conscious action as particularly valuable. However, Irwin Rosenstock, among others, is quick to point out that there may be a sort of zero-sum relationship among the values people attach to action: "[A]ny attempt to increase the value of health may first entail decreasing the value of other dimensions of life".[15] Emphasis on health education per se may have a similar effect as that of the health and medical experts' plea to heed their warnings as if to preach everything else matters less.

Moreover, even if the professionals' push for health awareness is necessary, it is only the beginning of a long process before the receptivity to that push takes roots in people's minds. Given the limited resources at their disposal, asking individuals to change by investing less time and energy in other demanding areas of their lives amounts to asking them to disrupt their lives as they know them. It only triggers another round of complex calculations of the gains and losses. If so, even accepting the primacy of health awareness is tantamount to being part of that "individualized" responsibility.

Thus, the overall circumstances in which the individualized responsibility is put into practice become a crucial focus of this observation.

"Individualized" responsibility as practised

Farmers in Phu Cat are in a very difficult position to make the right decision, one that is acceptable to health and medical specialists. The first obvious and oft-quoted reason is that they are poor. Buying health insurance as an investment in health is a luxury, especially when they do not recognize any problem with their health. A local newspaper reports that only 19% of poor households (accounting for 67%) in the whole province of Binh Dinh had health insurance in 2012. Phu Cat's performance in health insurance is among the lowest in the province. "I am still healthy and therefore I am not rushing to buy insurance just yet", remarked one farmer in Phu Cat.[16] The limited financial resources weaken the sense of urgency for health-conscious action as they make other daily concerns equally urgent. Securing their daily food intake is as important as what they eat.

Another, no less important factor that does not help them develop a sense of urgency where health is concerned is their location, that is, what their living environment offers. Frequent visits to hospitals and to medical doctors are the result both of health problems and of the predisposition to make use of these establishments. The predisposition, in turn, is a product of the sense of effectiveness of their visits in the past – the *efficacy* of their chosen action. Unlike Thanh Khe in Da Nang, Phu Cat's farmers are deprived of the opportunity to test the efficacy of their health-related action. Medical and health services, including the number of clinics and medical staff, are much more limited in Phu Cat and other similar rural areas. Phu Cat's farmers are thus doubly handicapped when faced with the need to make health-conscious decisions.

Farmers as decision-makers

To outsiders, the farmers in Phu Cat have lived a precarious life as if living next to an active "volcano", the dioxin-contaminated Nui Ba Mountains, its ponds, and its streams, even though the level of dioxin contamination has lowered sufficiently recently. Nevertheless, the presence of 2,000 victims of AO contamination hints at the likelihood that some human bodies may well still be carriers of the contaminants. As discussed in the previous chapter, risks to health have nonetheless never become salient parts of their daily concerns *because* the farmers "are still fine".

Asking these farmers to change and adopt preventive behaviour is a challenging task because its benefits in terms of health are not evident; they have not yet experienced disruptive "declines" in their health. Information, written on the labels of pesticide or herbicide containers, pieced together from rumours and mass media, is still not meaningful enough to influence their assessment of what risks they may have been exposed to or *are* facing. A medical doctor from a Hanoi Medical University team joked about one of Ministry of Labour – Invalids and Social Affairs' (MOLISA's) efforts to air warnings on the use of agrochemicals through a TV network. The farmers "just changed their channel". Symptoms like skin rashes or headaches are expected and readily tolerated as "trade-offs", and therefore do not help them think of the *worse*.

Neither the presence of the AO families nor the information they collected about the contaminated Nui Ba Mountains seemed to have much impact on them. It looks as though the ubiquitous "No Trespassing" signs by the ponds and reservoirs in the Mountains had erased the danger to health altogether. Behavioural economists, Richard Thaler and Cass Sunstein, argue that people assess the likelihood of risks by asking how readily examples come to mind. "If people can easily think of relevant examples, they are far more likely to be frightened or concerned than if they cannot". However, the AO victims' families who live right in the middle of the community are the "black swans", not "relevant examples" that "readily" come to the mind of these farmers. In addition, the AO complications are not "vivid and easily imagined causes" because of the delayed effects. What Thaler and Sunstein call "availability heuristic"[17] is not at work. The farmers do not have available (accessible) and emerging (salient) examples that they can think of in order to make a meaningful reference for their behaviours. Furthermore, Phu Cat's farmers have an indisputable explanation for the "black swan", i.e., that it is part of the distant past, the *war with America*, and/or the making of "bad luck". The distant past and the bad luck prevent the farmers from seeing a potential link between AO and the current use of agrochemicals.

Worse still, the efficacy of the farmers' action is particularly limited when their action is concerned with health. The habit of having a regular medical check-up is virtually non-existent among Phu Cat's farmers, including the AO families, due to the limited medical infrastructure for health services.

Table 6.1 shows that the number of health clinics in Phu Cat is double that in Thanh Khe (Da Nang). But these clinics and other medical facilities (24) have to cover a large area of 679 km^2, i.e., one health unit per 28 km^2, compared to one per 0.8 km^2 for Thanh Khe. Other major health services are also within their reach in the urban Thanh Khe. It is obviously easier for patients in this district to imagine the presence of medical services within their living environment. Given the limited number of clinics within commutable distance in Phu Cat, readiness to think of making use of the medical services is already limited among the

Table 6.1 Health Services in Thanh Khe and Phu Cat

	Thanh Khe	*Phu Cat*
Number of communes/wards	8	18
Size of area	9.3 km^2	679 km^2
Total population	160,582	210,100
Population density per km^2	17,267	286
Number of health units (clinics)	11	24
Medical staff	133	190
– Doctors with medical degree	51	45
– Assistant physicians	51	81
– Nurses	15	48
– Midwives	16	16
Pharmaceutical staff	9	7
– High-degree pharmacist	1	2
– Middle-degree pharmacist	4	3
– Assistant pharmacist	4	2

Source: General Statistics Office, 2006.

farmers. Quy Nhon General Hospital is even farther: a one- to one-and-a-half-hour drive away. Phu Cat's farmers are deprived of the conditions that otherwise would have primed them for making use of medical services.

From Table 6.1, we also see that the number of doctors is more or less the same in both areas. But the large size of Phu Cat conceals one important point that makes the presence of the medical staff even scarcer in Phu Cat than shown by the statistics. Usually more than 50% of the physicians with full medical degrees are stationed at Phu Cat District Health Centre. At the communal level, however, medical staff are mostly assistant physicians, a category of professionals slightly more advanced than nurses. They are products more of vocational training in auxiliary medical services, thereby severely limiting the services they are allowed to provide. Besides, as noted earlier in Chapter 3, sometimes they may not always be available for different reasons. Given these limits, Communal Clinics in Phu Cat are not installed or equipped to treat serious ailments.

Despite *representing* the medical and health authorities, Communal Clinics are no more than an infirmary, serving as a halfway stop. Serious cases must be sent to the District Health Centre (a 30-minute car ride for many villagers) in the Ngo May section of the District or Quy Nhon General Hospital, one and a half hours away for most.[18] The absence of sufficient medical services makes the cost of visiting the Centre even more taxing, which, in turn, makes people less inclined to rely on the medical establishment, unless their ailments become serious. Most of the parents of the AO victims in Phu Cat do not see the point of taking their children for regular check-ups or for rehabilitation. All such efforts, if any, are disruptions to their daily life. The great majority of the farmers are deprived of the opportunities to test the efficacy of health-conscious actions, even if they may wish to test them.

There is an additional factor that makes the physical and mental distance even greater. The *medical* staff at the Commune Clinics are well informed of the affairs of the farmers in their jurisdictions, a result of their efforts to familiarize themselves with the local villagers. Their presence is ubiquitous in the farmers' lives. Their efforts, however, may have won them the kind of authority that does not correspond to their status as *medical* professionals.

The story of Mr Phung, an assistant physician at Cat Trinh Commune Clinic and a constant companion of our research trips, is a case in point. He knows everyone in his Commune and almost every detail of the family affairs of the AO families and others. The villagers see him as representing not only the Cat Trinh Clinic, but also the Phu Cat District Health Centre and all the medical establishments above it. Mr Phung and others like him are all genuinely sympathetic to those parents with one or more disabled children. Their sympathy has its roots in their conviction that there is "no cure for Agent Orange complications". There is an unintended but ironical consequence of these staff's ubiquitous presence. Mr Phung's and others' casual statements carry the finality of the medical authority. In other words, the presence of the medical and health services in the rural villages through these Clinics and the staff does not offer an opportunity, but pre-empts the initial step, to test the effectiveness of the villagers' health-conscious action.

Left alone with all the health responsibilities, the farmers' choice for action is to stay close to what they have within their familiar reach – the use of *thay lang* (traditional health practitioners) to fix their health problems, or visits to local Commune Clinics just for simple medicines such as contraception devices. In other words, the efficacy of their health-related action is also tested only as far as the local medical and health services offer. These local conditions, contrary to the intention, serve as a "fundamental barrier" to nurturing a broader health consciousness.[19]

The following example may best illustrate how the limited local medical and health services prevent potential users from developing a reasonable health choice. During our first round of visits, one of the parents of the AO victims kept insisting that they would not have any more children because "it has been difficult enough" to take care of an older child with a birth defect. Her determination had led her to use contraceptive rings. In the second round of visits, a new baby, fortunately a healthy one, was there lying between the parents. Their explanation: "The [family] plan failed".

They meant that they had had the baby by accident. The use of contraceptive rings is still the most popular, and free, method, especially in rural areas of Vietnam. She became pregnant during a period when she had to remove the contraceptive device, because the ring had caused severe infection. Her honest explanation, when we pressed her, indicated more than a lack of prudence. She could have consulted with an obstetrician-gynaecologist, who would most likely have recommended an alternative such as condoms or pills in addition to careful infection treatment. However, the Clinic had only a mid-wife. The young mother had no past experience in consulting with a specialist. She works full-time in the rice paddies and taking pills regularly is more of a nuisance and additional chore in her daily routine; and the use of condoms is still embarrassing for the young couples. There was no apparent reason for breaking the habit.

Cost of choices

Professionals try to sell their options by emphasizing the benefits of adopting them and, similarly, the costs of not doing so. But as we tend to forget, the costs for these poor farmers are usually more extreme *either* way, choosing or not choosing the "right" option. A conventional view of being poor may prevent us from realizing that being poor has special meaning to the people who feel they are poor, regardless of their actual well-being. To borrow from another behavioural economist, Daniel Kahneman, "being poor is living below one's reference point", and therefore whoever feels he is poor is always "in the losses". A small gain that they make is therefore likely to be perceived as "a reduced loss, not as a gain".[20] An obvious incentive is not so readily perceived as such.

This observation helps us see how many of Phu Cat's farmers weigh an increase in earnings and how that "increase" matters to them. The perception of gains or losses hinges upon where their "reference points" are. Any gain is not an automatic gain to them. This perspective highlights an earlier point, by Rosenstock, about the lives of Phu Cat's farmers: any attempt to increase the value of health may first entail decreasing the value of other dimensions of life.[21]

If we expound on Kahneman's observation in real life, the effect of an incentive for action turns out to be even more complex. Let us bring in the earlier point that many factors and concerns collectively make up one's life. Each of these many factors and concerns demands an action, and that action will be derived on the basis of one reference point. Life, in other words, rarely allows one single reference point to dominate the others. Each reference point is likely to be skewed somewhat as it is integral to a set of tangled-up reference points. Take, for instance, the young couple whose "family plan" had failed. Who knows if one reference point prompting a cautious reproductive action may have been skewed by another that holds that farming families usually have many children.

The farmers are *at once* the producers and consumers of agricultural products, the parents of children, community members, and potentially patients. The roles they take on vary depending on whom and what they interact with. A role may require them to act rationally in one sense, and another role may require them to act rationally in another sense. Therefore, they are faced with multiple concerns that make it an unavoidable task for them to run a calculation to see if gains in one lead to losses in another. A likely result is a good "enough" choice that offers sufficient gains in one and satisfies some in another, the choice that is best described as "satisficing" by Herbert Simon.[22]

There is more to the farmers' "satisficing" decisions than what appears to be a product of random compromises. The professionals in medicine, economic development planning, and education, among others, especially in developing countries, are eager to promote changes by insisting more on the gains than the costs of their policies. These experts reach the same people as the "beneficiaries" of their policies. A reversal of an object-observer relationship occurs. The farmers are no longer "farmers" in the eyes of these experts. The farmers are what these experts make them out to be. The relationship between an elephant and six blind men in a Vietnamese folk tale is apt, if cynical, metaphor about highly specialized observers' view of an object that blinds the observers to the larger whole of which the observed object is a part.

> The blind man who feels a leg says the elephant is a pillar;
> The blind man who feels the tail says the elephant is a rope;
> The blind man who feels the trunk says the elephant is a tree branch;
> The blind man who feels the ear says the elephant is a fan;
> The blind man who feels the belly says the elephant is a wall; and
> The blind man who feels the tusk says the elephant is a solid pipe.

The farmers, on the other hand, are farmers. The demands of their lives prompt them to perform more than one "role" at any given time. They may pursue a course of action recommended by one professional but do so only to the point at which the action begins interfering with actions encouraged by professionals of other types or with other demands. Complete satisfaction of all demands rarely crosses the farmers' minds, given the limited resources at their disposal. Even an attempt at satisfying some is immensely taxing. The calculation of the costs of recommended actions, intersecting with each other, without the benefits of the promised results, is virtually impossible. The net result: the farmers are likely to disappoint any one of the professionals of diverse expertise.

However, the professionals' disappointment, bordering on condescension, is the other side of the same coin, that is, that of the farmers' satisfaction with life because of it, not in spite of it. Their life is proof that their decisions have not left the damaging drain on the precious resources needed to meet the demands on their life.

The farmers who grow cashew nuts adopt health-conscious behaviours, such as hiring somebody to spray chemicals for their cashew nut farm. They do so, however, not necessarily or only because of the health motive. Some of the swaying factors are incidental, such as too large a size of farm to take care of alone *and* the neighbours having the equipment and manpower. The young couples in Thanh Khe tend to have more birth space between disabled children and the next than is the case in the other two areas. The examples may be taken as a sign that they do not want to face the higher risk of having another handicapped child. This may be so, to some extent. But the higher living costs of having an additional member in the more urban Da Nang clearly have an impact on their decisions.

By contrast, regardless of the additional costs, having more children as a compensation for a lost child, lost to birth defects, stays in the minds of the AO families in rural areas like Phu Cat and Kim Bang. The medical experts try to push their preferred option – not to have more children – by emphasizing the costs of not taking that option. Farmers respond by considering the cost of taking that cautious option, which entirely removes even the slightest chance of their having a healthy child. A norm dictating the other demands of rural life such as having many children, even by default, retains its swaying power.

Decision-makers in action: Phu Cat's farmers

Chemical and medical professionals may find it an imperative to present an ideal choice of action in the clearest way that gains in one demand or facet of life can also be gains in another. After all, the farmers are not to be blamed if they fail to see the negative consequences of one choice because of the fear that the choice may cause unintended collateral damages elsewhere. The best conceivable way for the professionals is to show an instance of killing two birds with one stone.

There is an interesting report on a rice-producing village in the Mekong Delta by a pair of economists from Vietnam National University.[23] They found that the farmers spent about an extra 100,000 VND ($5) for 270 g of pesticide per hectare, resulting in its excessive use. Health costs due to pesticide exposure were calculated to be between 89,310 VND and 94,129 VND per farmer, per hectare. In order to reduce this excessive spending and use, the study proposes a tax of about 33% on current pesticide prices. This would lead to less use of the chemicals and decreased rice yields. It may also lead to savings on the inputs and reductions in health costs. In all, the researchers calculated that such a tax would bring a net benefit to the farmers of over 56,000 VND (a little over $2.5) per hectare, in addition to the government gain from the tax revenue.

Its feasibility aside, to the economists who conducted this research, a net benefit of 56,000 VND is obviously a gain for the farmers, even if it means a decrease from the previous crop. To the farmers who believe that they are poor, these estimates do not make much sense. As Kahneman would have concurred, the *reduced* gain for the poor is still merely a "reduced" loss. Besides, linking the gains in two different areas of wealth and health is an exercise in empty calculation since the gains in health are not readily discernible as mentioned before.

On the other hand, if the farmers pursue a higher productivity and do not take appropriate protection measures as suggested by the instructions for the use of chemicals, the cost (damaged health) could be extremely high when and if it happens. The AO victims' families are the living examples of how costly it could be, financially, mentally, and socially. Yet here, the presence of AO families may even have an opposite effect. Their presence, which is too exceptional, may decrease the others' caution against chemical contamination as the farmers may believe, mistakenly, that the chemicals they handle are not as bad as AO.

Nonetheless, an alarming reminder awaits the farmers. Arnold Schecter, who has been observing the effects of AO for a long time, saw a new development: the children of the new generation are born where their parents may have been exposed to dioxin contamination *other than* AO.[24] Robert Allen joins in: "We are all exposed to dioxin and *other contaminants*. Pesticides have exposed millions of people ignorant of the dangers and other contaminants"[25] (italics added).

Decision-makers in action: Agent Orange victims' families

Unlike the victims' families in Da Nang, among whom was one parent who had to quit their job to become a full-time care-giver to their handicapped child, none of the AO families in Phu Cat have stopped being farmers. If one of the parents decides to quit working on the farm in order to stay at home with their disabled child, it would jeopardize that much income, pushing them that much closer to a life of subsistence. Having a disabled child is already a great cost to these farmers. Hence the need for extra income, or protecting the current level of income, becomes critical. Knowing that disabled children are susceptible to lapses in their given health conditions, however sporadic they may be, the need becomes even greater.

Furthermore, the decision to have or not to have another child after a disabled child or two among these parents is also not an easy one to make. The desire to have a healthy child is *stronger* among them. If not stronger, it at least stays with them. If they go along with the advice from medical doctors (not to have more children or to have an abortion), they are concluding that they are not going to have another child, *any* child. This is a crucial cost that the AO families consider.

The doctors may try to tilt the AO families' attention in their favour by first pointing out the higher probability of birth defects, then the cost of having another disabled child. They pay less or no attention to the costs that these families have to weigh from not having any child, possibly a healthy child. Not having children, especially healthy children, goes against the dominant social norm in rural areas in which children are the source of three utilities for their parents (entertainment, labour, and security)[26] and the assurance that they are not isolated from the community. Having a disabled child may not make them look *different* from other families but having only one does. In other words, there is nothing particularly theatrical about Madame Nguyễn Thị Bình's statement about the soldiers returning from the war: "[W]hen the first child was born with a birth defect, they tried again and again". They were acting perfectly harmoniously with the long-standing norm that survived the war.

Deciding on a choice is a result of weighing up its costs and benefits. If the benefits outweigh the costs, the choice is a rational one to make. There is more to this simple equation. A choice made is another choice abandoned. In real life, there is more than one balance sheet of costs and benefits. What appears to be a rational choice on one balance sheet could well mean benefits abandoned on other balance sheets. As mentioned earlier, any decision would have to be made on a complex calculation of zero-sum relationships intractably entangling gains and losses "in many dimensions of life".

Phu Cat farmers' decisions, which appear to be far less responsive to the experts' plea to make the right decision, follow the complexity of this calculation. The resulting choices appear to be, at the very least, irresponsive to the experts. The farmers' decisions, however, are designed to avert the losses that matter most to them at decision times. This "compensatory strategy"[27] is the means for Phu Cat's farmers to be content with the choices they abandoned *and* with their unknown consequences.

A Missing link

There has been a plethora of efforts to contain, minimize, and even undo the negative consequences of toxic chemicals, AO included. Of these, the most notable is the joint Vietnam-U.S. effort to neutralize the AO contamination in the exposed areas. Phu Cat, together with the other two dioxin "hot spots", Bien Hoa and Da Nang, was the target of a $5 million UNDP and GEF (Global Environment Facility) project. The Ministry of Environment and Natural Resources' Committee 33 in close cooperation with the Ministry of Defence launched "Environmental Remediation of Dioxin Contaminated Hotspots in Viet Nam" in July 2010. Le Ke Son and Charles Bailey detailed this massive and coordinated effort to neutralize the contamination in the three strategically important sites.[28]

In August 2012, more than 7,000 cubic metres of highly dioxin-contaminated soil at Phu Cat Airbase were safely contained in landfill. This Phu Cat landfill was constructed in full compliance with national regulations and met international standards. The landfill stopped the spread of the dioxin to the surrounding environment and eliminated the exposure of the local population. In the words of Le Ke Son, Director General of the Viet Nam Environment Administration and Director of Committee 33, the Ministry of Natural Resources and Environment:[29]

> With the landfill's closing, the Phu Cat Airbase has been removed from the list of the three dioxin hot spots in Vietnam. Dioxin is no longer leaking from the site and dioxin will not have an impact on the environment and people living in the surrounding area.

After this, the project focussed on Bien Hoa and Da Nang.

However, the 7,000 cubic metres around Phu Cat Airbase was not the only place exposed to dioxin during the war. Local witnesses reported spraying in many parts along the long range of Nui Ba Mountains, with a surface area of over 100 km^2. Moreover, the contaminants do not reside only in the physical environment but are already inside at least some of the parents and kin of the almost 2,000 human bodies in Phu Cat. "Dioxin … will not have an impact on the environment and people living in the surrounding area" is true only for those who live around the airport. It is not the conclusion about the contamination issues.

Professionals and experts in corrective and preventive medicine have not been sitting idly around either. Some of their actions are circulated through popular media. Here is one such example: a controversial approach called the "Hubbard method" applied by Hanoi's military 103 Hospital.[30] It is aimed at cleansing the contaminated bodies. The method is a detoxification treatment developed by Scientologists and not internationally recognized. The patients in this programme receive treatment largely consisting of saunas, exercise, and vitamins. The treatment programme could take months. Currently (2012), about 24 people are being treated on a trial basis at Hanoi's 103 Hospital and most of them are residents of the area near Da Nang Airbase and have all tested positive for elevated levels of the highly toxic compound.

The more popular practise is a blood test for people living in the contaminated area. However, the practice has been mostly random and not consistent, partly because of the lengthy as well as costly examination process. Doctors also advise young couples in the areas to have regular check-ups, especially ultrasound examinations during pregnancy to detect any irregularity. Again, the issue goes back to whether or not the necessary equipment for the testing is readily available to residents. The distance between the residential area and decent hospital facilities matters. None of the Communal Clinics in any of the three Districts of our examination have an ultrasound device. Therefore, a lot still needs to be done before this preventive approach can make a difference in the farmers' life.

As regards agrochemicals generally, the government has focussed on the regulatory approach to monitor and supervise their market as well as their use since 1990 (Chapter 3). The main achievement of the government is the establishment of Plant Protection Centre stations at the lowest administrative units throughout the country. The Ministry of Agricultural and Rural Development (MARD) established the Plant Protection Department as early as 1961.[31]

These government's efforts aimed at improving the living environment as a way of containing and reducing health risks. These are the more conventional top-down approaches, concentrating on isolating and cleaning the living environment, accompanied by a host of regulations, such as enforcement of the standards and explicit instructions on chemical use. Along the way, the role of information and education is emphasized to increase the awareness of the risks involved in the use of pesticides and other toxic chemicals.

These efforts, however, leave the farmers with the ultimate responsibility of what to purchase and how, where, and when to use it. The experts and professionals in the matters of chemicals, health, and education remain in their own "trenches". MARD may claim exclusive jurisdiction over the matter of agrochemicals, and the Ministry of Health likewise over the matter of health, while environmental and ecological issues belong to the Ministry of Mineral Resources and Environment. The opportunities for testing the efficacy of the farmers' health-conscious behaviour are beyond the purview of these efforts.

Notes

1 Pimentel, *op. cit.*, p. 230.
2 Beck, *op. cit.*, p. xv.
3 Sven Ove Hansson, "Seven Myths Risk", *Risk Management*, Vol. 7, No. 2, 2005, p. 12.
4 Susan J. Simmons, "Health: A Concept Analysis", *International Journal of Nursing Studies*, Vol. 26, No. 2, 1989, p. 156.
5 Llyod Novick and Cynthia B. Morrow, "Defining Public Health: Historical and Contemporary Development", in Lloyd F. Novick, Cynthia B. Morrow, and Glen P. Mays, eds., *Public Health Administration: Principles for Population-Based Management* (2nd edn), Burlington, MA, Jones and Bartlett Publishers, 2008, p. 6.
6 *Ibid.*, p. 9.

7 *Ibid.*, p. 11.
8 *Ibid.*, pp. 16–17.
9 *Ibid.*, pp. 27–30.
10 These conditions constitute the "drive model" of the Yale Attitude Change Approach. See C. I. Hovland, I. L. Janis, and H. H. Kelley, *Communication and Persuasion: Psychological Studies of Obvious Change*, New Haven, CT, Yale University Press, 1953 as expanded in Kenneth H. Beck and Arthur Frankel, "A Conceptualization of Threat Communications and Protective Health Behavior", *Social Psychology Quarterly*, Vol. 44, No. 3, 1981, pp. 205–213.
11 Nancy K. Janz and Marshal H. Becker, "The Health Belief Model: A Decade Later", *Health Education Quarterly*, Vol. 11, No. 1, 1984, pp. 1–47. See also, Irwin Rosenstock, Victor Strecher, and Marshall Becker, "Social Learning Theory and the Health Brief Model", *Health Education Quarterly*, Vol. 15, No. 2, 1988, pp. 175–83.
12 For a representative work on this line of argument, see Beck and Frankel, *op. cit.* See also Steven Prentice-Dunn and Ronald W. Rogers, "Protection Motivation and Preventive Health: Beyond the Health Belief Model", *Health Education Research – Theory and Practice*, Vol. 1, No. 3, 1986, pp. 153–61.
13 Nuffield Council on Bioethics. *Public Health: Ethical Issues. London, Nuffield Council on Bioethics, 2007*, quoted in Alan Maryon-Davis and Rachel Jolley, "Healthy Nudges: When the Public Wants Change but the Politicians Don't Know It", *Policy Action Report*, 2010, Faculty of Public Heath, King's College, p. 4.
14 Lewis, *op. cit.*, p. 123.
15 Irwin M. Rosenstock, "What Research in Motivation Suggests for Public Health", *American Journal of Public Health* Vol. 50 (3 Pt 1), March 1960, p. 301.
16 *Binh Dinh News*, www.baobinhdinh. com.vn/viewer.aspx?macm=6&macmp =8&mabb =1144, reconfirmed on March 26, 2012.
17 Richard H. Thaler and Cass R. Sunstein, *Nudge: Improving Decisions about Health, Wealth, and Happiness*, London, Penguin Books, 2009, p. 25.
18 How the distance makes a major difference in the use of medical services by Phu Cat's farmers is well documented by Dr Truong Quang Dat, former director of the Phu Cat District Health Centre. His findings were presented in "Health Service Utilization of the Phu Cat District Residents", at the *Fourth Workshop for Human Security in East Asia*, February 25–27, 2007, at Keio University, Japan.
19 Maryon-Davis and Jolley, *op. cit.*, p. 5.
20 Kahneman, *op. cit.*, 2011, p. 298.
21 Rosenstock, *op. cit.*, p. 301.
22 See en. 7 and en. 8 of Introductory chapter. Herbert Simon's "satisficing" describes a decision-making tendency, which induces people to opt for a good enough choice. "Satisficing" combines "satisfy" and "suffice". A principal factor behind this tendency is people's limited cognitive capacity, which is severely limited by the limited information on choices, the decision-making environment, among others.
23 Nguyen Huu Dung and Tran Thi Thanh Dung, "Economic and Health Consequences of Pesticide Use in Paddy Production in the Mekong Delta, Vietnam", *Economy and Environmental Program for Southeast Asia Research Report*, 1999.
24 Schecter et al., *op. cit.*, 2001, pp. 435–43.
25 Allen, *op. cit.*, p. 138.
26 Leibenstein, *op. cit.*
27 Thaler and Sunstein, *op. cit.*, p. 97.
28 Son and Bailey, *op. cit.*
29 United Nations in Vietnam, www.un.org.vn/en/undp-agencypresscenter1-99/2247-phu-cat-military-airbase-removed-from-dioxin-hotspot-list.html
30 Yahoo News (September 7, 2012), http://sg.news.yahoo.com/vietnam-agent-orange-victims-scientology-detox-160516004.html
31 FAO, www.fao.org/docrep/008/af340e/af340e0m.htm#TopOfPage

7 Farmers' logic

Loss aversion

The actions of Phu Cat's farmers (including the Agent Orange families) do make sense, most of the time. That is a view that not many experts or professionals would readily agree with. However, a closer look at the farmers' behaviour may help us see the point of this view: their actions make sense because they are the result of incessant cost-benefit calculations in their everyday lives, without suspending it even for a moment.

If this is the case, then, the seeds of action that may satisfy the professionals, and experts too, would have to be rooted somewhere in these farmers' actions and how they come to act the way they do. The necessary step in this chapter is to reconstruct the farmers' behaviour from the perspective that nearly all actions are taken for reasons, and that not all actions are meant to *maximize* their utility. At the very base of this attempt at reconstruction is a simple proposition: if people find it difficult to recognize the utility of an action, they do not take that action; insistence upon taking that action tilts their attention more to the costs accompanying that action. In turn, the attention to the costs greatly influences their behaviour.

As we have discussed, the examples of the negative consequences of toxic chemicals, the AO families, are spread thinly across Phu Cat District. In the eyes of the majority of the farmers, families with disabled children are "rare" events. They represent exceptions rather than examples. If the utility of the recommended action were the protection of the farmers from these "rare" events or anything similar to them, the farmers would have a difficult time recognizing that utility. More intimate examples such as headaches and skin rashes do not help the farmers see the utility either. They do not help because they are either part of a normal health condition or examples deserving, possibly, of caution.

The utility that the professionals wish to emphasize remains elusive to the farmers. Yet the experts and professionals concentrate their efforts exclusively on refining and strengthening the basis for their preferred action, and illuminating and selling its utility. Oblivious to how little traction the utility of their "product" – a recommended action – has on the farmers, the professionals see the beneficiaries of their efforts in a simple framework, i.e., as either "unwise" (risk-taking) or "wise" (risk-averse) consumers.

Worse still, their efforts to make their product (a recommended action) more indisputable, as their vocational ethics rightly demands, only harden their positioning in their "trenches" of expertise. The likelihood that a zero-sum relationship may exist where the resources of one course of action cut into those of the others rarely crosses their minds. Consequently, an important consideration remains uncompelling and outside their purview. Take, for example, the situation where one considers whether or not to make a choice that is claimed to contain, neutralize, or remove a danger threatening to disrupt one's life. It is not an easy decision to make, as Sven Ove Hansson, a philosopher with a special leaning towards decision-making theories, has this to say: "If risk management took place in complete isolation from other decisions in [life], then the uniform price tag promoted by cost-benefits analysts would make sense" but "risk issues are dispersed over the whole social agenda, where they are parts of various larger and more complex issues". Thus, the idea of founding risk decisions on a "unified calculation for all [aspects of one's life] is insensitive to the different concerns and decision procedures of the various [aspects of life]".[1]

The farmers and professionals of various expertise may not be so far apart on one thing. Both count on the consequences – the proven utility or the lack thereof – of an action for its continuation, adjustment, or replacement by an alternative. The similarity, however, ends there. The old Vietnamese folk tale we cited in Chapter 6 helps illuminate the difference in expectation between the farmers and the professionals: an elephant and those who see the elephant through its parts only and exclusively. The professionals rarely, if ever, question whether what they see are merely parts of a whole and if that whole profoundly influences the behaviour of the parts they are concerned with. The professionals' presumption is much too strong that the farmers only need to heed their – disparate – prescriptions for action. Consequently, the farmers' reaction would have to appear to be irresponsive to the professionals' expectations, as it is directed more at the costs accompanying those expected actions.

In real life, samples abound where the professionals' prescribed action rarely reaches its "beneficiaries" and leads them to change and navigate their behaviours. Thousands continue to live dangerously close to a recently erupted volcano, as we see in the case of the villagers near Mount Merapi in Indonesia. It recently went through a series of devastating eruptions, leading to the government's push for evacuation. The villagers returned from the resettlement areas to their old living quarters within a short while and resumed their life as they knew it. One villager offered an explanation: the most recent lava flow bypassed his village. The great majority of the residents in and near Tokyo do not change their everyday life, even though the seismologists and other experts have increased the warnings about impending major earthquakes.

The soundness of the professionals' warnings is not what matters to these residents. What matters to them is that the warnings have little to do with the various costs they would have to bear if they were to heed even some of them. Furthermore, the professionals give very little consideration to the specific, and various, contexts in which the alleged beneficiaries come into contact with the warnings. To the professionals, that consideration is tantamount to *customizing* the warnings, and lies outside their "trenches", or else it contradicts the very nature of the warnings as a public policy. The beneficiaries are left with their counsel when they need to work out which action to take and not to take through the intricately connected costs any action might incur.

We pay closer attention to these farmers' winding decision-making processes that go through constant consultation with the resources they have at their disposal. The processes are distinctly different from those that are inspired and sustained by the ultimate utility of an action, or a series of consistent actions.

Risks as they see them

The most striking decision-making cases that betray the experts' expectation involves those who decided to have more children after a child was born with a birth defect(s). As the data (Tables 3.7, 3.8, and 5.1) show that the farmers exhibited no apparent caution against the risk of having a child with birth defects. There is no discernible difference in the spacing of time between the two births of healthy children and that between one with a birth defect(s) and another healthy child. Having a disabled child does not seem to have primed the parents for more cautious reproductive activities. Or, to these parents, a child with mental and physical disabilities appears to be more coincidental than an inevitable result of their action, and the fact that they had a child is the proof of their chosen action.

There are other, perhaps less dramatic, cases where we would not find motivation leading to an action or where we would have difficulties tracing the origin(s) of an action. Parents casually picking up their children from school for the household chores on the spur of the moment, or so it appears, is one example. Pushing a male child with a fairly serious mental problem to marry a healthy girl may be another. Consequently, we are making ourselves susceptible to an easy characterization of these actions as simply irrational or at least illogical. However, there are many cases where the result of an action is not a confirmation of its logical origin. Irwin Rosenstock notes, in the area where health-conscious behaviour matters, that "health-related motives may not always give rise to health-related behaviour, and conversely health-related behaviour may not always be determined by health-related motives".[2]

The first step at reconstructing how the farmers make decisions, then, is to place it in a process characteristically different from our conventional view of it. It is a step that is necessary to free ourselves from a presupposition that their decisions are parts of a seamless flow of thinking. This alternative perspective captures the decisions as they are made, at the junctures of their being made, and the farmers in a constant consultation with the resources at their disposal and their understanding of their needs. Their acts of decision-making look more disjointed efforts, each taking place within a distinct phase. We take the case of a young couple in Cat Trinh Commune, Phu Cat, for a reconstruction attempt (November 2016, August 2017, and every spring and summer since).

The husband, Luy (b. 1980), and his wife, Luu (b. 1978), run a small bike repair shop in Cat Trinh Commune off the railway track not far from Ngo May. They have a rice paddy (1,000 m^2) 4 or 5 km away from home in another district where the husband was born and grew up. They also have a few livestock. They have three girls: the oldest is 16 years old, and the youngest is 4 years old. The middle daughter, Tuyet, who is 8, was born prematurely and has a severe hearing impairment. Tuyet, who recently began coming to *Lop hoc Uoc Mo*, Dream Class I, is the link between the family and us.

The farm away from home provides the basis of the family's livelihood, but that is beginning to look less sufficient as the oldest is moving up through the school grades. The repair shop may bring in, as they testified, around 2,000,000 VND ($100) a month. This additional income is unpredictable and thus less dependable, as the demand for their service varies.

When Tuyet was three, they took her all the way to Ho Chi Minh City for a physical examination and were told that an operation might fix her problem. The cost, they were told, was estimated at $15,000 and the chance of her acquiring the ability to hear was 50%. For the parents who would rely for any contingency on the additional but unpredictable $100-a-month earnings from the bike shop, the choice of surgery was tantamount to non-existent. After the trip, they apparently stopped doing much for the girl apart from occasional visits to the commune clinic to pick up some medicines for her.

There was nearly a five-year hiatus before they took her to the Dream Class. "Can you help us financially?" was the first question Tuyet's father asked in one of the rare meetings between the parents of Dream Class I children and us a year earlier. They are financially struggling. The husband still hopes to have a son but is willing to concede in his wife's presence: "Oh, it's up to her". The wife is reluctant, if not rejecting the idea outright: "I'd rather not. I'm getting old".

In sum, there is not a single train of consistent thought detectable in the thinking of the young husband and wife. They had their youngest daughter soon after they were told that the one before her was conclusively diagnosed as having a disability, which to them is "incurable" – requiring a $15,000 operation with a 50-50 chance of improvement. The father is still hoping, though he is willing to compromise that hope for a son. They run a small repair shop that generates, at best, an incidental cash income. There is no sign of him or his wife advertising their repair services. They set up their shop 4, or 5 km away from their rice paddies in the first place, leaving very little time for running the shop. As it turned out, his request for financial support at a Dream Class parents' meeting was not for Tuyet's surgery but to cover the rising expenses for the oldest daughter's middle school.

There seem to be no health-related concerns. Nor are there signs of management efforts for running the repair shop. Not even a sense of time and labour allocation is present. Nearly all of their moves seem extemporaneous and look as though the couple has reacted to whatever push or opportunity presents itself.

Nonetheless, each decision, if taken as the result of a separate cost and benefit calculation, appears different. The three-year time lapse before taking Tuyet to

Ho Chi Minh City is part of the logical steps that they followed on an expected upward path, starting with the diagnosis at the Commune Clinic and consultation against the increasingly conclusive prognosis. The parents were faced with a firmer confirmation at each step concerning the difficulty of fixing or undoing the disability. The fact that they stopped medical consultations afterward is a logical conclusion from the failed efficacy "test" of their "health-conscious" steps. These steps did not leave the parents merely unimpressed. The steps made them more aware of the accompanying costs. Given the financially tight conditions, a smaller cost appears larger. They say that they go to the Commune Clinic to pick up the medicine for Tuyet. The medicines' effectiveness is not the motivation for the visit. "Oh, just once in five or six months", the parents testified. It is a move that often vacillates, depending on their financial and other conditions.

They had a third daughter after Tuyet, a move that would have irked some in the medical establishment. It is a logical move, however, of parents without a son, in line with the norm that no one in this rural community questions. Moreover, had they been left with only Tuyet and the older sister, who may well leave the family in a few years, they would have been deprived of a key resource just to protect their current well-being. Trying to have another child was a perfectly rational course of action to take. The only conceivable reason for *not* trying to have a fourth child (regardless of its gender) is the ceiling that the financial burden sets for a family of five.

Mr N. V. Thom, the land millionaire, is not too different from Luy and Luu, even with a family life he has no complaints about. As we saw it, they accumulated their assets (land) as opportunities presented themselves. They could afford to hire many people but they have not done so. They could improve their living quarters in the Mountains, such as with a better electricity supply, easily. They are not inclined to do so. They are happy with their dimly lit rooms even when they are entertaining some of their close relatives and friends. We once questioned him about the other house he kept at the foot of the Mountains where they used to live before moving further into the Mountains. He answered: "For savings, just in case". But he knows, as well as anybody else, that there is no such thing as a real estate market where he can convert this piece of real estate into a contingency fund or investment fund. To him, parting with what is already in his possession is, first and foremost, a loss, a cost that requires a sufficient benefit outweighing it. Mr N. V. Thom and his wife, who have lived with all the assets that made him a "millionaire", are happy with the way things are. There is very little margin for seeking an "additional benefit" that may make a meaningful difference to their lives.

It is tempting but too hasty to conclude that the two cases represent a kind of life with no apparent plan or goal to pursue, a life drifting with the tide. However, some essential characteristics across these cases make these decision-makers more than mere drifters.

First of all, they have an accurate grasp of, and routinely examine, the resources at their disposal at the decision-making junctures. Second, they do speculate about the gains that certain actions may bring about, but those are the gains that have left no mark in their actual life. Speculations remain speculations. The medical staff might have given the young parents a broad idea about the improvements in their daughter's health. But the parents saw no proof of the gains (the improvements) as they moved up the ladder of medical examinations and treatments. The land millionaire had the asset – the seldom-used house – sitting vacant. Yet, the house is not the *surplus* asset that his conscious effort at investment has produced. He had no proof in his life that an investment effort in the past brought about its expected return. The house is more a coincidence alongside his efforts to navigate through the post-*Doi Moi* changes.

These are decision-makers under conditions of incomplete information, as the rational choice theorists may put it. Some of the professionals share this diagnostic view as they often stress: "We need to educate them". This diagnostic view breathes life into the efforts to enrich the information about the "gains" from a specific action and to help the decision-makers increase their receptivity to the gains and their awareness of the increasing cost of ignoring the "gains". A genetic consulting effort at warning against the possibility of birth abnormalities, which we have referred to in Chapter 3, may be a case in point.

These efforts, however, gloss over the significance of the information that these farmers have. In the absence of necessary information about the "gains" that a certain action may produce, what the farmers know and have come to know become a powerful force swaying their decisions. The young parents know that their past health-motivated moves came up short of the expected gains. Their actions were not rewarded with the expected gains. The information sticks in their minds: they witnessed failure in the efficacy test of their actions. The failed test of the health-motivated action's efficacy, in turn, shifted their attention to the accompanying cost of the actions they took.

The case of the land millionaire may offer the opposite development, i.e., for better. But the implications are the same: the swaying power of a successful efficacy test of their action. They have built the current status of the household by seizing the opportunities as far as the resources at their disposal permitted. The family has had very little sense of investment – calculations of the cost from the perspective of uncertain gains – in their winding, but upward, move in building their wealth. The seldom-used second house is "for the savings", the millionaire says. However, he has not checked the market nor sent out feelers for possible buyers so he could have some basis for speculating on its market value. If anything, parting with that house is a "loss" to his existing assets.

These two cases representing the farmers, the AO families included, illustrate the individuals as decision-makers in action. They act only when calculating that the cost, a logical response to any risk-cum-uncertainty, is "neither frightening nor mysterious",[3] to borrow Herbert Simon's apt characterization of a decision-maker under the conditions of incomplete information. Simon's characterization may leave a strong impression that it gives a lot of weight to the subjective impression – frightening or mysterious – influencing a decision-maker. As such, it may sound justifiable to presume that there is an infinite variation in people's, the farmers', behaviour, leading to a refusal to give an explanation.

His characterization, however, also draws our attention to the decision-makers at the decision-making junctures. We see them as not inspired by the result of an action that consumes a period of time and resources, while its consequence remains largely uncertain except in the script prepared by the designer-promoter of the action. The psychologist-cum-behavioural economist Daniel Kahneman offers a point of departure for this shift in our interpretations of the farmers' behaviour.

Making sense: loss aversion

We start with a now well-known position. One has to choose between one of two alternatives.

A: 80% chance to win $100 and 20% chance to win $10
B: $80 for certain

If one chooses A over B, the loss of $80 is assured. A has a possibility of a larger gain but remains merely a possibility even with the assured $20 minimizing the damage when $100 is not achieved. Even an expected utility theorist would go for B, and would offer the explanation that choice B is perfectly rational as it is guided by a promised utility – going after an assured outcome that is larger than the assured minimum of $20 for A. B is a choice of avoiding risk (risk aversion). One point whose significance we may lose sight of is the *assured* $80. The $80 becomes an endowment for the decision-maker the minute it is assured. It ceases to be the measurement of a gain. It has become the yardstick against which the decision-maker measures losses and gains. Kahneman and others call it a "reference point". What if all the alternatives are bad?

A: A certain loss of $900
B: 90% chance of losing $1,000

An expected utilitarian expects everyone to go for A because of the assured *smaller* loss. Yet he is oblivious to an important human trait: the certain loss of a large sum of $900 runs deeper, prompting people to develop some ways (or *any* way) of averting the loss – loss aversion. Many in the experiment opted to make a risk choice – gambling on B. As Kahneman concludes, "[w]here a certain loss is compared to a larger loss that is merely probable, diminishing sensitivity causes risk-seeking".[4] These two cases highlight the prominence of our inclination towards loss aversion with regard to both risk aversion and risk-taking.

We also need to note how this prominence works *at* the decision-making junctures. With this "loss aversion", we have a shift from viewing people responding to the promised value of an action to viewing people responding to a delicate calculation between gains and losses accruing on taking the prescribed action. Kahneman observes that human beings are "guided by the immediate emotional impact of gains and losses, not by long-term prospects of wealth and global utility".[5] In fact, this sensitivity to "losses" may be more potent than an expected utilitarian wishes to believe. On capturing decision-makers over a longer span of time, Nassim Taleb has this to offer: "People tend to be sensitive to the presence or absence of a given stimulus rather than its magnitude. This implies that *a loss is first perceived as just a loss, with further implications later*". With this, Taleb presents what we know only unconsciously: "the agent [human being] would prefer the number of losses to be low and the number of gains to be high, rather than optimizing the total performance".[6]

A little more on how decision-makers work at the decision-making junctures and how that perspective is elusive to many of us: we usually evaluate a loss and a gain exclusively based on the cost-benefit calculation. We are often utilitarian theorists: we evaluate the utility of a gain by comparing its two states. Here is an example involving wealth. The utility of an increase of $50 to the current wealth of $500 is the difference between the utility of $500 and that of $550. By the same token, the utility of a loss of $50 to the current wealth of $500 is again the difference between the utility of $500 and that of $450. We casually assume that an increase of $50 and a loss of $50 only differ in the signs, + and –. Anyone's reference point easily suggests where the *optimized* wealth is, as guiding a choice. Kahneman adds, "Possible differences between gains and losses were neither expected or studied".[7] Within this frame of mind, there is nothing clouding our conclusion about which choice to make, provided that we have "a complete and consistent system of [choices]", as Simon might warn.

Kahneman shows that "the decision weights that people assign to outcomes are not identical to the probabilities of these outcomes".[8] Note here in the table below that both figures increase, but the increase in the decision weight is not proportionate to that in the probability (Table 7.1).

The decision weights are identical to the corresponding probabilities between the two extremes: 0 and 100. The decision weights are smaller as the probability gets closer to 0. Kahneman calls it the "possibility effect". It is easy to see that unlikely events carry smaller weight in influencing our thinking. It is a reminder of Taleb's *Black Swan*. The opposite is also true. A higher probability generates a larger weight swaying the decision-maker to make the choice. Kahneman calls it the "certainty effect", which can help explain the preference for *assured* outcomes. Caught between these two extremes, our motivation to take an action is not as finely tuned as a precision tool. "The combination of the certainty effect and possibility effects at the two ends of the probability scale is inevitably accompanied by *inadequate sensitivity* to intermediate probabilities [5%–95%]" (italics added).[9] Note also the obvious inclination to take the probability seriously when

Table 7.1 Kahneman's Decision Weights

Probability (%)	*0*	*1*	*2*	*5*	*10*	*20*	*50*	*80*	*90*	*95*	*98*	*99*	*100*
Decision weight	0	5.5	8.1	13.2	18.6	26.1	42.1	60.1	71.2	79.3	87.1	91.2	100

Source: Kahneman, op. cit., pp. 315.

it approaches zero, giving more weight not to act. The calculation at work makes the decision-makers more conscious of the cost than the benefit. Here, the behavioural economist's two factors are at work in swaying the decision-maker: the *reference point* that is derived from the decision-maker's understanding of what is in his or her possession (*the endowment effect*).

The figure below summarizes Kahneman's cost-benefit calculation of an act where a decision-maker responds more sharply to losses (endowment effect). The attention to the effect of changes in one's endowment allows us to explain people's behaviour, which appears to be infinitely various. We see that people do not respond the same way to a gain of $100 and a loss of $100. An increase of $100 results in an increase of one utility unit but a similar loss results in a loss of up to four utility units. This makes the curved line in the losses area much steeper than that in the gains area (Figure 7.1).

Against this frame of observation, Phu Cat farmers' behaviour now appears to follow a pattern. Kahneman's observation helps our efforts to reconstruct the farmers' behaviour: "Being poor [...] is living below one's reference point [...] Small amounts of money that they receive are therefore perceived as a *reduced loss*, not as *a gain*" (italics added).[10] It is debatable whether the majority of the farmers in Phu Cat are poor. It does matter whether or not they consider themselves poor, i.e., they consider themselves in the "loss" so that they see even small gains as merely reduced losses.[11] If we translate this "poor" to mean "want", then we may have an explanation as to why AO families' try to have more child(ren).

Losses as they see them: the Agent Orange victims' families

The group of families of the children with AO-induced physical and mental disabilities have already experienced the negative impacts of exposure to pesticides

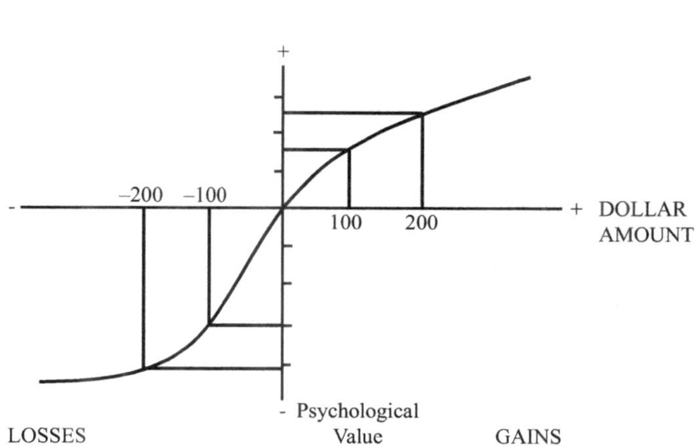

Figure 7.1 Diminishing Sensitivity for Gains and Losses in Prospect Theory.
Source: Kahneman, op. cit., p. 283.

and/or AO. In facing the decision of whether or not they should have more children after the first disabled child, they are similar to those who have gone through a massive evacuation campaign away from an active volcano that has been dormant for a long time, facing a high risk of another eruption. One experience of a Black Swan – the child with birth abnormalities – could discredit their own belief that this "rare event" will never happen to them again. Risk aversion is expected to be the rational, and also the only, choice for these families.

However, there are more cases where the parents deviated from the utilitarian expectation of the health experts. The medical professionals see their reproductive activities as no more than risk-taking, and the parents are ignorant of their prescriptions. The preceding efforts at reconstruction of the farmers as decision-makers force us to reconsider the power of utilitarian expectation.

The deviation suggests different perspectives in the parents' decision-making as they face a choice with grave consequences. Ralph Hertwig and his colleagues[12] warn that different kinds of information may lead those who would otherwise follow a similar course of action to often stand at odds with one another. This certainly is the case for the AO parents and the medical specialists. Whether or not the latter's information is squarely based on scientific research and findings may not matter that much. The parents are more inclined to decide based on the information they themselves have obtained through their "experiences". The experiences, regardless of how the parents interpret them, are a powerful resource on which they rely for navigating their decision-making. With this in mind, we go through another round of reconstruction of the AO families' behaviour.

To the doctors or health experts, with over 2,000 cases of AO victims in the community, having a disabled child is not a "rare event". They offer and push the choice that eliminates any chance of the families' having a child with physical and mental disabilities. An acceptable compromise for the medical doctors and the parents is the insistence upon the use of every possible measure of contraception. Further along the line of compromise, from the medical perspective, is an ultrasound examination to detect any sign of abnormal births during the pregnancy so that they can have a timely abortion. This progression in compromise is still within the ***risk aversion*** mode of reasoning. The reference point of these doctors suggests two opposing results: a disabled child on the one hand, and a healthy child and/or no child on the other, as shown in Figure 7.2. The former is a "loss", and the latter is a "gain", as far as the medical doctors are concerned.

To the AO families with a disabled child(ren), their desire to have more children is informed by a growing hope of having a healthy child after having

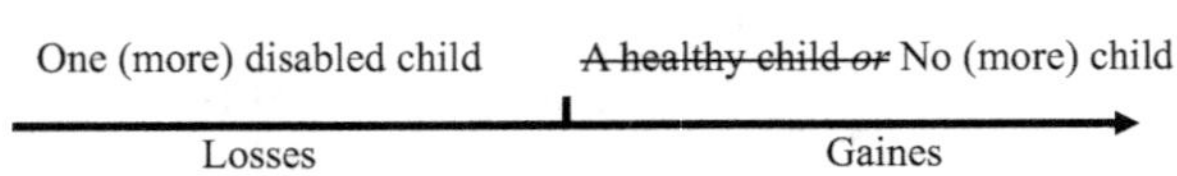

Figure 7.2 Health Experts' Losses and Gains.

experienced the loss of a healthy child, i.e., a child with congenital deficiencies; the social pressure from the living environment where having a few children is still the norm; pressure to pursue a son; and even simply an acceptance of the three expected utilities of having a child in normal families – Leibenstein's entertainment, labour, and security.

Here is another observation from our visit to one family, that of Thao, in September 2010: another child, a six-year-old daughter, was born soon after the parents had told us that they were not planning to have any more children. "It was an accident", said the mother referring to Tao's younger sister. She didn't forget to add quickly: "It turned out to be a blessing because she can keep an eye on her [older] sister when we have to go out". A 6-year-old girl taking care of her 12-year-old disabled sister was a difficult sight but it was obvious that Thao was much more animated than the first time we saw her in 2005. Having a disabled child in the family, without any access to rehabilitation facilities, brings some of the parents close to tears with one particular concern: "who will take care of my child when we are gone?" Having a healthy sibling for a disabled child is a great relief for a family that already has one or two disabled children. Trying to have another child, against the likelihood of another disabled child, is a natural desire to the point that "why" is not the question in their mind but rather "why not".

Borrowing Kahneman's definition of the poor as those always "in the losses", their efforts are first and foremost to reduce those "losses". In other words, the parents may wish to have more children *because*, and not despite, the fact that, they already have a disabled child or two. Their wish is not necessarily aimed at a gain but at reducing the "loss".

That underlying wish of the AO parents sets them further apart from the medical professionals. The latter's reference point makes the action leading to "no child" indisputable. On the other hand, the AO parents' reference point and their intimate experiences around them give them a choice of a somewhat more complex loss-and-gain pairings. A desire to compensate for the lost child (disabled child) is just as, or even more, powerful. The observations of other families living in the *same* environment and still doing well make them *under*value the possibility of having another disabled child. Finally, there is nothing discrediting the belief that a "rare event" (bad luck) is unlikely to knock on their door twice.

They are *less preoccupied* with the "disabled" and "healthy" distinction than with another between "having" and "not having" a child at all. The medical professionals' prescribed choice is no prescription for the parents who cannot afford to underestimate even the smallest possibility of having a healthy child. The case of the three Phu Cat mothers who refused to abort illustrates the strength of the desire to have a child. They are among the mothers who are diagnosed as having more than an 80% chance of having an abnormal birth, including stillbirth.[13] To use Kahneman's language, the desire is so strong that the possibility effect outweighs the certainty effect. Figure 7.3 shows how the AO families see "losses".

The burden of having a disabled child, of course, follows the parents. It is not a burden, however, that the parents willingly attribute to their effort to have a child. Nor is it a burden accompanying any efforts to undo the previous misfortune.

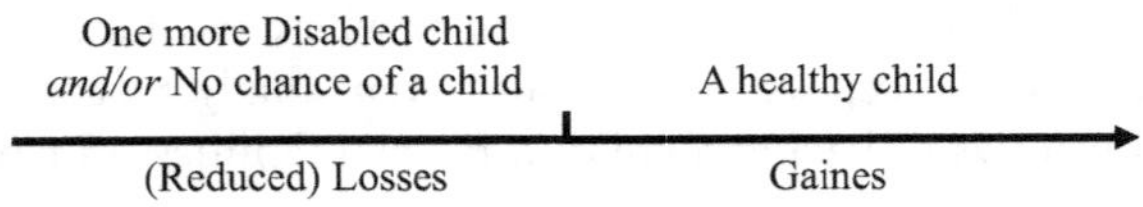

Figure 7.3 AO Families' Losses and Gains.

It is a burden that accompanies the efforts of parents and the remaining family members to make it "unproblematic", or in Kahneman's language, reducing the "losses"[14] in their life. Sensitivity to the loss (loss aversion mode of thinking) continues to rule the AO families' behaviour over the receptivity to the gains prescribed by the medical professionals.

For instance, the AO families rarely make use of District Health Centres and Commune Clinics. When they do, their visits are not really aimed at achieving improvements in their disabled children's conditions. Their reference point for any health-related action is clearly defined by the repeated statement by the medical professionals: "Agent Orange? No cure". In their mind, they are *poor* in the world of health, and always in the "losses".

There is a reason for their behaviour that appears to be health-motivated. Tuyet's parents visit their Commune Clinic for her medicine. But what is that medicine for? The price tag of the unreachable $15,000 with a 50-50 chance of any significant improvement makes Tuyet's disability permanent, the possibility effect nearing zero. They say they visit the Clinic once every five or six months. The visits look more like a courtesy call to the Clinic staff, some of whom are more like their neighbours with nearly full knowledge of the family's affairs. The visit may be an investment in keeping a good rapport with the Clinic staff.

"I don't trust the district hospital". Nihn is straight to the point. He has a younger sister with Down's syndrome and mild cases of additional mental and physical deficiencies. His denunciation has come after years of looking after his disabled sister and his own family alone while his mother was trying to make ends meet in Ho Chi Minh City. His caring efforts have left no improvements in his sister's health. Nevertheless, he makes use of herbal medicine for his sister. His answer to our query reflects his motivation, which is unrelated to medical effects. He admits that giving herbal medicine to his sister makes him feel better in that he is doing something for his unfortunate sister. It is more than a self-serving act as it meets the important need to reduce "the loss" at least in Nihn's consciousness.

Throughout the years of our research in Phu Cat, we have witnessed many similar efforts by disabled children's parents and siblings. There is a lot more to what appears to be an obvious act of familial obligation to the unfortunate ones. Their act is an effort to reduce the "loss", an act that follows a choice among only bad choices.

The attempt to reconstruct the AO families' behaviour is incomplete until we locate a powerful role for a casual resort to fate, *so phan*, within the framework of their "loss aversion" mode of thinking. The word pops up too often and too casually for it to reflect anything other than a cosmetic addition to the conversation. However, when it follows the birth of a child with birth abnormalities, it becomes a target of ridicule by the medical professionals to whom there is no room for an unexplainable factor – *so phan* – to play a part. They have all the necessary correlations among the factors that support the high probability of an abnormal birth. Or the professionals join the parents when the latter utter *so phan*. The professionals are more than willing to empathize with the parents' resignation that they cannot do anything about the child's misfortune.

However, there is something else that the medical professionals, or for that matter any risk professionals with scientific findings backing them, cannot do anything about: determination of when, where, and to whom the probability turns into reality. The existence of over 2,000 cases of congenital deficiencies is hardly sufficient to "determine" who else among the others in the same living environment may meet the same misfortune. Someone who drinks heavily and smokes incessantly may live long while a jogging vegetarian may die young. Here the professionals' use of risk comes close to fate, *so phan*: when what happened in the past may happen in the future under similar conditions is beyond anyone's control. Anthony Giddens sees the irony: risk is the "substitute for fate in [the] modern period".[15]

Finally, *so phan* may be an expression of resignation to a given misfortune. It describes the AO families' and the medical professionals' understanding that nearly all birth abnormalities cannot be undone. Beyond this, the resignation carries different implications. For the medical professionals, a distinction is at least conceivable between what is and what is not possible for physical and mental disabilities, and they have their ways of coping at least with "what is possible", however remote it may be, such as sending the child to a better hospital or to a better specialist.

For the AO families, that distinction does not make sense in the first place. For them, the resignation is tantamount to abandoning the child, a decision as unlikely as seeking a $15,000 surgical operation. In other words, there are few choices left for the families other than embracing the disabled child(ren) as integral to their life. *So phan* signals to them a resolve to embrace a misfortune that cannot be undone. The least they could do is to protect the reduced "loss" from becoming larger. Nihn's and the young parents' efforts incorporate anything even faintly relevant to the disabled children as part of their routine. Their actions may not reduce the "loss", but at least they survive their efficacy tests, as the disabled children are no longer a source of pressure on them to do more.

Losses as they see them: the farmers

We make use of the preceding framework to reconstruct the behaviour of AO families to evaluate other farmers who are spared direct damages to their family members.

Doi Moi and the accompanying reforms, especially in the early 1990s, made the land available to the farmers, who were liberated from the production line of the cooperatives. The forestland, which used to belong to and be managed by the state in the Mountains, was an opportunity to test the farmers' investment curiosity and readiness. With all sorts of incentives such as government subsidies notwithstanding, not many Phu Cat farmers exhibited signs of changing behaviour. Some of the farmers in lowland Phu Cat who did not seize the opportunity inadvertently expressed their envy when calling the farmer who did "land millionaire".

A closer look shows that the land millionaire acted on an opportunity dictated by what may be close to Kahneman's "endowment effect". Mr N. V. Tom had the allocated land in his possession through the earlier land reforms. Additionally, he had worked in the Mountains through the shifting responsibility of management from the state to the local people's committee. Then, when the majority of Phu Cat farmers showed little or no interest in the forestland that the people's committee made available to the residents, Tom stayed on and kept occupying the adjacent land for only a token cost. He could do so because he did not need to relinquish the right to the allocated land he had at the foot of the Mountains in the process either.

At every decision-making juncture, the choice appeared to be between what he had accumulated (endowment or assured outcome) and the probable increase in wealth, which was unknown to him. The fact remained that any addition did not come with collateral damage to his endowments. By the same token, those with little endowment had very little "endowment effect", ***blocking*** an action leading to an untested result, as shown in the cases of Mr H. H. Gian and Mr N. N. Tien, who were just starting their lives with their newlywed spouses when the forestland became available. Staying with what little they had would have been as uncertain as trying to add more land, regardless of its productivity being unpredictable.

The use of important capital goods, agrochemicals, presents a somewhat more complex picture since the losses-gains calculation works across two different areas of concern for the farmers: wealth and health. The use of chemicals is especially important for commercial agriculture such as, in the case of Phu Cat, cashew nuts.

As we noted earlier, the Phu Cat farmers' attitude towards the use of pesticides and other toxic chemicals is, at best, lax. In purchasing and using the chemicals, they often ignore the instructions on the containers' labels, disregard appropriate protective measures, casually purchase chemicals of unidentifiable origins, and rely heavily on their admittedly well-tested instincts. Even with behaviour that may fit the "risk-averse" mode, such as the use of other people to do the chemical spraying, the sense of protection of health is not distinct. It was the availability of the labour and spraying equipment that counted and prompted the farmers to make use of them.

Health risk does not figure prominently in the minds of the farmers. The presence of a large number of AO families represents the collateral damage of the war in the distant past, and not an extreme case of chemical abuse in general. We have witnessed empty chemical bags of unknown origin even along the rice paddies and peanut farms in and around the AO families' houses. Given this, the recent and more intimate experiences among the farmers with any sign of their negative effects rarely help deepen the farmers' wariness towards such capital goods. As discussed earlier, we are inclined to understand health more easily in its absence or negative state. These regular farmers, too, tend to take being healthy more as a given than a result of health-conscious actions. Health as an endowment whose presence can be detected only when it is damaged makes the cost-benefit calculation a little more complex where health is concerned.

Two perspectives on the farmers' behaviour as decision-makers are now loosely discernible. The important criterion to evaluate their behaviour at decision-making junctures is shown in Figure 7.4 (see also Chapter 5).

The first of these, approximating an expected utilitarian position, belongs to the medical and chemicals professionals acting in their official capacities. In their supposition, if the farmers ignore the recommendations on the use of toxic chemicals, they are risking a high likelihood of health damages. These professionals assume, as their expertise dictates, that the emphasis on the damaged health alone is potent enough to the neglect of the remaining possibility that health might survive the abuse of chemicals.

They are ready to attribute the abuse to the farmers' preoccupation with maintaining or elevating production level. They may not deny the contribution of any use of chemicals to the increased productivity, i.e., the gains in wealth. But the perceived cost in health should easily overshadow any gain in wealth, they argue. They take the gains in health as unequivocal.

The second of the two perspectives is one broadly shared by the farmers. In place of the professionals' expert knowledge, the farmers have their own experiences. These experiences with the chemicals stretch from the sustained level of production to unthreatening anomalies in health, such as skin rashes, headaches, and temporal losses of appetite. For them, these are "normal" health conditions. Anything that may improve these conditions are still in the area of no gains as shown in Figure 7.4.

The presence of AO families, scattered all over the vast District, is hardly a reminder of the threat to health that the use of chemicals may generate. Even if the farmers happen to know one or two AO families in their neighbourhood, these families are just the evidence of "bad luck" that may set off sympathy. The AO families, a "rare event", have a reason(s) to be rare and stop short of even hinting that AO might be within the broader group of toxic chemicals which the farmers use routinely. In other words, the farmers' use of chemicals that appear

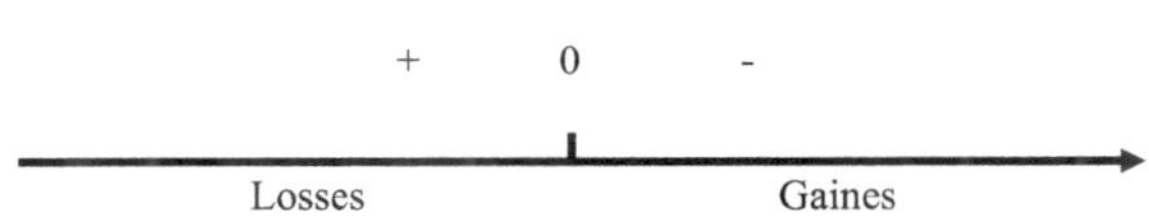

Figure 7.4 Gains and Losses in Health and Wealth.

to reflect their concern with production (gains in wealth) is an action not by their own choosing but by default. Health as an area of concern has little place in the famers' mind.

These two perspectives leave a room for one more, third, perspective, that captures the farmers' behaviour without either health or wealth consuming their attention. All these farmers have survived the constant changes in their living environment since before and after the *Doi Moi* reforms. For the older farmers, the changes they have survived extend back as far as the preunification era. Surviving these changes, which seemed to have no end, alone is the efficacy test of their chosen action. The life they have is the net result of the choices that have gone through the test of efficacy, that is, a complex of productive and reproductive activities, mutual and reciprocal observations of communal obligations, among others. A third perspective to capture the farmers' behaviour consists of what approximates Kahneman's "endowment effect" and the action that has survived waves of its efficacy test.

*Losses as they see them: Pre-*Doi Moi *farmers*

The reference point of the pre-*Doi Moi* farmers is especially difficult to locate for reasons over which the farmers had very little control. Most of the time, the government enforced the major decisions concerning the farmers' life while the farmers had very little say in them. The farmers went through waves of changes that the leaders designed and pushed, from their liberation as tenant farmers under French colonial rule to their reorganization as "workers" in a cooperative's production line. The farmers in the North, in particular, went through these changes when the war demanded that they sustain the supply of war material and manpower through the cooperative.

Reorganization as "workers" in a cooperative started soon after Japan's surrender in August 1945. But it took another ten years to have an effect, on any scale, on the farmers, especially in the North. The liberated farmers welcomed the decision at the top to organize them first into mutual-help organizations (*to doi cong*) but did so less the government's further push into "lower-level cooperatives" (*Hop Tac Xa bac thap*). Two key factors that swayed the farmers' reference point were in the offing: farmers' belief in the possession of farmland (the endowment effect) and the establishment of families as the primary promoter–protector of their own well-being.

Their less than enthusiastic reactions to the government's push to organize the farmers into low-level cooperatives came just as they were beginning to bask in their status as independent farmers. For them, the promotion of *to doi cong* was more a resumption of communal practices, with the only difference from the past being that they were no longer tenant farmers. On the other hand, the farmers would have to evaluate the impact of the move further toward *Hop Tac Xa* based on what they already had in their possession – gains or losses to their newly acquired freedom of production on their own farmland. Outright resistance was probably not among their options due to the lack of resources to sustain it. Besides, the government leaders saw no point of leaving any margin for liberal interpretations of its intent. Nevertheless, their immediate response to this move towards collective farming was far less cooperative than the government's expectations (Chapter 2).

There were a few reasons for the government to pressure the farmers to join the cooperatives in the even more rigorous form of *hop tac xa ba cao* in the closing years of the 1950s and the early years of the 1960s. The establishment of socialist rule, at least in the North, was an unmistakable goal, increasing the pressure on farmers to join the cooperative. Recovery of the war-torn economy (even in the North alone) ranked among the top priorities for the new socialist rule. Thus, the improvement of agricultural productivity by way of collective farming could well have been a stone aiming at two birds. Then, the impending preparation for the liberation of the South and the likelihood of confrontation with its protector, the United States, left little choice for the leaders other than one through which to tighten the control of the farmers. The last of these reasons helped the government to achieve a near-100% rate of organization of the farmers by the beginning of the 1960s.

The farmers were left with very little resources to resist the push towards collectivization. However, two developments moderated the inhibitive presence of the production cooperatives. One was the expansion of the cooperatives' activities into other significant areas of the farmers' lives, such as medical services and education. The cooperatives began managing the greater portion of the residents' welfare, not unlike the current version of a "people's committee". The farmers ceased to see the cooperatives as merely making use of their labour.

The other was the worsening of the war following its Americanization during 1964–1965. The increasing confrontations with the vastly superior United States and its allied forces in the South turned the cooperatives in the North into the principal vehicle for mobilizing young people to the battle front. The farmers' support for the cooperative's work now became indistinguishable from the farmers' *patriotic* support of the war efforts. The efficacy of their action – support for the war efforts – often returned, ironically, in the form of casualties among their friends, relatives, and family members. The farmers' experience of the cooperatives now overlapped with that of surviving war, which was raging not too far from their everyday lives.

These developments, however, did not leave the farmers entirely without a distinct realm of action in which their familiar reference point remained intact. The government authority, from the very beginning of collectivization moves, set aside around 5% of the cooperative land (*dat nam phan tram*) as "household plots". The farmers were to use the plot to grow whatever they deemed fit to complement their income. The psychological impact of having the household plots must have been significant as their activities in the plot would result immediately in the improvement or failure of the household economy. A high productivity on this small portion of land easily surpassing that of the remaining collective land was the reward for the farmers who exercised the cost-benefit calculation of their choice *independent* of the agricultural cooperatives.

Household plot management may well have been the precursor to "contract farming" (*khoan*) – the assignment of a product quota to a farming family while the means to achieve the quota was left entirely to the family's choosing. As mentioned in Chapter 2, a case where such autonomy was granted to the farmers was reported in a province in the North as early as 1968. If not on a cooperative scale, similar practices survived the war, and the unification of the North and South as the idea of this "contract farming" resurfaced in the years of *Doi Moi* reforms.

In sum, the behaviour of the farmers in the North before the unification and before the *Doi Moi* reforms exhibited a choice aimed at protecting, or at least minimizing the damage to, what they believed was inherently theirs – autonomy in managing the household economy and, more broadly, the family's well-being. Their behaviour can best be characterized as one of loss aversion.

Changes for enduring farmers

Farmers have exhibited a remarkable consistency, especially at the junctures where their decisions counted most for them. This consistency still escapes the watchful eyes of professionals with various expertise, including some of the professional cooperative managers. The professionals tend to evaluate the end results of the farmers' behaviour. The fact that there was no significant attrition among the farmers from the agricultural cooperatives in the North is evidence that the merits of the collective mode of production motivated the farmers to stay committed to the cooperatives. The same cooperative's manager rarely speculated about the possibility that the farmers may have stayed in the cooperatives for merits that may have lain elsewhere: the assurance of the family-centred production within the small 5% of land. Similarly, preoccupied with the very utility that their choice of action promises, the professionals look down on the AO families' behaviour, especially those with multiple birth abnormalities, as the failure to achieve that utility. The medical professionals conclude that there are no grounds on which birth abnormalities are acceptable. They are blinded to the alternative to a disabled child(ren), i.e., the possibility of a healthy child that never leaves the parents' mind.

The consistency in the farmers' behaviour is the product of their cost-benefit calculation where they view one action, first and foremost, from its burden (loss or cost) that it levies on the very basis of their life. Their choice of one action over others is attributable to Kahneman's endowment effect, winning over the speculation of a delayed effect of the action prescribed by the professionals.

The professionals are faulted not on defending their choice but on underestimating the worth of the farmers' reaction, and how it is shaped, in the face of alternatives pushing them to choose. Indeed, the farmers' life often exhibits no signs of improvement and may even remain unchanged over a long time. Either way, the farmers' lives appear to be unfulfilled promises, especially in the eyes of many professionals: the farmers forsake the reachable goal. The unfulfilled promise, however, is that of the professionals, not of the farmers. The lack of attention to the farmers at their decision-making junctures makes many of the professionals unsuccessful at selling their product (their choice of action).

The attention paid to the decisions at the juncture of their making uncovers the developments or factors that any effort to lure the farmers into a preferred action cannot ignore. The attention is vital for both the farmers and the professionals as both task themselves to change whenever the necessity to do so arises.

The first point to note that the attention to the decision at its making helps illuminate is the weight of the experiential knowledge of past accomplishment and failure. Tuyet's parents followed the steps that the medical staff suggested that they should pursue. The experience of pursuing the steps is the accumulation of greater disappointment and that the disappointment stays close to any health-conscious behaviour. In the broadest sense of the term, the endowment effect (including negative endowment = bitter lessons) comes to life at the very time of decision-making. Second, given the endowment effect, the decision-makers are most sensitive to the limitation of the resources at their disposal, facing a set of alternatives to solve a problem. The utility of the action fades in the mind of the decision-maker as he or she simultaneously calculates the cost of that action cutting into the resources necessary to cope with other problems or issues of his or her life. Third, the awareness of the cost accompanying any course of action alerts the decision-maker to the availability of any supplemental resources that may moderate the weight of the endowment effect. Finally, with very few exceptions, the fact remains that the farmers have survived the constant changes in the living environment over the generations. That is a powerful factor leading the farmers to act as though they were acting against their better judgment, or they were ignoring the need to act.

The revelation of these developments in the farmers by no means implies that they are reluctant to change. On the contrary, it reveals how the farmers endure the temptations to deviate from the dictates of experiential knowledge. It illuminates the conditions under which the farmers interpret what is and is not conceivable given the resources at their disposal and their past experiences.

The remaining task is to examine the formation of an action as inspired by the result of the previous action, and not by the promises of a "good result", which usually remain in the decision-makers' imagination or wishful thinking.

Notes

1 Hansson, *op. cit.*, p. 12.
2 Rosenstock, *op. cit.*, p. 299.
3 For Herbert Simon's observations, see en. 7 of Introductory Chapter.
4 *Ibid.*, 2011, p. 285.
5 *Ibid.*, pp. 286–7.
6 Nassim Taleb, *Fooled by Randomness: The Hidden Role of Chance in Life and in the Markets*, New York, Random House, 2004, p. 111.
7 Kahneman, 2011, *op. cit.*, p. 279.
8 *Ibid.*, p. 312.
9 *Ibid.*, p. 315.
10 *Ibid.*, p. 298.

11 *Ibid.*
12 Ralph Hertwig et al., "Decisions From Experience and the Effect of Rare Events in Risk Choice", *Psychological Science*, Vol. 15, No. 8, 2004, pp. 534–9.
13 Phan, *mimeo*, *op. cit.*
14 Kahneman, *op. cit.*, p. 298.
15 Giddens, *op. cit.*, 1999.

8 Seed for action, seed for change

The farmers are slow in reacting to the instruction or recommendation for actions by various professionals. They prefer to either ignore the instruction or to observe their way of doing things stubbornly. The promoters of the instruction, be they cooperative managers, medical professionals, or agrochemical specialists, resign themselves to their view of the farmers that they are ignorant or that they need to be educated. Some farmers rightly deserve these characterizations. More than once, we came across a narrow path between the rice paddies littered with empty pesticide bags with Chinese characters listing their contents. We doubted if the farmers, or whoever used the chemicals, could read the labels. Due to such scenery, we often suspected that the farmers were ill-informed about the contents and their proper use. The use of a mosquito net in the field sounded to us almost like a joke. The net had been soaked in the chemical, which was supposedly in use for malaria prevention in the highlands. "It works like a miracle" was the response, with very little concern over the health risk for the user (Chapter 4). Often, medical or any other specialists are not the only ones who encounter many flabbergasting scenes.

These characterizations, however, overlook one crucial point in the professionals' appeal enticing the farmers to act in the way they recommend. The appeal is usually oblivious to the importance to its audience of the presence of the intervening period for its recommended action to produce its effects. The slow reaction by the farmers is a reaction to the unknown effect of the prescribed choice, which leaves a large margin for the farmers to count more on what they *already* know in place of the appeal. In other words, the sub-textual message by the professionals to educate or enlighten the farmers, unilateral empowerment, also falls on deaf ears in a manner much like the professionals' appeal itself does.

The gap between the farmers and the professionals is not solely the result of the former's lack of education or intelligence. Both, after all, are knowledgeable: the former with the practical knowledge tested through the changing living environment and the latter with the knowledge through formal education, training, and practice in their areas of specialization.

Rather, the cause of the unbridgeable gap between the two parties lies in the very nature of the instructions and recommendations by the professionals. The professionals' instructions presuppose the broadest possible beneficiaries within the problems clearly defined by their expertise. It is the fundamental tenet of any public policy that targets the broadest possible population while minimizing the necessity to customize its use for specific cases within the targeted population. Customization of policy implementation, making it susceptible to the ever-rising cost or to the lure of nepotism, is anathema for any policy with a large population as its target. In other words, the farmers and the professionals face the not-so-uncommon barrier standing in the way of effective policy implementation.

Health, in particular, is just such a problem area of specified expertise where any policy presupposes the clearly defined beneficiaries. It is also the problem area in which the gap is widest between the ordinary people and the professionals, mainly because health, as we examined earlier, is an area where any gain is difficult to recognize and is also an area of highly specialized expertise. The distance between the ordinary people and the professionals is nearly unbridgeable. That is an area where the latter tends to see the absence of that action as a failure on the former's part. A shift in thinking is needed, away from one that emphasizes the importance only of the result of action.

There are arguments for different thinking that tolerates a broad margin of trial and error *for* the targeted population. Rosenstock, as cited before, reminds us that "health-related motives may not always give rise to health-related behaviour, and conversely health-related behaviour may not always be determined by health-related motives". That draws attention to the importance of a view that sees the accumulation of actions collectively, and even coincidentally, accomplishing a result that the professionals consider is their projected goal (utility). The specific reasons for individual actions may matter less.

Rosenstock's view has much broader implications beyond the area of health. For the sake of clarity, we stay with health as the primary focus. The first thing is to establish the nature of the distance that formal health policy sets itself apart from its beneficiaries.

Health: paternalistic and public responsibility

The state is the ultimate authority responsible for delivering the necessary services for the health of the nation. The exercise of that authority is tailored to provide these services on an equal basis at least within the population in a specific expertise problem area. An example of this equality principle among the policy's broadest beneficiaries is the preventive health policies against lifestyle-induced diseases ranging from the physical education and annual physical check-ups at schools to the annual regular physical check-ups that municipal governments require residents to observe. There is a paternalistic strain in this kind of health policy as the authority, in a father's or mother's role, prepares a wide range of services where there is no discrimination among their children; the authority, like the usual parents, expects the children (the residents) to act responsibly in receiving the benefits while the children receive at least similar benefits. The more thorough the services become, the broader the net of services becomes, and the less weight of responsibility to choose or not to choose remains with their beneficiaries. The differences among the beneficiaries vary only to the extent to which they are willing to receive the benefits. The burden on the authority's purse, of course, is proportionate to the extent of the services.

The case of Vietnam follows the turns expected of a developing nation, with some unique ones. Up to the mid-1980s, the state of Vietnam played this crucial role in providing health services to its population. It was along the lines of the "collectivist" ideal. In post-unification Vietnam, as in the pre-unification North, the agricultural cooperatives took upon the principal role in rural Vietnam of "financing the activities of commune-level health workers, while medicine, materials, and labour were allocated through the planned economy".[1] The collapse of the planned economy by the end of the 1980s decimated the foundation of the state-financed health system. Since then, the burden of health management has gradually shifted from the state to households,[2] in much the same way as the households surged as the independent and dominant players in production.

In 1989, the government introduced user fees (Decision No. 45), which "formally permitted the 'collection of partial expenses' in public clinics and hospitals".[3] This decision marked the beginning of the system where the government prepares the services while their beneficiaries have the choice of whether to make or not to make use of them, at a cost.

Since the closing years of the 1980s, with the economic recovery and improvement, Vietnam has also invested more in the health management system. The most noted effort is the development of a system of safety nets "to protect certain segments of the population from the vagaries of a marketized health system". The targets of these safety nets (health-care fee exemption and reductions) have been gradually expanded to cover the disadvantaged, the poor, children under five, and members of certain political "priority groups" (contributors to the War of Independence and Unification such as certain veterans, mothers of certain fallen soldiers, and their children and orphans).[4]

The paternalistic strain is most apparent in this notion of the "priority" group. The 2005 Ordinance on Preferential Treatment for Persons with Meritorious Activities in Assisting the Revolution classified its beneficiaries into 12 groups in two categories: the contributors to the whole process of independence and unification; and their immediate family members.[5] It aimed at once to secure a whole group of beneficiaries and customize the services within the group. The Law on Persons with Disabilities in 2010 upgraded the contents of the services by including improvements in the parametric conditions for the disabled such as education, vocational training, promotion of employment, among others.[6]

Compared with other countries at similar or higher stages of economic development in the region such as Laos, Cambodia, Philippines, Thailand, Indonesia, and China, Vietnam does well in terms of total health expenditure (7.2% of GDP in 2008).[7] During the period 1998–2008, the annual growth rate of the increase in total health expenditure reached 9.8%, surpassing that of GDP, which was 7.2%.[8] During the first round of our research, Vietnam was in the midst of rapid growth in per capita health expenditure – approximately quadrupling the less than $20 per capita spending in 1999 to reach $66 in 2008.[9]

However, the spending by the state on public health did not increase as a proportion of GDP (0.9% in 2005), while state expenditures increased in other social policy areas such as education (3.5%, 2005).[10] On the other hand, the out-of-pocket (OOP) health spending of households also increased and accounted for the biggest share of the total health expenditures (55.5%) in 2007, and there was not much change as it showed over 50% in 2015. The spending from the government purse (at the central level, 3.7% and provincial level, 6.3%) remained a distant second. Social health insurance contributed 14.2% of total health spending as of 2007 (Table 8.1).

How this overall health-relevant environment appears to the Vietnamese is best captured by the low rate of insurance coverage, 65% of the population as of 2013 and 89% as 2019, even though the official target was 100% coverage by 2014. There is no record of improvement in OOP spending. The low rate of insurance users among the Vietnamese and high rate of out-of-pocket spending are part of a vicious circle that traps the health-conscious moves among the population.[11]

One direction of the vicious circle linking the two may go as follows. There is an immensely complex procedure involved in the use of public hospitals where the users can use health insurance, and there are only a few private hospitals that accept the insurance. The cumbersome procedure and the limited availability of medical establishment keep the potential insurance beneficiaries away from making use of any medical establishment. Consequently, the potential beneficiaries prolong their hospital visit as long as possible, leading them eventually to rely on their own out-of-pocket spending when a hospital visit becomes the last resort. The out-of-pocket reliance deprives the potential beneficiaries of the opportunity to test the efficacy of their health-conscious behaviour, including signing up to, or purchasing, health insurance.

This vicious circle hits low-income families the hardest. Alerted by the plight of poor families not covered by any form of insurance, the World Health Organization characterizes the plight of these families as being hit by "catastrophic spending", which is:

> ...when people have to pay fees or co-payments for health care, the amount can be so high in relation to income that it results in "financial catastrophe"

Table 8.1 Sources of Total Health Expenditure in 2007

Sources of Total Health Spending as of 2007	*(%)*
Out-of-pocket	55.5
Provincial government budget	19.0
Social health insurance	14.2
Central government budget	3.7
ODA	1.3
Other private spending	6.3

Source: Tran Van Tien et al., "A Health Financing Review of Vietnam: With a Focus on Social Health Insurance", WHO (2011), www.who.int/health_financing/documents/oasis_f_11-vietnam.pdf, p. 10.

> for the individual or the household. Such high expenditure can mean that people have to cut down on necessities such as food and clothing, or are unable to pay for their children's education. Every year, approximately 44 million households, or more than 150 million individuals, throughout the world face catastrophic expenditure, and about 25 million households or more than 100 million individuals are pushed into poverty by the need to pay for services.[12]

The same report also points out that few households face catastrophic spending where OOP spending is less than 15% of the total health spending.[13] The point is clear that the promotion of some form of safety net, including public health insurance, is needed. Short of the financial resources, efforts are needed to make people aware that the higher cost and heavier burden on them follow their earlier neglect of health-conscious moves.

Another direction of the vicious circle linking the two – the high OOP rate and the low insurance coverage – has this look: (1) the uninsured people have far fewer opportunities to test the efficacy of hospital visits; (2) even a very few visits relying on the out-of-pocket payment easily cuts into their thinning purse, turning any thought of another hospital visit or of any use of medical facilities into a reminder of mostly its cost; and (3) back to the beginning where people have few, if any, opportunities to test the efficacy of hospital visits or any health-motivated action.

Short of compulsory physical check-ups or insurance premium payments, there seems no place for the seeds for a desirable action to be planted other than in the very conditions that leave people with no other choices.

Local conditions can easily aggravate the difficulties in luring the potential beneficiaries to act as the service providers wish. As we discussed earlier, Phu Cat's farmers need to stop and think first about the distance they have to travel to a medical establishment with adequate facilities. For them, the time spent and opportunities invested in making use of the services are the time and opportunities lost for other equally important concerns and demands of everyday life. Generally, with little surplus resources, the endowment effect is already prohibitive. The farmers may not be entirely without a choice of medical services, yet the most immediate contact with a medical establishment takes place at its lowest end, the Commune Clinics. The contact may be much less demanding on their resources, but the effect of the contact itself is much less rewarding as it often means merely the first step upwards along the medical establishment, with increasingly prohibitive costs. An observation by Alan Johnson, the United Kingdom's former Health Secretary, captured the core of the problem: "[T]he causes of poor health are not so much about the choices people make but the choices that they are unable to make".[14]

Nonetheless, one thing stands out throughout the years of observation. All these farmers rarely stop doing things the way they do unless unexpected events or incidents call a moratorium on their routinized life. There is a common thread running through these farmers, including those in need of health-conscious behaviour, that keeps them going. Behavioural economists

Daniel Kahneman's, Richard Thaler's, and Cass Sunstein's observations give us a hint as to what this thread is, which is also running through all of us: "[Men] are guided by the immediate emotional impact of gains and losses...",[15] and they are most reluctant to select the choices for action "that have delayed effects...".[16] The farmers' life, in other words, is a culmination of actions where one action feeds its result back into another – i.e., actions dictated by a short-term action-appreciation tandem. The same tandem either stimulates or stifles moves towards action.

Seed for action

It is tempting to call a life dependent upon the short-term action-appreciation tandem a short-sighted one. The temptation resonates with an expected utilitarian obsession that an action is always part of a series of actions leading to an indisputable destination, *regardless* of the time lapse before reaching the destination.

The attention to the short-term action-appreciation tandem, however, is a different framework for capturing an action. It also allows us to see an action capable of achieving more than one result, or contributing to produce a result with the effects broader than one *intended* effect. There are cases where a desirable state of affairs is achieved by the accumulation of actions, while the motivation for each may have nothing to do with that state. Fastening a seat belt is one such case. Some drivers who have developed the habit of fastening their seat belt just want to ensure that the annoying warning beep will not start, or want to avoid embarrassing warning by the police or a fine for not fastening their seat belt. Neither of these has anything to do with the drastic decline in the deaths caused by traffic accidents, when the drivers begin making it a habit to fasten seat belts.

This attention to the short-term tandem is also a way of observing any action as part of a larger set of actions, dispersed among many dimensions of everyday life. It is virtually impossible for anyone to be conscious of the contribution of one of his actions to what the larger set collectively achieves. One's consciousness of the overall goal of keeping everyday life free of disruptions plays a very small role in motivating a specific action. The attention is the guard against the tendency – prevalent among the professionals of specific expertise – to assign disproportionate weight to a particular action. The end result does matter, but not as the goal that sustains a consistency in actions but as a culmination of various acts over time.

For the farmers in Vietnam, the end result is the stability of a household-centric management of everyday life. It is a culmination of actions variously managed in the constantly changing living environment: the use of a 5% "household plot" under the pressure of collectivist production, its expanded version in the form of "contract farming" following the unification, and finally the acquisition of the right to produce on their own allocated farmland since the early nineties. The inspiration to act did not originate in the distant goal of collectivist production, nor in the exploitation of a commercializing mode of agriculture. The force at work was the short-term action-appreciation tandem dispersed among many spheres of household-centred life.

The preceding observation is a defence of the short-term action-appreciation tandem. It suggests an alternative to the costly and often ineffective promotion of a policy with a relatively large and well-defined population as its potential beneficiaries. As such, it is a different way of appreciating the farmers' actions and how they have come to where they are now.

Nor does this alternative deprive the professionals of their role. On the contrary, their role remains squarely founded on the clearest grasp of a desirable state – be it higher agricultural productivity or physical resilience in the health-unfriendly environment. It instead presupposes an additional task for them – the breaking down of an entire process from the beginning to the end of an action or a series of actions into parts. Each part is small enough for an actor or a group of actors to benefit from the action-appreciation tandem.

It is an alternative to "trying to shove people *in a certain direction*" (italics added).[17] The professionals need to be aware of their vocational hazard – hastiness in making a conclusive judgement on the process at any of its points too quickly and only from the perspective of the final result of the process.

There is one intriguing series of changes in Phu Cat, which may lead eventually to the desired result with only a little interference by a specialist, while all concerned parties appeared to mind their own business. One small change, however, plays a significant role.

There is a nearly 10 km-long stretch of Route I linking Phu Cat Airport and the Ngo May section of the district. Earlier in our research, Route I was a two-lane road with broad shoulders on both sides. The road was, and is, well-travelled. There were only two traffic lights at the beginning and end of the stretch. The residents made as much use of the shoulders of the road and ignored, which was the wrong or right side. The packed side was the wrong side, and the open side was the right side to ride their motorcycles and even drive their cars. The farmers with a huge pile of various products in the baskets on their backs almost freely crossed Route I at spots of their choosing. On several occasions, we witnessed near-collisions between motorcycles going in opposite directions on one side. The farmers, with their years of experience, either patiently waited for the motorcycles to pass them from wrong directions, or skilfully wove through among the moving vehicles.

A little later, they expanded Route I to four lanes, making it that much more difficult for the farmers to cross it at whatever crossing point they chose. The drivers drove as freely as before. Soon, with the expanded road came a central divider. It is a chain of cement blocks, each of which is about 2 m long, 1 m tall, and 70–80 cm wide at the bottom. On top of each block sits a 50 cm-tall and 2 m-long duckboard-like steel panel. With this addition, drivers became more cautious about driving in the wrong direction; the farmers had a harder time crossing the road with the added burden of climbing over the divider, with a near-impossible choice of walking a long distance to either end of the stretch where the lights were. There was no choice for the farmers but to stay with the much-accustomed crossing spots.

Soon after that, our eyes caught several gaps, each about 50 cm deep and 2 m wide, cutting into the divider. There was no space at regular intervals between the gaps. Some of them were bunched up within 1 km. A few of them were more than a kilometre apart. The farmers and other residents now climb over the divider through these gaps to cross the road with a little less difficulty. The irregular intervals reflect spots on the road close to those that the farmers used to cross it long before they built the central divider. Somebody must have removed, or suggested the authority to remove, those steel panels atop the cement blocks. The farmers' road-crossing is now better regulated as they choose their spot within a much-narrowed stretch (between where they are and the closest gaps). Traffic safety consciousness is beginning to emerge among the residents.

There are no statistical data available concerning traffic accidents, but an argument can be made that the gaps in the central divider, which were not part of the original plan for widening the road nor for the plan for regulating traffic, helped push the farmers and the residents to make better judgements when crossing the well-travelled national road. The man-made gaps are a "nudge", in Thaler and Sunstein's parlance, a small push in the right direction.[18]

The illustration above suggests the significance of the self-restraint by the professionals and their tolerance towards certain behavioural deficiencies such as the slowness with which the farmers part with the habit. At the same time, as suggested in this example, the short-term action-appreciation tandem helps professionals of various stripes: it frees them from the temptation to make a hasty judgement of action from the perspective of their desired state of affairs that may require a long time before its achievement. More importantly, by taking the deficiencies as given, the professionals see the need for, design, and build compensatory responses in the living environment. The additional role of the professionals is to discover and predict the opportunities for a "nudge" and design these compensatory responses, without compromising their professionalism – the professionals are the "choice architects", as Thaler and Sunstein call them.

Thaler and Sunstein suggest six types of opportunities for a "nudge" to intervene in people's behaviour: Defaults, Expect error, Give feedback, Understand mappings, Structure complex choices, and Incentives.[19] They all take behavioural deficiencies as being integral to human nature, the correction of which may well be immensely time-consuming and costly.

On any busy weekday morning, an office worker rushes out to catch a commuter bus. Only a few minutes after the bus has left the bus stop, the worker realizes that he or she forgot to turn off the cooking stove boiling water in the kitchen. Carelessness or forgetfulness could easily cause a major disaster in a place like Japan, where earthquakes of various scales are nearly daily occurrences. A few seconds of panic grab the office worker and stay with him or her. But the office worker does not get off the bus and return home. The cooking stove automatically turns itself off at its main valve when it detects the emptying pot as the water evaporates. The cooking stove is designed by a "choice architect". A similar compensatory device is a fuse that goes off automatically in a house when one turns on a TV, an electric heater or two, a vacuum cleaner, or an air cleaner, while forgetting to turn off lights in rooms no one is using, all at once, pushing the use of electricity beyond the allocated capacity.

These compensatory devices are not there merely to prevent small mistakes or forgetfulness turning into a major disaster. These devices, when activated, remind ordinary people of their behavioural deficiencies. They also help ordinary people become conscious of their own missteps without the cost of significant disruptions while pursuing whatever may be the demands of the day, of the month, or the year. An additional merit of compensatory devices is the time they secure for their beneficiaries to narrow the scope of missteps or to reduce the frequency with which they commit missteps. Time for learning is a precious resource that a "nudge" or a series of "nudges" can offer.

These measures to compensate for missteps have another function: simplification of a set of choices one routinely faces. If one were to check everything between the time in one's bedroom in the morning to the time back in bed every night, the pressure of making sure that one makes the right choice at decision-making junctures would become so overwhelming that the chances of mistakes and carelessness would multiply. These devices lighten the burden of decision-making by simplifying the otherwise complex set of choices for the decision-makers. In other words, the role of the choice architects is to encourage individuals to help themselves "effortlessly" reach wherever they are headed for.

Kahneman attributes similar missteps to acquired habits. When we are too busy or lazy, or too preoccupied with something else, an instinctive or emotional response in our mind usually rules our reaction at decision junctures. He calls it the "System-1" mode of response at decision-making times. System-1 responses are faster because the decision-makers' predispositions have been shaped through similar circumstances in the past. The responses are more habitual. That contrasts with the System-2 mode of thinking, which generates slower, more deliberative, and logical responses. Missteps are likely when the System-1 mode of thinking dominates the decision-makers facing a situation demanding action. Missteps do *not* necessarily represent a wrong understanding of the situation by the decision-makers. They happen under the pressure of time. The gap between System-1 action and System-2 action appears to be huge but is not unsurmountable. Learning – be it in the classroom or in real life – occurs as one action produces a result contrary to the expectation. When the result betrays the expectation a few times, the actor begins to give a second thought before acting. Here, too, the frequency of missteps gradually declines. It is a result of a process by which the dominance of the System-1 mode of response gradually gives way to System-2, and the latter begins to modify the former in due time. More importantly, the System-1 mode of thinking, if that dominates people's behaviour, is something that the professionals need to take into consideration when promoting policies in their expertise.

Seedbed for action

Any human being is a seedbed for action. What remains for an action to become meaningful, i.e., capable of generating positive results, hinges upon the awareness that any action can be informed of the benefits it produces. The awareness does not need to belong to the actor alone, who may remain unaware of the presence of that goal, especially if it lies too far ahead in time. The awareness also embraces certain behavioural deficiencies as given, not as something that needs to be removed or corrected.

Here is a revealing example. The Cameron administration (2010–2016) in the United Kingdom installed a Behavioural Insight Team (BIT) in 2010, the first of its kind, which put the idea of "nudge" to the practical test. The overall purpose is to "generate and apply behavioural insights", its website declares, "to inform policy, improve public services, and deliver positive results for people and communities".[20]

The examples that the website offers include the case of pushing delinquent taxpayers to pay what they owe. The official notification or report circulated among the residents, including delinquent taxpayers, merely mentioned that the majority of the residents ***had already*** paid their due. The payment rate went up by a large margin. There was no mention of civic duties, nor an outright threat against the delinquent behaviour. A push, a nudge, works best when applied to the spot where people react quickly and see its result instantaneously. This is a case that makes best use of the System-1 mode of thinking.

Another case is even more illuminating. Energy-saving efforts have a clear goal to achieve. Cutting down on the use of electricity or the use of public transportation is part of those efforts. Nevertheless, these are efforts where one finds it difficult to see their contribution to the goal and thus are hardly an incentive to act accordingly. Then there was an effort enabling one to recognize one's contribution to the goal – the application-based financial aid to reinforcement and/or instalment of insulation by individual house owners. People responded very little to the financial aid, which puzzled BIT. A package was then offered with the suggestion that insulation firms would clear the attic, dispose of unwanted items, install insulation, and restore the attic to its pre-installation conditions (minus the unwanted items). The applications for financial aid tripled.[21] A push (a nudge) helped the residents to overcome the otherwise overwhelming thought of even just clearing the attic, or of the cumbersome process of selecting the right insulation firm. One act of grant application produces its effect without the applicant being bothered by the otherwise cumbersome and time-consuming moves towards the energy-saving result.

These cases, however, are illuminating in another sense. The residents in the two cases live in an environment more or less typical of a developed society with a solid history of welfare policies. Their living environment is loaded with institutions and organizations that were invented and have grown for citizens at large as their beneficiaries. They cover vast areas of services, ranging from the public transportation system to public utility management, and from public health insurance and public medical services to public schools.

The residents are not new to the workings of these institutions and organizations. They are, instead, the products of these institutions. The sense of civic duty, not entirely unlike its traditional counterpart of communal obligations, has grown out of their experiences with the workings of these institutions and organizations. In short, various services and the infrastructure for them are already in place, awaiting their use by anyone in need of them. Nudge is a little push to reach what is already available.

On the other hand, short of these services, there are few opportunities for a "nudge". The living environment has made a choice for the people already. The choices left for the people to consider often concern how to deal with that living environment itself. The living environment directly dictates people's actions, and the opportunities in it for a "nudge" intervention appear characteristically different.

A far greater responsibility falls upon the individuals at decision-making junctures, which, in turn, begets either inaction or a scramble for a quick fix for immediate results. Improving that living environment, of course, is a long-term policy goal. It is a goal that most developing societies are struggling to achieve, Vietnam included. It is under the conditions of this interim that the greater portion of the population would have to live with the dictate of the changing living environment.

An AO family in an urban environment, Thanh Khe in Da Nang, offers a glimpse of the immensely inhibitive living environment, to which they had to adapt their family life at considerable cost (Chapter 3). The parents, both of whom were office workers, had two disabled sons within a short period in 1987 and 1989. The younger of the two began showing signs of severe epilepsy four years after his birth. The symptoms – 20 or more seizures a day – were bad enough for the parents to send him to a mental hospital to stay. Four years later, in 1997, the parents risked another, which turned out to be a healthy child. However, with the husband being an office worker in a different district, the wife had no alternative but to quit her job at a People's Committee office and open a grocery shop at home. The growth of the remaining two children reduced alternatives even more. The parents asked the mother's sibling to adopt the healthy child. By this time, there were very few marks left of the family when the parents began building what seemed to them to be a normal family life.

The years 1987, 1989, and 1997 still saw precipitous changes as the post-*Doi Moi* land reforms were sweeping through Vietnam, and the United States lifted its embargo and recognized Vietnam. Contamination of the environment by the herbicide and its human consequences were the issues that occupied the minds of medical and agrochemical professionals. The 2004 lawsuit of Vietnamese AO victims was still yet to come.

When the parents made critical decisions – having two disabled children in quick succession, having a third child, and sending the second disabled child to the hospital – there were few opportunities for anyone to intervene with a set of alternatives. The parents were *solely* responsible for the consequences of their decisions. It was merely fortuitous that the mother's brother's children were already grown-ups when he took in the youngest from his sister.

The case of the Thanh Khe parents, however, does not represent all people in transitional Vietnam. A living environment without any public services is a rarity. First of all, when there are public services available, however limited they might be, they open up opportunities for nudge intervention. One of the services that were installed relatively early in the *Doi Moi* reform years is the Plant Protection Centre, a local branch of the Ministry of Agriculture and Rural Development (MARD). The purposes of the Centre are the quality control and distribution of seeds and seedlings, and the procurement and distribution of WHO-sanctioned agrochemicals.

"Oh [the farmers] have no choice", the director of the local Plant Protection Centre testified, "they have to buy the chemicals we recommend when they buy the seeds" (September 2009). Access to legitimate agrochemicals is packaged with the distribution system of a whole set of agriculture-related goods.

The effect is uncanny. The farmers go to the Plant Protection Centre to purchase seedlings and seeds and return home with them *and* the recommended chemicals. They are freed from the pressure of choosing the right chemicals. If they are far from the Centre, they purchase chemicals of the same brands at other retail shops.

The case of H. H. Gian (Chapter 4) uncovers a wide range of effects from the act of purchasing the seedlings at the Centre. He used to rely on chemicals of unknown origin in China and of unknown quality at retail shops. He could not read the Chinese written all over the packages. He began to doubt the effectiveness of the chemicals of unknown origin, and around the same time, the retail shops he used to rely on were closed.

Mr Gian is one of a few with a memory of the unknown substance he picked up in the Mountains. He had a frightening experience with the toxic substance when he threw it in the lake and saw hundreds of dead fish. However, the fear of toxic chemicals played little role in his shift to using the Plant Protection Centre. He chose the Centre and its package of goods, including the recommended chemicals, by default. Packaging the recommended chemicals *is* the nudge, a reminder of the packaged deal for installing insulation in the United Kingdom.

Second, the poverty of social and other services in the living environment still does not leave the residents entirely at its whim. As we have observed, the AO families in Phu Cat manage to keep their life afloat, which hints at the presence of some form of "services" installed in the living environment.

After the initial shock of having their newborn babies diagnosed as being struck by "incurable" disabilities had subsided, most of the AO families settled back to their routines as farmers. They allocate special time for their disabled children before reaching the point of altering their life as they know it. For the urban AO families, nearly all of whom rely on their monthly payment as office workers, having disabled children has a more disruptive impact on their life as one or both parents often need to stop working. By contrast, the rural AO families work in the rice paddies and other fields for other produce. Rice production consumes much of their time since Phu Cat usually has a twice-a-year harvesting schedule. At high-production times, they become part of the mutual-help network in the community, which aims for maximum use of its labour force.

They allocate any surplus time to raising pigs and chickens, growing vegetables for family consumption, opening a small grocery shop in front of the house, and making leaf hats for a fraction of cash earnings, herding cows, and collecting firewood. During the off season, away from the fields, some of them even travel to distant places for additional cash earnings. Seeking seasonal employment is an additional alternative to the routine but is usually limited for the Phu Cat farmers as they have less time off from the paddies because of the rice harvesting twice a year. They all calculate the help, time, and other resources at their disposal to meet the demands of their life. The demands may change as some may fall ill unexpectedly, or as children grow to school age. They always count on the help (among other resources) offered among themselves.

An unmarried woman adopted a child, Binh, with disabilities from another unmarried woman who had another disabled child, Mai (introduction). Binh's adopted mother grows rice in the rainy season (the beginning of summer) on her allocated land and auction land. In the off season, until recently, she had left Binh with her neighbours and gone to Dak Lak (a coffee plantation centre in the central highland, 150 km south of Phu Cat) to work as a hired labourer in a coffee plantation for two months. Three or four women in her neighbourhood kept coming by to cook for Binh and take care of her. The mother always made sure she would be with Binh for the Tet, the Lunar New Year.

At first glance, the adoption did not make sense initially. Why adopt a girl with disabilities if she were to be left alone? On second thoughts, nothing is unusual about this "family", or the mother and the daughter. In much the same way as Ninh and Tam's mother spent years in Ho Chi Minh City to support herself, Binh's mother did everything she could to support their household. The demands of this family of two dictate the mother's behaviour and the demands are elastic with the changing employment conditions in the highland or with Binh's growth. Tam's mother relied on Ninh, Tam's brother, to look after Tam; Binh's mother relied on the neighbours and her relatives for Binh's care. The relatives and the neighbours *are* the "social service" providers – on whom Binh's mother counts for protecting her household in much the same way as the people do in a service-rich, developed society. The presence of these "informal" services is integral in rural life. Any efforts at improving social services would have to be as part of the farmer's living environment.

There is a notable, if unwitting, service that these service providers offer beyond the help for the mothers who were obviously in need of extra hands to keep their life afloat. They signalled the ***approval*** of the mothers' management of their being a "mother". A "nudge" here does not involve any distinct act. The nudge is the acquiescence by the family members, the neighbours, and the friends to these mothers' efforts to support their households in much the same way as they helped each other in the busy harvest time, in communal events such as funerals, weddings, and small gatherings commemorating full-moon occasions. They are sending the message to the mothers that it is okay to be like anyone else, *with or without* disabled children.

These observations leave a few questions that nudge strategists usually do not address. The first concerns the goal. What is a nudge for? A nudge is justified by an unquestionable goal. In the instances of successful nudge interventions in the UK mentioned above, no one questioned the legitimacy of the goal – desirable results that the nudges steer people to achieve. The goals are indisputable and are perfectly agreeable to the professionals who are given the task of overseeing, not interfering with, the steering process. In much the same way, the mothers' goal to support their households is just as agreeable to their neighbours, friends, and family members. Then, the second question: who is entitled to entertain a goal that justifies some, if not all, of the mothers' actions, especially when the necessary services such as daycare services for the disabled are woefully insufficient? These two questions, combined together, raise a fundamental question: what is the right, or wrong, goal?

The neighbours', friends', and relatives' acquiescence is a nudge. It is a small push for the mothers to pursue a goal that is *normal* to anyone else in the rural Phu Cat community. The push also suggests an important assumption on the part of these service providers about the differences between having and not having children with mental and physical deficiencies. The medical professionals consider the birth of a disabled child an irretrievable loss. These service providers consider a disabled child a "given" to be embraced in life. That position of service providers also underlies that of the parents with one or two disabled children, as we examined in Chapter 3, who did not stop wanting to have more children.

Seed for action: reversing the recipe

The gap between the professionals and the ordinary people in rural Vietnam appears to be insurmountable. The former continues to accuse the latter of being ignorant, stubborn, or uncooperative. In their eyes, the latter is irresponsible with their lives. The latter, on the other hand, respond to the push by the former with resistance or indifference as they see no immediate relevance of the recommended action to their life. The professionals stay behind their "trenches" of expertise, and the ordinary people are usually left with their counsel. There are very few opportunities for either side to narrow the gap. A meaningful contact occurs only when the contact is too late. The situation is a reminder of the medical doctors and healthy individuals. Warnings against, and recommendations for, specific actions make little inroads into those who think they are healthy, those who think their life is reasonably acceptable as it is.

This gap, however, is a seed for action to trigger changes in the routinized life. The parties on both sides of the gap recognize the limit of their routinized actions. They recognize a threshold, or a limit, when their routine action fails to produce an expected result. Farmers see the threshold when they need more than just helping hands. The recognition of the threshold may be even sharper if they need reassurance from a medical doctor that the lingering headaches or skin rashes are not an indication of anything worse than the usual reactions to the chemicals they routinely use. The medical professionals recognize their threshold when they need more refined expert knowledge when facing unfamiliar symptoms in a patient. It is a threshold, to paraphrase a public health specialist's view on health, below which the present state of well-being falls short of "satisfying the demands of life".[22]

No one is without this threshold, which is both common and unique to everyone as diverse elements contribute to the formation of each individual's threshold. Furthermore, everyone's threshold is also variable commensurate with changing physical and mental strengths, good or bad neighbourhood relationships, good or bad professional training, and exposure to the diverse lifestyles of others, among others.

The gap remains intact when the parties on both sides remain below this critical threshold, or when they refuse to recognize its presence. A failed warning for the farmers against the abuse of chemicals using a TV broadcast best illustrates the persistent gap. The farmers apparently responded by changing the TV channel carrying a warning message against the abuse of the chemicals. A medical doctor made light of that move (Chapter 6). The doctor's casual remark says more about the unchanged stance on the part of the medical profession that their responsibility ended when they prepared the warning. The farmers see no point in watching the warning, which appears to be irrelevant to the demands of their life. The inclusion of the presence of the Plant Protection Centre in the warnings would have been a small "nudge". Alternatively, a reference to exemplary farmers in their cautious use of the chemicals, like the indirect warning to delinquent taxpayers above, would have produced a more positive response. These extra messages, however, are definitely outside the medical doctors' expertise. The doctors did not see, or refused to see, their own threshold.

An effective push does not lie in louder warnings, nor in a penalty for the failure to heed the warnings. The family planning policy had cases where the penalty did not produce the expected result. The policy was launched with the specific purpose of reducing the pressure of the increasing population upon the economic growth in the closing years of the 1980s, a part of broader *Doi Moi* reforms. The residents, especially in rural Vietnam, responded by accepting a penalty (a few kilograms of rice) for a third child more as a one-time fee and continued to have more children.[23] The penalty of a few kilograms of rice might have worked only on those who were on the verge of reaching the threshold. Even for those families at the subsistence level, there are informal social services – local officials willing to turn away from their obligations to enforce the penalty. Finally, there is an unwarranted assumption on the penalty enforcer's part that having more than two children may lower the farmers' threshold.

An intriguing example is a short-lived genetic consulting effort for young couples where the concerned parties may have been on the verge of recognizing the threshold.[24] The ultimate goal, as the planners envisioned, was to reduce the incidence of birth abnormalities. The target was a group of young parents in the living environment contaminated by the wartime use of toxic chemicals. The result: among a dozen nearly 100% chances of abnormalities, two disregarded the recommendation for abortion and ended up having children with birth abnormalities.

A record of this consulting effort has not been made public. It is also easy to see that the effort itself was treading on very thin ethical ice if the abortion was recommended based on *less than* 100% chances of abnormal birth or regardless of what types the abnormalities were. These difficulties aside, the consulting effort contains the possibility of a different scenario.

The consulting process could consist of an expanded series of actions: (1) invitation to a well-defined population to a consultation; (2) suggested use of contraception, especially for the period when the pregnancy rate is high; (3) the use of ultrasound examination after the wife becomes pregnant; and (4) an offer of abortion as a choice if irregularities are detected in the foetus. One important, unintended, result of the consultation for both parties is the time invested in making the decision at each juncture. We are not sure of the total number of days or even months spent in preparing and completing the entire process. Regardless, in each of the steps from (1) to (4), the targeted couples would pause to think of the effect of the decision. The young couples may consult with their friends and relatives. The professionals, likewise, would reconsider, following step (1), for example, wondering if the threat of birth abnormality alone should suffice to lure the young couples into having a consultation, or on the timing of step (3). Each step is a precious learning opportunity for both parties.

There is, however, a significant precondition that needs to be met for each decision juncture to devote sufficient time to learning: both parties need to be unfettered by, or freed from, the pressure to reach the ultimate goal of "reducing birth abnormalities". Without this freedom, the pressure makes the medical professionals see each step merely as one stepping stone necessitating the next. Without it, the young couples do not see each of the steps as an opportunity to give thought to where their threshold lies, and to what constitutes it. It is a process that ends only when the result appears, leaving no more responsibility for the professionals to even think about. Likewise, the pressure deprives the young couples of opportunities to explore alternative ways of meeting the demands of their young life.

Facing only the message insisting on the elimination of all birth abnormalities, the choices for the young couples are entirely inhibitive, as shown below. The remaining possibility, however remote, stays in their minds as indicated by Δ in Table 8.2 below, swaying their final decisions.

Freed from the weight of the ultimate goal, the promoter and the young clients take time to reconsider all "apparent" implications of the choices at different stages of consulting, and even to contemplate alternative goals. Although their presence is not prominent as they are scattered throughout the vast Phu Cat District, there are AO families who have been meeting the demands of "family" life while making use of various *informal* social services. The question lingers on if

Table 8.2 Choices

Before the Consultation	*During the Consultation*	*Goal of the Consultation*
Promoters of the consulting services		
X Child with birth defects	X Child with birth defects	X Child with birth defects
○ no child	○ no child	○ no child
Young couples		
X Child with birth defects	X Child with birth defects	X Child with birth defects
X no child	X no child	X no child
○ a child	○ healthy child	○ healthy child
	Δ Child with or without birth defects	

○ acceptable, X not acceptable, Δ undecided.

their presence is evidence that having a disabled child terminates life as desired, or evidence that life does continue, albeit with altered demands to meet.

For the medical doctors, too, are the AO families to be used only for warning against birth abnormalities? Do the AO families not have anything else to offer? The steps in the consulting efforts are opportunities for nudge intervention. They are also opportunities to free all concerned parties from the weight of a goal that they may have rarely questioned. The beneficiaries of the freedom from an unquestionable goal are many, such as the house owners in the UK cited above. Freedom also enables actions to fulfil more goals than one, as in the case of fastening a seat belt. Action is versatile as it is capable of producing a result for more purposes than one.

In Phu Cat, as in many other places, the "birth abnormalities" are the mark of something that cannot be undone, or of an area where no one other than medical doctors with highly refined expertise is entitled to do or say anything. The vast majority of the farmers in Phu Cat see that there is nothing they can do *about* the mental and physical deficiencies. Helping the disabled children, of course, does matter to them. But they do not see any role in the *medical* treatment of disabilities. In an ironical way, they have the mindset of genetic consultants – their role ends when they see the birth of a child with disabilities. They share the resignation expressed in the oft-heard statement by clinic staff: "No cure for Agent Orange victims". The role that ended, however, is merely one role.

This resignation frees them from the impossible goal of medical solutions and redirects their attention to things they *can* do. It helps the parents of these disabled children *in spite of* the disabled children, and *not* because they can do anything about the disabled children. What they are capable of determines what they do for the AO families. Action defines its goal. They offer help to the parents in the same manner that they do with any other family in the community.

An increasing number of Phu Cat residents are finding the freedom of action unfettered by the conventional understanding of "help" for the AO victims, which they believed belonged exclusively to the medical profession's jurisdiction.

Their actions find them a goal that they can reach, and that may make a small difference to the disabled children.

"Oh that, even I can do", an owner of a stationery shop in the Ngo May section was overheard saying. He was looking over at us purchasing a large quantity of notebooks, painting books, and crayons. We were explaining to the shop worker the purpose of the purchase: the goods were for the education of the disabled children who gathered every weekend in a primary school classroom, *Lop Hoc Uoc Mo*, a Dream Class.

Another case of the freedom of action is a group of Dream Class volunteer teachers. Many of them earlier expressed their hope to us that we could offer financial support for hiring disability specialists. Some of them are still caught in the trap that anything to do with disabled children must deal with the disabilities first and foremost. With the time spent with the children, other teachers began to pay more attention to what the disabled children *could* do, replacing their earlier preoccupation with what the disabled children *could not* do. Volunteer teachers in Dream Class II in Cat Thanh now take the disabled children to roadside cafés and allow them to spend time in their broader community, beyond their home, the neighbourhood, and the class. Their presence has become much less eye-catching even for the volunteer teachers. More importantly, the teachers are also freed from their unquestionable task (goal) as the teachers of a formal school – to maintain and raise the school's performance and reputation, which is often based on the children's graduation rate.

The ring of people who are freed from their earlier view towards the disabled children has expanded to include at least some, if not all, of the AO families. Many of the parents of the Dream Classes are still trapped by their inability to do anything *about* the children's physical and mental deficiencies. They do exhibit signs of relief at the sight of their children's efforts to paint, or sing, or play with their classmates. The children remain as "handicapped" as before since their disabilities have not changed. The mother of Hanh, a girl with Down's syndrome and learning disabilities, has not changed her view towards Hanh. "Ah, but she is handicapped" was the mother's conclusive view as she watched Hanh ably serving cups of tea to visitors. Hanh being in the Dream Class is the time for the mother to be relieved from the worries about the *disabled* child. The difficulty in freeing themselves from the absolute inability to do anything *about* the disabilities is often too much and prohibitive to inspire some of the parents to do anything but bring the children to the Dream Class every weekend.

Liem's father, a war veteran on the side of the South at the close of the war, rarely connected the war and his daughter's mental and physical deficiencies. The refusal to see the connection between the war and his daughter's misfortune is still with him almost 15 years after our first visit. His first visible reaction to our frequent visits was relief at the assurance that we would not simply walk away once the research was done. The second reaction, earlier in the second round of research, was a little more involved. He felt relieved of one persistent worry about Liem after he and his wife went: "The Dream Class will look after her".

Then, more recently, he found himself relieved of the burden of futile speculation about what he could do *about* Liem's disabilities. He confided, "You know what I can do for Liem?" To our puzzled silence, he said: "I can help the Dream Class". He apparently contributes to the Dream Class, the honorarium that we occasionally offered him for his being a willing witness. He was relieved of a persistent sense of utter inability and began acting with a new goal in mind. He stopped helping Liem commute to the Dream Class.

These changes are not the token merely of the goodwill of a few. They are the product of a realization that what they are capable of doing does produce a desirable result, which satisfies the demand for a goal different from the old, impossible goal of fixing, or improving, the disabilities. They suggest an essential shift in the farmers' thinking: what they can do, and not what they should do, determines what they do. It is a reversed recipe for inspiring action – the order is reversed from a goal-induced action to an action-induced goal.

In this reversed recipe, attention to the short-term action-appreciation tandem, too, earns its rightful place in contemplating, designing, and implementing long-term policy goals. As witnessed in the use of the 5% family plot and its expanded version in the contract farming, the short-term action-appreciation tandem has much to offer in terms of enduring the constant changes in their living environment.

There are many areas of social and other public services that require long-term planning and implementation. There are many such policies, with the well-defined populations as the beneficiaries in the areas of our research concern alone. Access to better-equipped and better-manned medical services may top the list. Improvements in public safety measures are not too far down the priority list. These and other improvements in various areas of needed services require long-term planning and the allocation of scarce financial and human resources. A sub-textual message in all these long-term projects is the need for the patience: some of the needed improvements are part of the trickle-down effects that the improvement in an overall economic performance eventually produces.

There is a problem accompanying this conventional recipe – goal-induced action. It tends to make light of some of the drawbacks simply as collateral damages. The increase in agricultural productivity, a stationary argument of development economists and planners, is a case in point. As we observed earlier, the damages caused by the abuse of agrochemicals cost Vietnam the equivalent of 2% of GNP in the early 2000s. The farmers who are released from agricultural production find jobs in the cities, mostly in the informal sector. Given the technology-intensive (labour-saving) investment tendency, the informal sector will only grow to the point that aggregate data such as GNP per capita no longer conceal its grave implications.

The reversed recipe, on the other hand, releases many of the future beneficiaries from a long-term and indisputable goal, whose quality and arrival time remain unknown to most of them. Freedom from the pressure to reach that goal, in turn, alerts them to the working of the short-term action-appreciation tandem in their life. The reversed recipe offer neither an outright rejection or blind conformity with the promoters of a long-time goal follows. Instead, it encourages them to do what they can within the limit of the resources they employ to satisfy all other demands and goals of life. What they can do determines what they do even along the path towards a long-term goal. The reversed recipe for action most likely slows the progress towards one long-term goal. However, it does so with much fewer collateral damages, if any, to the resources to be employed for other goals and demands of life.

In the recent past, Vietnamese farmers did not endure the wait for the benefits that long-term policies promised to deliver. They have endured, instead, the test of their action, which has ensured the surest return on their action. Within the span of two generations since the division of Vietnam in 1954, there have been many opportunities for such a test, from the collectivization era in the North through the contract farming phase in unified Vietnam, to the family-centred life with the informal "social" services of their neighbours and friends at their disposal. The reversed recipe may suggest that the benefits for a larger population come with a slower progression towards the goal as long as its beneficiaries have the freedom to test the efficacy of their chosen action.

Notes

1 Jonathan D. London, "Reasserting the State in Vietnam: Health Care and the Logics of Market-Leninism", *Policy and Society*, No. 27, 2008, p. 117.
2 *Ibid.*, p. 115.
3 *Ibid.*, P. 117.
4 *Ibid.*, p. 121.
5 Ordinance 26/2005/PL-UBTVQH11.
6 Ordinance 51/2010/QH12.
7 World Health Organization, *World Health Statistics*, 2011, p. 134; the average total health expenditure of South-East Asia was 3.8% of GDP in 2008.
8 Tran Van Tien et al., "A Health Financing Review of Vietnam: With a Focus on Social Health Insurance", WHO (2011), p. 9, www.who.int/health_ financing/documents/oasis_f_11-vietnam.pdf.
9 *Ibid.*, p. 9.
10 London, *op. cit.*, p. 119.
11 Vietnam Health Insurance Website, News from August 13, 2013, www.baohiemxahoi.gov.vn/?u=nws&su=d&cid=397&id=7984, and *Finance Digital News* (Ministry of Finance), http://thoibaotaichinhvietnam.vn/pages/tien-te-bao-hiem/2019-06-05/ty-le-bao-phu-bao-hiem-y-te-da-dat-89-dan-so-72302.aspx
12 WHO, *Technical Briefs for Policy Makers No. 2 – Designing Health Financing System to Reduce Catastrophic Health Expenditures*, Geneva, 2005, p. 2, accessed at http://apps.who.int/iris/bitstream/10665/70005/1/WHO_EIP_HSF_PB_05.02_eng.pdf, p. 2.
13 *Ibid.*, p. 3.
14 Quoted in Dominic Upton and Katie Thirlaway, *Promoting Healthy Behaviour: Practical Guide for Nursing and Healthcare Professionals*, London, Routledge, 2010, p. 356.
15 Kahneman, *op. cit.*, p. 287.
16 Thaler and Sunstein, *op. cit.*, p. 79.
17 *Ibid.*, p. 70.
18 *Ibid.*, Chapters 4 and 5.

19 *Ibid.*, pp. 83–102. For further information on diverse "nudges", see also Chapter 19, called "Bonus Chapter: Twenty More Nudges".
20 UK Cabinet Office, www.cabinetoffice.gov.uk/behavioural-insights-team.
21 *The Economist*, March 24, 2012, www.economist.com/node/21551032, also see www.gov.uk/government/publications/fraud-error-and-debt-behavioural-insights-team-paper.
22 Bircher, *op. cit.*, p. 336.
23 There is an ironical twist in the family planning policy. Earlier, the emphasis on depressing the high growth rate uncovered people's uncanny ways of evading the penalty, which became progressively harsher against one additional child after two. The growth rate then hit an alarmingly low rate towards the closing years of the 1990s. The planning shifted its emphasis from less to more. The language for more is subtly curtailed: "Each family should fulfill the quota of two children". Resolution 21 NQ/TW (by the Sixth Plenum Party Central Committee VII) issued on October 25, 2017.
24 Correspondence and conversations with Dr Tran Duc Phan, a disciple of the late Dr Bao, first at the Vietnam Red Cross Society's Agent Orange Victims Fund and then at Hanoi Medical University in 2005 and 2006. See also Phan, *mimeo*, *op. cit.*

Bibliography

Allen, Robert, *The Dioxin War – Truth and Lies about a Perfect Poison*, London and Ann Arbor, MI: Pluto Press, 2004.

Beck, Ulrich, *Risk Society towards a New Modernity, London*, Newbury Park, CA and New Delhi: SAGE Publications, 1992.

Beck, Kenneth H., and Arthur Frankel, "A Conceptual of Threat Communications and Protective Health Behavior," *Social Psychology Quarterly*, Vol. 44, No. 3, September 1981, pp. 204–217.

Beck, Ulrich, and Elisabeth Beck-Gernsheim, *Individualization: Institutionalized Individualism and its Social and Political Consequences*, London: SAGE, 2002.

Beck, Ulrich, Anthony Giddens, and Scott Lash, *Reflexive Modernization: Politics, Tradition and Aesthetics in the Modern Social Order*, Stanford, CA: Stanford University Press, 1994.

Binh, Nguyen Thi, "An Interview by Guardian," *The Guardian*, March 29, 2003.

Binh Dinh Department of Labour, War Invalids and Social Affairs, "List of AO Victims in Binh Dinh Province," (*mimeo*) August 20, 1999.

Binh Quyen, Pham, Duc Dang Nhan, and Nguyen Van San, "Environmental Pollution in Vietnam: Analytical Estimation and Environmental Priorities," *Trends in Analytical Chemistry*, Vol. 14, No. 1, 2007, pp. 383–387.

Bircher, Johannes, "Towards a Dynamic Definition of Health and Disease," *Medicine, Health Care and Philosophy*, No. 8, Spring 2005, pp. 335–341.

Boivin, Thomas, et al., "Agent Orange Dioxin Contamination in the Environment and Human Population in the Vicinity of Da Nang Airbase, Viet Nam," unpublished paper presented at *Dioxin 2007: International Symposium*, Tokyo, September 2–7, 2007.

Buckingham, William A. Jr., *Operation Ranch Hand- Herbicides in Southeast Asia 1961–1971*, Washington, DC: Office of Air Force History, United States Air Force, 1982.

Byron, Michael, "Satisficing and Optimality," *Ethics*, Vol. 109, October 1998, pp. 67–93.

Cao Dai, Le, *Agent Orange in the Viet Nam War: History and Consequences*, Hanoi: Vietnam Red Cross Society, 2000.

———, *Memoirs of War: The Central Highlands, A North Vietnamese Journal of Life on the Ho Chi Minh Trail 1965–1973*, Hanoi: The Gioi Publishers, 2004.

Chanda, Nayan, *Brother Enemy: The War after the War*, New York: Harcourt, 1986.

Chi, Vu Le Thao, "Farmers in Developing Countries: An Inquiry into Human Insecurity of the Many," *Journal of Human Security Studies*, Vol. 1, No. 2, Summer 2012, pp. 94–108.

———, "Risks and Farmers' Behaviors in Vietnam," unpublished doctoral thesis, Keio University, 2014.

Commission of Human Security, *Human Security Now*, New York: The Commission of Human Security, 2003.

Dapice, David, "Vietnam at the Starting Point: Just Another Successful Asian Economy?" in Borje Ljunggren, ed., *The Challenge of Reform in Indochina*, Cambridge, MA: Harvard University Press, 1993, pp. 167–181.

Dasgupta, Sasumita, et al., "Pesticide Poisoning of Farm Workers: Implications of Blood Test Results from Vietnam," *World Bank Policy Research Working Paper*, no. 3624, 2005.

Duc Phan, Tran, "The Consequence of Agent Orange in Human, Some Methods Supporting Agent Orange Victims," n.d., *mimeo*.

Duc Vien, Tran, *Forestland Management Policies in Vietnam: An Overview*, Center for Agricultural Research and Ecological Studies (CARES), Hanoi University of Agriculture, n.d., www.cares.org.vn/webplus/Article/Forestland%20management%-20policies%20in%20VietNam%20An%20Overview.pdf

Duc Vien, Tran, and Pham Van Hoi, "Pesticide Uses in Agriculture: Food and Water Contamination and Health Impacts in Vietnam," unpublished paper presented at *4th workshop for Human Security at East Asia*, Keio University, Tokyo, February 25–27, 2007.

Dung, Nguyen Huu, and Tran Thi Thanh Dung, "Economic and Health Consequences of Pesticide Use in Paddy Production in the Mekong Delta, Vietnam," *Economy and Environment Program for Southeast Asia (EEPSEA) Research Report Series*, Singapore, 1999, http://idl-bnc.idrc.ca/dspace/bitstream/10625/25143/10/113557.pdf

Eckstein, Harry, "Case Study and Theory in Political Science," in Harry Eckstein, ed., *Regarding Politics: Essays on Political Theory, Stability, and Change*, Berkeley and Oxford: University of California Press, 1992, pp. 117–176.

Environmental Protection Agency (EPA), *2000–2001 Pesticide Market Estimates: Historical Data*, www.epa.gov/oppbead1/pestsales/01pestsales/historical_data2001.htm#table5_1

Fforde, Adam, and Stefan de Vylder, "Part Three: Vietnam," in Pradumna B. Rana and Naved Hamid, eds., *From Centrally Planned to Market Economies: The Asian Approach, Volume 3 Lao PDR, Myanmar and Vietnam*, Hong Kong: Oxford University Press, 1996, pp. 335–466.

Figueroa, Mark, "W. Arthur Lewis versus the Lewis Model: Agricultural or Industrial Development?" *The Manchester School*, Vol. 72, No. 6, December 2004, pp. 736–750.

Food and Agriculture Organization (FAO), *Report of the First External Review of the Systemwide Programme on Integrated Pest Management (SPI-IPM)*, Chapter 1, August 2003, www.fao.org/WAIRDOCS/TAC/Y4847E/y4847e05.htm

———, Proceedings of Asia Regional Workshop on Implementation, Monitoring and Observance. International Code of Conduct on the Distribution and Use of Pesticides, Bangkok, Thailand 26–28 July 2005 (Food and Agriculture Organization of the United nations, Regional Office for Asia and the Pacific), http://www.fao.org/3/af340e/af340e00.htm#Contents

———, *FAO Statistical Year Book*, 2004 and 2010.

Fukuyama, Francis, "The End of History?" *The National Interest*, Summer 1989, pp. 3–18.

General Statistic Office, *Socio-Economic Statistical Data of 671 Districts, Towns and Cities under the Authority of Provinces in Vietnam*, Hanoi: Statistical Publishing House, 2006.

Giddens, Anthony, *Modernity and Self-Identity: Self and Society in the Late Modern Age*, Stanford: Stanford University Press, 1991.

———, "Living in a Post-Traditional Society," in Ulrich Beck, Anthony Giddens, and Scott Lash, eds., *Reflexive Modernization: Politics, Tradition and Aesthetics in the Modern Social Order*, Cambridge: Polity Press, 1994.

———, "Runaway World," The Reith Lectures, 1999. *BBC Radio*, www.bbc.co.uk/programmes/p00ghvgj

Glewwe, Paul, "An Overview of Economic Growth and Household Welfare in Vietnam in 1990s," in Paul Glewwe, Nisha Agrawal, and David Dollar, eds., *Economic Growth, Poverty, and Household Welfare in Vietnam*, Washington, DC: The World Bank, 2004, pp. 1–26.

Glewwe, Paul, Michele Gragnolati, and Hassan Zamanet, "Who Gained from the Vietnam's Booms in the 1990s?" *Journal of Economic Development and Cultural Change*, Vol. 50, No. 4, 2002, pp. 773–792.

Graham, John D., and Jonathan Baert Wiener, eds., *Risk vs. Risk: Tradeoffs in Protecting Health and the Environment*, Cambridge, MA; London: Harvard University Press, 1995.

Hansson, Sven Ove, "Seven Myths of Risk," *Risk Management*, Vol. 7, No. 2, 2005, pp. 7–17.

Hertwig, Ralph, et al., "Decisions from Experience and the Effect of Rare Event in Risky Choice," *Psychological Science Journal*, Vol. 15, No. 8, 2004, pp. 534–539.

Hill, Polly, *Development Economics on Trial – The Anthropological Case for a Prosecution*, Cambridge: Cambridge University Press, 1986.

HM Government, *Healthy Lives Healthy People: Our Strategy for Public Health in England*, presented to Parliament by the Secretary of State for Healthy by Command of Her Majesty, November 30, 2010, www.official-documents.gov.uk/document/cm79/7985/7985.pdf

Hovland, C. I., I. L. Janis, and H. H. Kelley, *Communication and Persuasion: Psychological Studies of Obvious Change*, New Haven, CT: Yale University Press, 1953.

Huan, Nguyen Huu, and Dao Trong Anh, "Increased Demand for Locally Adapted Hybrid Fruit and Vegetable Varieties in Vietnam," an unpublished paper presented at the *Workshop on Quality Management in Food Hygiene and Safety*, organized by the Food Administration of the Ministry of Health in Hanoi, September 9, 2000.

Human Security Commission, *Human Security Now*, New York: Human Security Commission, 2003.

International Monetary Fund (IMF), *Vietnam: Poverty Reduction Strategy Paper*, Washington DC, January 2004, www.imf.org/external/pubs/ft/scr/2004/cr0425.pdf

International Plant Protection Convention, www.ippc.int/file_uploaded/1310182292_26_vietnam.pdf

Janz, Nancy K., and Marshal H. Becker, "The Health Belief Model: A Decade Later," *Health Education Quarterly*, Vol. 11, No. 1, 1984, pp. 1–47.

de Jong, Wil, et al., *Forest Rehabilitation in Vietnam: Histories, Realities and Future*, Center for International Forestry Research (CIFOR), 2006.

Kahneman, Daniel, "Maps of Bounded Rationality: Psychology for Behavioral Economics," *The American Economic Review*, Vol. 93, No. 5, 2003, pp. 1449–1475.

———, "The Riddle of Experience vs. Memory," February 2010, TED website www.ted.com/talks/daniel_kahneman_the_riddle_of_experience_vs_memory.html?quote=655

———, *Thinking, Fast and Slow*, New York: Farrar, Straus and Giroux, 2011.

Kahneman, Daniel, and Amos Tversky, "Prospect Theory: An Analysis of Decision under Risk," *Econometrica*, Vol. 47, No. 2, 1979, pp. 263–292.

Kerkvliet, Benedict J. Tria, *The Power of Everyday Politics: How Vietnamese Peasants Transformed National Policy*, Ithaca, NY: Cornell University Pres, 2005.

Kunstadter, Peter, ed., *Pesticides in Southeast Asia- Environmental, Biomedical and Economic Uses and Effects*, Chiang Mai: Sanga Sabhasri Research Foundation, Silkworm Books, 2007, pp. 139–148.

Lane, Christopher, "What is Health? Increasingly, the Absence of Abnormality," *Psychology Today*, www.psychologytoday.com/blog/side-effects/201012/

Le Skaife, Jane, "Vietnam No Longer an Underdeveloped Country," *Newgeography*, 2011, www.newgeography.com/content/002154-vietnam-no-longer-underdeveloped-country

Leibenstein, Harvey, "An Interpretation of the Economic Theory of Fertility: Promising Path or Blind Alley?" *Journal of Economic Literature*, Vol. 12, No. 2, 1974, pp. 457–479.

Levy, Jack S., *Annual Meeting Focus: The Decade of Behavior Lecture*, "Daniel Kahneman: Judgement, Decision, and Rationality," https://pdfs.semanticscholar.org/ 47b0/312 fb97a83e3f9bb639f3309e960e5037664.pdf

Lewis, H. W., *Technological Risk*, New York: W. W. Norton & Company, 1992.

Lewis, W. Arthur, "Economic Development with Unlimited Supplies of Labour," *The Manchester School*, Vol. 22, No. 2, 1954, pp. 139–191.

———, "Reflections on Unlimited Labor," in L. DiMarco, ed., *International Economics and Development*, New York: Academic Press, 1972, pp. 75–96.

———, "Autobiographical Note," *Social and Economic Studies*, Vol. 29, No. 4, 1980, pp. 1–4.

London, Jonathan D., "Reasserting the State in Vietnam: Health Care and the Logics of Market-Leninism", *Policy and Society*, Vol. 27, 2008, pp. 115–128.

Lupton, Deborah, *Risk*, London and New York: Routledge, 1999.

Maitre, Jacque, and Bernard Doray, "The Experience of the Families of AO Victims," a paper presented at *International Scientific Conference: "Victims of Agent Orange/ Dioxin in Vietnam – The Expectations,"* Hanoi, March 16–17, 2006, http://ffrd.org/ AO/CGFED/03Impact.pdf

Martin, Lee R., ed., *A Survey of Agricultural Economics Literature (Vol. 4): Agriculture in Economic Development 1940s to 1990s*, Minneapolis: University of Minnesota Press for the American Agricultural Economics Association, 1992.

Martini, Edwin A., *Agent Orange: History, Science, and the Politics of Uncertainty*, Amherst and Boston: University of Massachusetts Press, 2012.

Maryon Davis, Alan, and Rachel Jolley, *Healthy Nudges: When the Public Wants Change but the Politicians Do Not Know It*, London: Faculty of Public Health, King's College London, 2010, www.fph.org.uk/uploads/Healthy%20nudges%20-%20final%20final.pdf.

McRae, Rob, "Human Security in a Globalized World," in Rob McRae and Don Hubert, eds., *Human Security and the New Diplomacy: Protecting People, Promoting Peace*, Montreal: McGill-Queen's University Press, 2001.

Meier, Gerald M., *Biography of a Subject: An Evolution of Development Economics*, New York: Oxford University Press, 2005.

Mellor, John W., "Agriculture on the Road to Industrialization," in J. P. Lewis and V. Kallab, eds., *Development Strategies Reconsidered*, Washington, DC: Overseas Development Council, 1986, pp. 67–89.

Mellor, John W., and Mohinder S. Mudahar, "Agriculture in Economic Development: Theories, Findings, and Challenges in an Asian Context," in Lee R. Martin, ed., *A Survey of Agricultural Economics Literature (Vol. 4), Agriculture in Economic Development, 1940s to 1990s*, Minneapolis, University of Minnesota Press, 1992, pp. 331–542.

Micheal, Kirk, and Nguyen Do Anh Tuan, "Land Tenure Policy Reforms: Decollectivization and the Doi Moi system in Vietnam," *IFPRI Discussion Paper 00927*, International Food Policy Research Institute, 2009.

Morris, Stephen J., *Why Vietnam Invaded Cambodia: Political Culture and the Causes of War*, Palo Alto, CA: Stanford University Press, 1999.

Nhan Dan, "British Man Still Seeking Justice for Vietnamese AO Victims," 2007, www.nhandan.com.vn/english/life/170707/life_b.htm

Novick, Lloyd, Cynthia B. Morrow, and Glen P. Mays, eds., *Public Health Administration: Principles for Population-based Management*, Sudbury, MA: Jones and Barlett Publishers, 2008.

PAN-UK, "Current Pesticide Spectrum, Global Use and Major Concerns," www.pan-uk.org/briefing/SIDA_Fil/CHapl.htm, 2003.

Perkins, John H., *Geopolitics and the Green Revolution, Wheat, Genes and the Cold War*, New York: Oxford University Press, 1997.

Pham, Ngoc Quang, Bui Trinh, and Thanh Duc Nguyen, "Structural Change and Economic Performance of Vietnam 1986–2000: Evidence from the Three Input-Output Tables," presented at *Intermediate Input Output Conference*, Sendai, 2006, www.iioa.org/pdf/Intermediate-2006/ Full%20paper_Ngoc%20Pham.pdf.

———, "Economic Performance of Vietnam, 1976–2000," *DEPOCEN* (Development and Policies Research Center) *Working Paper Series*, 2017, 2007/13, pp. 1–45, http://www.depocenwp.org/upload/pubs/PhamQuangNgoc/Structural_change_&_econonmic_perfomance_of_VN_DEPOCENWP.pdf.

Phat, Nguyen Tan, and Ngyuen Tien Dung, "Vietnam's Land Policy in the Transition Period," *Tokyo Jouhou Daigaku Kennkyuu Ronsou*, Vol. 15, No. 1, 2011, pp. 9–25.

Pike, Douglas, "Vietnam during 1976: Economics in Command," *Asian Survey*, Vol. 17, No. 1, 1976, pp. 34–42.

Pimentel, David, "Environmental and Economic Costs of the Application of Pesticides Primarily in the United States," *Environment Development and Sustainability*, Vol. 7, 2005, pp. 229–252.

Prentice-Dunn, Steven, and Ronald W. Rogers, Protection Motivation and Preventive Health: beyond the Health Belief Model, *Health Education Research: Theory and Practice*, Vol. 1, No. 3, 1986, pp. 153–161.

Prybyla, Jan S., "Soviet and Chinese Economic Aid to North Vietnam," *The China Quarterly*, No. 27, July–September 1966, pp. 84–100.

Quang, Nguyen M., *An Evaluation of the Chemical Pollution in Vietnam*, September 2001, a Web Report, www.mekonginfo.org/mrc_en/doclib.nsf /0/1D952C500BE72DC587256B74000703C8/$FILE/FULLTEXT.pdf.

Quang Dat, Truong, "Health Service Utilization of the Phu Cat District Residents," paper presented at *4th workshop for Human Security at East Asia*, Keio, Tokyo, February 25–27, 2007.

Rosenstock, Irwin M., "What Research in Motivation Suggests for Public Health," *American Journal of Public Health*, Vol. 50 (3 Pt 1), March 1960, pp. 295–302.

Rosenstock, Irwin M., Victor Strecher, and Marshall Becker, "Social Learning Theory and the Health Brief Model," *Health Education Quarterly*, Vol. 15, No. 2, 1988, pp. 175–183.

Schecter, Arnold, Le Cao Dai, Olaf Päpke, Joelle Prange, John D. Constable, Muneaki Matsuda, Vu Duc Thao, and Amanda L. Piskac, "Recent Dioxin Contamination from Agent Orange in Residents of a Southern Vietnam City," *Journal of Occupational and Environmental Medicine*, Vol. 43, No. 4, 2001, pp. 435–443.

Schecter, Arnold, Hoang Trong Quynh, Marian Pavuk, Olaf Papke, Rainer Malisch, and John D. Constable, "Food as a Source of Dioxin Exposure in the Residents of Bien Hoa City, Vietnam," *Journal of Occupational and Environmental Medicine*, Vol. 45, No. 4, 2003, pp. 781–788.

Sen, Amartya, *Commodities and Capabilities*, New York: Oxford University Press, 1999 (1987).

———, *Development as Freedom*, New York: Knopf, 1999.

Sethurman, S. V., "The Urban Informal Sector: Concept, Measurement and Policy," *International Labour Review*, Vol. 114, No. 1, July–August 1976, pp. 69–81.

Shultz, Theodore W., *Transforming Traditional Agriculture*, New Haven, CT: Yale University Press, 1964.

Simon, Herbert A., "Bounded Rationality and Organizational Learning," *Organization Science*, Vol. 2, No. 1, 1991, pp. 125–134.

———, "Rational Choice and the Structure of the Environment," *Psychological Review*, Vol. 63, No. 2, 1956, pp. 129–138.

———, *Administrative Behavior: A Study of Decision-Making Processes in Administrative Organizations*, 4th edn, Glencoe: The Free Press, 1997 (1947).

Simmons, Susan J., "Health: A Concept Analysis," *International Journal of Nursing Studies*, Vol. 26, No. 2, 1989, pp. 155–161.

Skranabek, Petr, *The Death of Human Medicine and the rise of Coercive Healthism*, Suffolk: The Social Affairs Unit, 1994.

Smith, Adam, *The Wealth of Nations*, R. H. Campbell and A. S. Skinner edition, Oxford: Oxford University Press, 1976 (1776).

Son, Le Ke, and Charles R. Baily, *From Enemies to Partners: Vietnam, the U.S. and Agent Orange*, Chicago, IL: G. Anton Publishing, 2017.

Stellman, Jeanne M., *Video Map of Herbicides in Vietnam 1963–1970*, Columbia University, 2003, www.columbia.edu/~jms13/video.html

Stellman, Jeanne M., Steven D. Stellman, Richard Christian, Tracy Weber, and Carrie Tomasallo, "The Extent and Patterns of Usage of Agent Orange and Other Herbicides in Vietnam," *Nature*, Vol. 422, 2003, pp. 681–687.

St John, Ronald Bruce, *Revolution, Reform and Regionalism in Southeast Asia: Cambodia, Laos and Vietnam*, London and New York: Routledge, 2006.

Stockholm International Peace Research Institute (SIPRI), ed., *Ecological Consequences of the Second Indochina War*, Stockholm: Almqvist & Wiksell, 1976.

System of Vietnamese Legal Documents, Information Gate authorized by Ministry of Justice, www.moj.gov.vn/vbpq/Lists/Vn%20bn%20php%20lut/View_Detail.aspx?ItemID=10661

Taleb, Nassim Nicholas, *Fooled by Randomness: The Hidden Role of Chance in Life and in the Markets*, Random House: New York, 2004.

———, *The Black Swan: The impact of the Highly Improbable*, New York: Random House, 2007.

Tan Phat, Nguyen, and Nguyen Tien Dung, "Vietnam's Land Policy in the Transition Period," *Tokyo Jouhou Daigaku Kennkyuu Ronsou*, Vol. 15, No. 1, 2011, pp. 9–25.

Thaler, Richard H., and Cass R. Sunstein, *Nudge: Improving Decisions about Health, Wealth, and Happiness*, London, Penguin Books, 2008.

Than, Mya, and Joseph L. H. Tan, *Vietnam's Dilemmas and Options: The Challenge of Economic Transition in the 1990s*, Singapore: Institute of Southeast Asian Studies, 1993.

The U.S Veterans Dispatch, "The Story of Agent Orange," *US Veteran Dispatch Report*, November 1990, Issue, www.usvetdsp.com/agentorange.htm

Thi Que, Tran, "Economic Reforms and Their Impact on Agricultural Development in Vietnam," *ASEAN Economic Bulletin*, Vol. 15, No. 1, "Development Strategies, Agricultural Policies and Agricultural Development in Southeast Asia," April 1998, pp. 30–46.

———, "Land and Agricultural Land Management in Vietnam," in Ha Huy Thanh and Shozo Sakata, eds., *Impact of Socio-economic Changes on the Livelihoods of People Living in Poverty in Vietnam*, IDE ASEDP Series, no. 71, 2005, pp. 175–196.

Todaro, Michael P., *Economic Development in the Third World*, 5th edn, New York: Longman, 1992.

Tuan Anh, Vu, *Development in Vietnam: Policy Reforms and Economic Growth*, Singapore: Institute of Southeast Asian Studies, 1994.

Tung, Nguyen Khac, and Bui Xuan Dinh, "Sideline Occupations of Peasant Households in Vietnam," in Huy Le Phan, et al., eds., *The Traditional Village in Vietnam*, Hanoi: The Gioi Publishers, 1993, pp. 369–374.

Tversky, Amos, and Daniel Kahneman, "The Framing of Decision and the Psychology of Choice," *Science*, New series, Vol. 211, No. 4481, January 30, 1981, pp. 453–458.

Umegaki, Michio, and Vu Le Thao Chi, "Agent Orange-Dioxin Contamination: Human and Social Dimensions," unpublished paper, presented at *Dioxin 2007: International Symposium*, Tokyo, September 2–7, 2007.

Umegaki, Michio, Vu Le Thao Chi, and Tran Duc Phan, "Embracing Human Insecurity: Agent Orange and the Legacies of the War in Viet Nam," in Michio Umegaki, Lynn Thiesmeyer, and Atsushi Watabe, eds., *Human Insecurity in East Asia*, Tokyo and New York: United Nations University Press, 2009, pp. 21–46.

United Nations Development Program, *Human Development Report*, New York: United Nations Development Program, 2006, 2008 and 2012.

United Nations – Vietnam, www.un.org.vn/en/undp-agencypresscenter1-99/2247-phu-cat-military-airbase-removed-from-dioxin-hotspot-list.html

Upton, Dominic, and Katie Thirlaway, *Promoting Healthy Behaviour: Practical Guide for Nursing and Healthcare Professionals*, London: Routledge, 2010.

U.S. Department of Health, Education and Welfare, *Healthy People: The Surgeon General's Report on Health Promotion and Disease Prevention*, 1979, http://profiles.nlm.nih.gov/ps/access/NNBBGK.pdf

Van Bao, Trinh, Tran Duc Phan, and Nguyen Ngoc Hung, "National Project on Establishing a Genetic Consulting Model for the Families Affected by Warfare Chemicals," *mimeo*, 2003.

Van Mele, P., Nguyen Thi Thu Cuc, and A. van Huis, "Farmers' Knowledge, Perception and Practices in Mango Pest Management in the Mekong Delta, Vietnam," *International Journal of Pest Management*, Vol. 47, 2001, pp. 7–16.

Van Tien, Tran, et al., "A Health Financing Review of Vietnam: With a Focus of Social Health Insurance," World Health Organization, www.who.int/health_financing/documents/oasis_f_11-vietnam.pdf, 2011

Vien, Tran Duc, "Forestland Management Policies in Vietnam: An Overview," Center for Agricultural Research and Ecological Studies, 2006, *mimeo*, www.cares.org.vn/webplus/Article/Forestland%20management%20policies%20in%20VietNam%20An%20Overview.pdf

Vu Hanh, ed., *Agent Orange-Tragedy and Consequences*, Ho Chi Minh: Van Nghe Publisher, 2004.

Westing, Authur H., "Herbicides in War: Past and Present," in Arthur Westing, ed., *Herbicides in War –The Long-term Ecological and Human Consequences*, London and Philadelphia: Taylor & Francis, 1984, pp. 1–24.

Wiegersma, Nancy, *Vietnam: Peasant Land, Peasant Revolution: Patriarchy and Collectivity in the Rural Economy*, New York: St. Martin's Press, 1988.

Woodside, Alexander, "Nationalism and Poverty in the Breakdown of Sino-Vietnamese Relations," *Pacific Affairs*, Vol. 52, No. 3, Autumn 1979, pp. 381–383.

World Bank, *World Development Report, 1982*, Washington, DC: World Bank; New York: Oxford University Press, 1982.

———, "Vietnam Food Safety and Agricultural Health Action Plan," *Document of World Bank*, Report no. 35231 VN, 2006.

World Health Organization, *Ottawa Charter for Health Promotion 1986*, www.who.int/healthpromotion/conferences/previous/ottawa/en/

———, *Technical Briefs for Policy Makers No. 2- Designing Health Financing System to Reduce Catastrophic Health Expenditures*, Geneva, 2005, http://apps.who.int/iris/bitstream/10665/70005/1/WHO_EIP_HSF_PB_05.02_eng.pdf

———, *World Health Statistics 2007*, Geneva: World Health Organization, 2007.

———, *World Health Statistics 2011*, Geneva: World Health Organization, 2011, www.who.int/whosis/whostat/EN_WHS2011_Full.pdf.

Young, Marilyn, *The Vietnam Wars: 1945–1990*, New York: Harper Collins, 1991.

Zumwalt, Admiral Elmo R. II, and Elmo Zumwalt III, "Agent Orange and the Anguish of an American Family," *The New York Times Magazine*, August 24, 1986.

Zumwalt, Admiral Elmo R. II, *Report to Secretary of the Department of Veterans Affairs on the Association between Adverse Health Effects and Exposure to Agent Orange*, May 5, 1990, www.gulfwarvets.com/ao.html.

Vietnamese secondary sources

Dang, Trung, *Vietnam's Post-1975 Agrarian Reforms*, Canberra: Australian National University Press, 2018.

Phong, Dang, *Lich Su Kinh Te Vietnam 1945–2000*, Tap 1, Hanoi, Nha Xuat Ban Khoa Hoc Xa Hoi, 2002.

———, *Lich Su Kinh Te Vietnam 1945–2000*, Tap 2, Hanoi, Nha Xuat Ban Khoa Hoc Xa Hoi, 2005.

———, *"Phá Rào" Trong Kinh Tế Vào Đêm Trước Đổi Mới* (Breaking the economic barriers on the night before Doi Moi), Tri Thuc Publishers, 2009.

Sinh Cuc, Nguyen, *Nông nghiệp Việt Nam 1945–1975* (Agriculture of Vietnam 1945–1975), Hanoi: Thong Ke Publishers, 1995.

Thao, Van, *Bí Thư Tỉnh Ủy- Từ Cuộc Đời "Cha Đẻ Khoán Hộ" Kim Ngọc* (People Committee Chairman- From the life of the "Father of Contract Farming"- Kim Ngoc), Tre Publishing House Co. Ltd., Ho Chi Minh, 2010.

Van Linh, Nguyen, *Nguyen Van Linh: Tong Bi thu thoi dau doi moi*, Hanoi: Nha xuat ban Thong Tan, 2009.

Online sources

ASEM Connect, http://asemconnectvietnam.gov.vn/infodetail.aspx?infoid=11184

Binh Dinh Industrial Zone, http://kktbinhdinh.vn/default.asp?id=0&ID_tin=1963

Binh Dinh Online, www.baobinhdinh.com.vn/

The Economist, www.economist.com/

FAO (Food and Agriculture Organization of United Nations), www.fao.org/home/en/

Global Issues, www.globalissues.org/article/26/poverty-facts-and-stats.

Hệ Thống Văn Bản Quy Phạm Pháp Luật (System of Legal Documents) from Ministry of Justice, www.moj.gov.vn/Pages/vbpq.aspx

Inudgeyou website, www.inudgeyou.com/green-nudge-the-classic-social-comparison-experimen-by-opower/

Ministry of Natural Resources and Environment, www.monre.gov.vn/v35/default.aspx?tabid=673

National Assembly of the Socialist Republic of Vietnam, www.na.gov.vn/htx/English/C1330/#FSkJx8h4WGZ7

Nhândân, www.nhandan.com.vn/english/life/170707/life_b.htm

The New Yorker, www.newyorker.com/

Pháp Luật (Laws), http://phapluattp.vn/

Science and Technology Department of Binh Dinh, www.dostbinhdinh.org.vn/Magazine NewsPage.asp?TinTS_ID=495&TS_ID=48

Tạp Chí Tài Chính (*Finance Magazine*), www.tapchitaichinh.vn/

Technology, Entertainment and Design, www.ted.com/pages/about

Thanh Nien News, www.thanhniennews.com/

Thư Viện Pháp Luật (Library of Legal Documents), http://thuvienphapluat.vn/

Tuoi tre (Youth) online, www.tuoitre.com.vn/United Nations in Vietnam, www.un.org.vn/Vietnam Bank for Social Policies

U.K. Cabinet Office, www.cabinetoffice.gov.uk/behavioural-insights-team

U.S. Department of Veterans Affairs, *Agent Orange and Vietnam Veterans*, www.vba.va.gov/bln/21/benefits/herbicide/

Vietnam Cashew Nut Association, www.vinacas.com.vn/

Vietnam Central Coastal Region, http://binhdinh.vietccr.vn/xem-tong-quan/thong-tin-kinh-te-xa-hoi-binh-dinh-default.html

Vietnam Health Insurance, www.baohiemxahoi.gov.vn/

Vietnam Ministry of Foreign Affairs, www.mofa.gov.vn/en/nr040807104143/nr040807105039/ns050912160102

Index

Note: Page numbers followed by "n" denote endnotes, **Bold** page numbers refer to tables and *italic* page numbers refer to figures.

For Product Safety Concerns and Information please contact our EU representative GPSR@taylorandfrancis.com
Taylor & Francis Verlag GmbH, Kaufingerstraße 24, 80331 München, Germany

www.ingramcontent.com/pod-product-compliance
Lightning Source LLC
LaVergne TN
LVHW011126300926
849160LV00008B/531
* 9 7 8 1 0 3 2 1 7 3 3 8 2 *